Society and Institutions

in Early Modern France

Edited by Mack P. Holt

Society and

Institutions in

Early Modern

France

The University of Georgia Press   *Athens & London*

© 1991 by the University of Georgia Press
Athens, Georgia 30602
All rights reserved
Set in Sabon
The paper in this book meets the guidelines for
permanence and durability of the Committee on
Production Guidelines for Book Longevity of the
Council on Library Resources.

Printed in the United States of America

95   94   93   92   91   5   4   3   2   1

Library of Congress Cataloging in Publication Data
Society and institutions in early modern France / edited by Mack P.
   Holt.
         p. cm.
   Dedicated to J. Russell Major.
   "Bibliography of the works of J. Russell Major": p.
   Includes bibliographical references and index.
   ISBN 0-8203-1311-4 (alk. paper)
   ISBN 0-8203-1328-9 (pbk.: alk. paper)
   1. France. Etats généraux. 2. Representative government and
representation—France—History. 3. France—Nobility—History.
4. Authoritarianism—France—History. 5. Monarchy—France—History.
6. France—Politics and government—16th century. 7. France—
Politics and government—17th century. 8. Major, J. Russell (James
Russell), 1921– . I. Major, J. Russell (James Russell), 1921– .
II. Holt, Mack P.
JN2413.S63 1991
306.2'0944—dc20   90-11247
                           CIP

British Library Cataloging in Publication Data available

Essays presented to
J. Russell Major

Contents

Acknowledgments

I wish to record here my thanks and appreciation to a number of people without whom this volume would not have been possible. Karen Orchard of the University of Georgia Press comes first to mind, as without her enthusiasm and support from the very beginning it is unlikely that I would have persevered in my effort to get this collection of essays into print. Her encouragement and professional advice were exemplary, and I have nothing but praise for her editorial supervision. Al Hamscher also deserves special mention, since by right his name ought to be on the title page as coeditor alongside mine. He and I initially discussed this project some five years ago, and the impetus for getting it off the ground was as much his as mine. Moreover, he read every word of the manuscript and offered countless suggestions for improvements, for which every contributor owes him a debt of thanks. I would also like to thank Jack Censer, a colleague at George Mason University, who read and commented on the introduction, as well as offered useful suggestions of various kinds. And last but by no means least, I wish to express my gratitude to Blair Major. She has not only been a principal part of Russell Major's life ever since his career as a historian began, she has also been an always gracious and sympathetic friend to his graduate students. I am grateful for all her advice during the early stages of planning this volume, as well as for managing to keep its existence a secret from Russell for so long. But most of all, I appreciate her cheerful spirit and sympathetic concern for all of us who passed through Emory. She and Russell have always made us welcome.

Introduction

MACK P. HOLT

This collection of essays seeks to bring together some of the most recent work focused on an area increasingly popular among historians of early modern France: that is, the interconnections between political and social history. Such a focus is hardly novel, but that such a mutually beneficial union should have taken so long to seize the imagination of professional historians is nevertheless striking. The so-called scientific history of the late nineteenth and early twentieth centuries necessarily resulted in an emphasis on political history that concentrated almost exclusively on institutions and diplomacy, a development fueled and abetted by a contemporary world caught in the grip of the collapse of European empires and the First World War. When Marc Bloch and Lucien Febvre first reacted against this type of history in the 1920s and 1930s by emphasizing the social and economic factors on which political institutions rested and founded a new journal that would eventually become the *Annales,* an alternative emerged that would later become almost a new orthodoxy to replace the old. Ironically, the second generation of *Annaliste* scholars who emerged after the Second World War—men such as Fernand Braudel, Pierre Goubert, and Emmanuel Le Roy Ladurie—tended to focus on what they called *la longue durée* in order to write "total history." Their emphasis on long-term social and economic factors, which they viewed as clearly more important than surface events (or traditional political history), was a breath of fresh air that cleared the way for an exciting new way to study history. Within this "total history," however, political history came not only to take a back seat to social and economic history, but often to be omitted altogether. In these massive, multivolumed studies that were all originally *thèses d'état* in French universities, little place was found for political institutions, political policy, and the history of the state.[1] Thus, for all its breadth and vigor, this new kind of history was not truly total history at all. This is somewhat surprising given the interests of the founders of the *Annales.* The best example of genuinely total history is probably still Lucien Febvre's *Philippe II et la Franche Comté* (Paris, 1912); in the same vein, Marc Bloch wrote what is considered one of the most intelligent books on medieval kingship and the French monarchy, *Les rois thaumaturges* (Strasbourg, 1924). The result of the *Annalistes*' prevailing singlemindedness was that by the 1970s political and social history were no more closely integrated than they had been a century earlier.

Recently, historians on both sides of the Atlantic have made a more explicit attempt to integrate the best of both kinds of history. Eschewing the narrowly focused diplomatic and institutional histories of an earlier age as well as the overtly quantitative and serial methodologies of *la longue durée*, the new history attempts to understand the connections between state and society rather than to emphasize the boundaries separating them. Although this process has witnessed a variety of different methodologies, from the cultural (incorporating methods from social theory and cultural anthropology) to the linguistic (aided by linguistic and literary theory) to the sociopolitical (largely non-Marxist), the result has been the insistence that political and social history can no longer be viewed as distinct parts of the whole but must necessarily be understood in terms of one another if "state and society" are to mean anything at all in relation to early modern France.[2] One early pioneer of this trend in the United States was J. Russell Major of Emory University.

To be sure, Russell Major's first published work did not entirely presage what was to come. *The Estates General of 1560* (Princeton, 1951) was his revised doctoral dissertation at Princeton University, where he studied with Joseph R. Strayer and E. H. Harbison immediately after distinguished service in Europe during the Second World War. Although it was a tantalizingly brief book, and almost the only work in English on the subject of the French Estates General, it demonstrated the significant impact that Roman law had made on early modern representative assemblies. Nevertheless, this book offered little evidence that its author would one day emerge from the confines of institutional history to challenge the accepted orthodoxy of his day as well as to participate in the resurrection of a new post-Marxist, post-*Annaliste* view of early modern France. That Major had such designs as well as a broader and much more fully developed view of how French institutions like the Estates General fit into early modern society became apparent a few years later when he launched his own model of what he called the "Renaissance monarchy" in a brief article published in 1957. It exploded like a bombshell and was designed to have the same effect on current opinion about the early modern state.[3]

The orthodoxy that had long been prevalent primarily concerned the century following the Hundred Years' War, when European population gradually recovered after a century of ravages by war and plague, and a series of "new monarchies" emerged to replace the feudal monarchies of the Middle Ages. Unlike the feudal kings so dependent on their barons for arms, power, and authority to control their decentralized kingdoms, "new monarchs" such as Ferdinand of Aragon, Louis XI of France, and Henry VII of England, for just three examples, took the first steps to consolidate their power and to assert an unprecedented degree of control over their people in the late fifteenth century. Implementing the new secular principles later analyzed by Machiavelli, these Renaissance princes made significant strides toward increasing royal power at the expense of their nobles as well as ruling over the birth of the modern state. Thus, after 1500 princes such as Charles V of the Holy Roman Empire and Henry VIII of England governed with greater power and authority than had any of their predecessors.[4] As for France, Georges Pagès had written as early as 1928 that "perhaps no kings of France were ever more powerful than Francis I and Henry II, and it was at the beginning of the sixteenth century when absolutism had triumphed."[5]

To this interpretation Russell Major offered a powerful riposte that not only challenged the current orthodoxy but presented a new model for the periodization of French history. Far from viewing the late fifteenth- and early sixteenth-century monarchy as the progenitor of a modern, centralized, absolutist state, he argued that from the end of the Hundred Years' War to the Wars of Religion the French monarchy was neither medieval nor modern, but a unique amalgam of the Renaissance and its peculiar social, economic, and political forces. Kings such as Louis XI, Charles VIII, and Louis XII governed by bargaining and negotiating with their subjects through various representative institutions: principally the local and provincial estates in much of the realm and the Estates General, a body rarely convoked in the past but an institution that experienced a revival between 1484 and 1614. Thus, in Major's view the Renaissance monarchy was popular and consultative, unlike the medieval monarchy that preceded it, though still inherently weak, unlike the absolute monarchs of the seventeenth century, because the Renaissance kings lacked a large bureaucracy or royal army to implement their policies. In other words, Renaissance kings still depended on the will of their subjects; and above all, they still relied heavily on the loyalty of the French nobility, the class that continued to dominate French politics and society throughout the sixteenth and seventeenth centuries. So in contrast to the traditional view of a modern state emerging from the feudal monarchy of the Middle Ages around 1500, Major offered the new model of a distinctly Renaissance monarchy that differed from both its predecessors and its successors, and he emphasized the significance of representative institutions between the reigns of Charles VII (1422–61) and Henry IV (1589–1610).[6]

Old orthodoxies die hard and Major's entire schema drew criticism from various quarters, particularly from abroad.[7] In a moment of unusual candor, unusual in the historical profession, at least, Major himself noted in 1980 that "to my knowledge the only textbook to adopt my point of view is my own."[8] To be sure, Major's "Renaissance monarchy" did not become the new orthodoxy, and influential scholars continued to cling to various versions of the older point of view.[9] What Major was too modest to proclaim in 1980, however, was that even if scholars did not agree with his entire schema, various components of it had become part of a growing consensus on the need to reevaluate the nature of the early modern state. The concept of absolutism, to take just the most obvious example, has come under much closer scrutiny since Major's first query about when the absolutist state first emerged. Not only has periodization come into question, but what the absolute monarchy was, how it functioned, and the larger issue of whether absolute monarchs really were more powerful than their predecessors are subjects that have long dominated academic debate. Some scholars have even suggested that the term "absolutism" be dropped altogether from the historical vocabulary, much as "feudalism" has been discarded by medievalists, as its meaning can no longer be defined with consistency or widespread agreement. Even some of his critics have been forced to admit that a reexamination of the older view was mandatory, and they and a host of others have already begun a revision that is far from complete.[10] So, though Russell Major may not have convinced other scholars to adopt his own views in their entirety, he has certainly played a crucial role in getting historians to redefine their thinking on the relationship between state and society in early modern France. That redefinition is still going on, as many of the essays in this volume will attest, and there can be no doubt that Russell Major's role in influencing a number of later ideas is significant.

More specifically, Major's assertion that the aristocracy, or landed nobility, in France did not decline economically or politically in the Renaissance period has become an accepted part of current historical thinking. Eschewing the traditional view that the nobility in France declined significantly after the Hundred Years' War because it was unable to adapt socially and economically to a changing world no longer based on the feudal system, Major argued convincingly in 1964 that the aristocracy was hardly undermined by a rising bourgeoisie who replaced it through the sale of public offices and other forms of social advancement, but that as a group the nobility coped well with the changing social climate of the sixteenth and seventeenth centuries. Nobles managed to adapt and to hold onto the reins of social and economic power in the provinces, he argued, by substituting a patron-client network of political power for the lord-vassal relationship of the Middle Ages. To be sure, there were always cases of noble families who failed to keep abreast of the changing climate and ended up going bankrupt, selling off their fiefs, or both. And there clearly were tensions between older noble families and the newer ones who were making progress up the social ladder at the former's expense. The result, however, was not a declining but a replenished aristocracy that remained a potent political force in early modern France, and one that the crown was continually compelled to reckon with.[11]

Various students of the period have now documented this fact in various ways. Not only has it been shown that the aristocracy survived into the seventeenth century as a potent political, social, and economic force —often demonstrating surprising ingenuity in adapting to changing economic forces such as population stagnation, price inflation, and the like —but it is equally clear that the superficial quarrels between old aristocratic families and those newly ennobled that dominated political discourse throughout the period in fact masked a surprisingly united outlook and sense of common purpose, as well as a broad range of ties that linked robe and sword together in striking ways.[12] Thus, although Russell Major's schema has never been adopted as a new orthodoxy, a fundamental component of it clearly has been accepted. More important, Major's demand for a complete rethinking of the relationship between state and society in early modern France has led to a wave of new research and ideas that has completely reoriented our understanding of the "Age of Absolutism."

All the essays in this collection in some way attempt to deal with the relationship between the state and society in France in the sixteenth and seventeenth centuries, and in particular to emphasize the links between political and social history that Russell Major has done so much to bring to our attention.[13] The diversity of approaches and opinions in this volume alone should serve to underscore that no new consensus has quite yet emerged to replace fully the traditional orthodoxy. Although some of the present essays corroborate many of Major's findings, others either refine his approach or branch out into entirely new directions. James B. Wood writes on the royal army during the Wars of Religion and illustrates Major's contention that the Renaissance monarchy was too weak to implement its policies by force. Wood asks why the royal army was so unable to defeat the Huguenots militarily when it had far larger resources and manpower at its disposal, and his conclusions concern the institutional, structural, and logistical weaknesses of the early modern state. Sarah Hanley considers the relationship between representative assemblies and the French monarchy during this same period, concentrating on an important though often overlooked political tract of the 1570s: the anonymous *Discours politiques des diverses puissances* (1574). Like Major, she views representative assemblies as playing a significant role in the French constitution and shows how a theory of resistance emerged to challenge royal authority during the religious wars of the sixteenth century. Two other essays explore the social and economic power of the French nobility, and both support Major's point that the newer nobles of the robe did not supplant the power and authority of the older military aristocracy, but rather both groups shared a common outlook and similar function as elites in early modern society. Donna Bohanan argues that the nobles in the two provinces she has studied—Provence and Brittany—do not reveal a nobility divided between robe and sword, but demonstrate a united elite that intermarried and soon became indistinguishable. Gayle K. Brunelle shows how the two groups in Normandy shared a common outlook regarding trade and commerce. Contrary to the older view that landed nobles suffered an economic demise because they either refused or were unable to profit from commerce, Brunelle's Norman nobles demonstrated a remarkable capacity to engage and succeed in commercial activity.

Another pair of essays focuses on the changing relationship between municipalities and the crown. Annette Finley-Croswhite analyzes Henry IV's efforts to restore royal authority in the league towns that had rebelled against him during the 1590s. Examining a revolt in Limoges in 1602 as an illustration, she argues that the king had a clear and precise plan to bring autonomous municipal magistrates under royal control, and she uses this argument to support Major's general contention that the Renaissance monarchy of the sixteenth century gave way to the absolute monarchy of the seventeenth through the subversion of local privileges. One of the most visible municipal privileges that Henry IV and his successors sought to curtail was a town's right to elect its own mayor without royal interference. I myself examine the mayoral elections in the Burgundian capital of Dijon and have focused on a hidden facet of their significance. I argue that these elections had a social dynamic all their own to those who participated in them—largely winegrowers and artisans—and that the right to participate in the elections and the rituals surrounding them seemed to matter as much to the populace as the ability to control the result. A further pair of essays concerns the mid-seventeenth-century crisis of the Fronde, and both go a long way toward revising the older view of the Fronde as a social and political crisis that nearly undermined an emerging absolutist state. The Fronde played such a crucial role in the traditional orthodoxy of the development of absolutism that reinterpretations of this crisis are relevant to Major's work even though he wrote little about the event. Orest Ranum reexamines the revolts of the judges of the Parlement of Paris and many of the leading princes of the blood to show how the political divisions of the princes resulted in efforts to solicit support from the judges in Parlement. By analyzing the resulting patronage networks formed between the royal court and the judicial court, he is able to show that the success or failure of the revolts hinged in large measure on the ability of the princes to win the judges to their cause. William Beik goes even further in his study of the Fronde in Toulouse, where he takes a provincial look at the crisis from the "bottom up." The result is that the traditional interpretation of the Fronde gets turned on its head as Beik demonstrates how it was the Frondeurs who were the "absolutists" in their struggle with the crown.

Finally, three essays explore the concept of absolutism and the emerging centralized state in the seventeenth century from a variety of perspectives. Ellery Schalk's essay shows that the traditional view of absolutism, thoroughly revised by most of the other essays in this volume, is not entirely dead. He maintains that the recalcitrant nobles of the sixteenth-century Wars of Religion fell under the hypnotic spell of the absolute monarchy in the seventeenth century, with the 1590s being the watershed in this process. By analyzing the work of the seventeenth-century writer Molière, Schalk argues that much of the theoretical support given by the elites to the absolutist regime of the seventeenth century stemmed from their fear of reliving the horrors of the civil wars of the sixteenth century. Donald A. Bailey reexamines the career of Louis XIII's chancellor, Michel de Marillac. According to Russell Major, it was Marillac rather than Cardinal Richelieu who was the principal architect of Louis XIII's absolutist policies aimed at wresting away the fiscal privileges of the *pays d'états,* and Bailey's reassessment lends credence to that view. Finally, Albert N. Hamscher explores how the legal system actually worked during the reign of Louis XIV. Concentrating on the judicial aspect of the relations between the king's councils and the leading law courts of the realm—the parlements—he modifies the traditional picture of the absolute monarchy by emphasizing some of the institutional limitations on royal authority and the role that accommodation, consensus, and goodwill played in the crown's policies toward its traditional officials.

Has a new consensus emerged out of the destruction of the old? Probably not, at least none as simple as the older view. But if he has not inspired a new consensus, Major has been powerfully influential in reorienting our thinking and ideas. Standing on the shoulders of giants not only allows one to see farther; it also affords the chance to look around in many different directions. Russell Major's contribution to scholarship has been truly significant; and even if all those influenced by his work have not followed directly in his own footsteps or even adhered to all his interpretations, they have been encouraged to rethink and reshape the agenda he established. The essays included here are a reflection of that diversity. If some readers still find themselves wistfully longing for the good old days when interpretations concerning the emergence of the French state and royal absolutism were simpler and easier to teach, they should be comforted by the knowledge that what we now know is a great deal more convincing and closer to the reality of the Old Regime. Moreover, if anything has become part of a new consensus, it is surely what has always been one of Russell Major's central concerns: the understanding of the state and society as interdependent rather than autonomous forces in early modern France.

All of the essays in this volume were written by students or friends of Russell Major. That he directed fifteen Ph.D. dissertations and acquired such a wide variety of friends and acquaintances since he first went to Emory University in the fall of 1949 made it an easy task to solicit contributions for this volume.[14] Everyone who was solicited to contribute was delighted to take part in a work to celebrate the contributions of such a generous and articulate scholar. No one who has ever known Russell needs reminding of his professionalism, his humility and respect for others, his infectious enthusiasm for his work as teacher and scholar, or his concern for his students. His work habits are beyond reproach: mornings during term time spent teaching and seeing students, and afternoons until six (and all day Saturday) spent in the library researching and writing. He was the model graduate supervisor. Not only did he provide just enough prompting and nurturing to keep all his students on track so that they could begin their own professional careers as soon as possible, but he also encouraged intellectual independence and self-assertiveness. Upon graduation every student discovered that Russell's interest and concern had only just begun. Apart from scores of letters he wrote and phone calls he made in order to secure employment for his students, he was always pleased to advise and comment on their ongoing work.

As a Ph.D. student of Russell Major from 1978 to 1982, I am long enough removed from graduate school to have a realistic perspective about my graduate training as well as some insight into how beneficial that preparation was. The entering class of history graduate students at Emory University in the autumn of 1978 was unusually large, and I for one was not altogether confident of my ability to survive in the midst of such a talented and articulate group. Since my very first class was Russell's seminar on Renaissance France, within days of my arrival on campus I encountered him as teacher and mentor. Having been armed beforehand with a Gargantuan reading list for each class of the term, I expected the seminars to be intense and lively. I was completely unprepared, however, for the shock of Russell Major's opening gambit at the first meeting of the term. He went around the table of about a dozen students firing the same salvo of questions at each: "What did you read? How did you like it? And what did you learn?" Within minutes of the beginning of my first class with Russell Major, as one student after another became stunned, disarmed, and tongue-tied, I decided never to arrive unprepared for class again. This opening ritual, I soon learned, was not only the way Russell began all his seminars, but it was also a useful way for his students to learn from each other in a sort of trial by combat. Despite my initial reservations, I soon came to enjoy and look forward to those seminars. They were among the most intensly intellectual experiences of my life, and I shall not soon forget them.

To dwell on the intellectual nature of Russell Major, however, is to overlook his personal side. Not only did he come to take a strong interest in all his students, as any graduate supervisor might, he sacrificed his own precious time for research for their benefit. Unlike some graduate mentors, who tend to dawdle over dissertation chapters as if they are chores to be completed, Russell read all his students' work with enthusiasm and invari-

ably finished it and was ready to talk about it within twenty-four hours.
I recall when I was finishing up my own dissertation in the summer of
1981 that Russell was abroad for most of the summer. When he returned
in August, I handed him the last three chapters with great relief the very
day he returned to his office—a manuscript of about 175 pages. I should
not have been surprised when he was ready to discuss it with me the very
next afternoon. As one of his colleagues in the Emory history department
remarked, "No one in the department works harder than Russell."

If Russell's personal side is to be discussed at all, however, one has to
mention his wife, Blair. Serving as wife, mother, and occasional researcher,
Blair has closely intertwined her life with Russell's. She always took great
care to ensure that hospitality and friendship were offered to Russell's students in equal doses with the expected intellectual stimulation, and Russell
and Blair have always generously welcomed students and friends into their
home for food, drink, conversation, and friendship.

For all these reasons, I think I can say that students and friends of Russell
Major have a special appreciation of the real legacy he has left to the profession. But the mention of legacies has an unwarranted sense of finality
about it. Russell Major may be retiring from the Charles Howard Candler
Professorship in the Department of History at Emory University, but he is
hardly finished as a historian. He clearly has far more to say on the subject
of early modern France, and we can all be grateful for that.[15]

NOTES

1. Some of the earliest examples were Fernand Braudel, *La Méditerrannée et le
monde méditerranéan à l'époque de Philippe II,* 2 vols. (Paris, 1949; 2d rev. ed.,
1966); Pierre Goubert, *Beauvais et le Beauvaisis de 1600 à 1730: Contribution à
l'histoire sociale de la France du XVIIe siècle,* 2 vols. (Paris, 1960); and Emmanuel
Le Roy Ladurie, *Les paysans de Languedoc,* 2 vols. (Paris, 1966). Braudel's work
was the only one with any appreciable political history in it at all, as he added a
separate section of "histoire événementielle" as an afterthought. It was the least
successful part of his tripartite work on the Mediterranean.

2. Just a few of the many examples of these trends are Pierre Goubert, *L'Ancien
Régime,* 2 vols. (Paris, 1969, 1973); Roland Mousnier, *La plume, la faucille et le
marteau: Institutions et société en France du Moyen Age à la Révolution* (Paris,
1970); idem, *Les institutions de la France sous la monarchie absolue,* 2 vols. (Paris,

1974, 1980); Natalie Zemon Davis, *Society and Culture in Early Modern France* (Stanford, 1975); Robert Muchembled, *Culture populaire et culture des élites dans la France moderne: XVe–XVIIIe siècles* (Paris, 1978; English ed., 1985); William Beik, *Absolutism and Society in Seventeenth-Century France: State Power and Provincial Aristocracy in Languedoc* (Cambridge, 1985); and Jean Delumeau, *Rassurer et protéger: Le sentiment de sécurité dans l'Occident d'autrefois* (Paris, 1989).

3. J. Russell Major, "The Renaissance Monarchy: A Contribution to the Periodization of History," *Emory University Quarterly* 13 (1957): 112–24. This article received much greater notoriety when it was reprinted in a collection of essays and texts edited by A. J. Slavin, *The "New Monarchies" and Representative Assemblies: Medieval Constitutionalism or Modern Absolutism?* (Boston, 1964). His argument was further developed in a later article, "The French Monarchy as Seen Through the Estates-General," *Studies in the Renaissance* 9 (1962): 113–25.

4. For this consensus of opinion, see Slavin, ed., *New Monarchies*, introduction.

5. Georges Pagès, *La monarchie d'Ancien Régime en France* (Paris, 1928), 3. A more sophisticated statement of the same basic argument was later published by R. J. Knecht in *Francis I and the Absolute Monarchy* (London, 1969).

6. Major, "Renaissance Monarchy," 112–24. This argument was further elaborated in two books Russell Major published in 1960: *Representative Institutions in Renaissance France, 1421–1559* (Madison, 1960), and *The Deputies to the Estates General in Renaissance France* (Madison, 1960). Two seminal articles in the *American Historical Review* further strengthened his claim that the aristocracy was the dominant social class in the sixteenth century and that the nobility had not been displaced either by a rising bourgeoisie or by economic mismanagement; rather, it remained in power because of a powerful patron-client system: "The Crown and the Aristocracy in Renaissance France," *American Historical Review* 69 (1964): 631–45, and "Noble Income, Inflation, and the Wars of Religion in France," *American Historical Review* 86 (1981): 21–48. Major published the most comprehensive discussion of his argument in his magisterial *Representative Government in Early Modern France* (New Haven, 1980).

7. See particularly Salvo Mastellone, "Osservazioni sulla 'Renaissance Monarchy' in Francia," *Annali della fondazione italiana per la storia amministrativa* 1 (1964): 421–30. Mastellone noted that by emphasizing the popular support of the monarchy Major "runs the risk of ignoring all the history of the Middle Ages." Also see two articles by the French historian Bernard Guenée: "L'histoire de l'état en France à la fin du Moyen Age vue par les historiens français depuis cent ans," *Revue historique* 232 (1964): 331–60, and "Espace et état dans la France du Bas-Moyen Age," *Annales E.S.C.* 23 (1968): 744–58.

8. Major, *Representative Government*, 1.

9. For several of the many examples that could be cited, see Richard Bonney, *Political Change in France Under Richelieu and Mazarin, 1624–1661* (Oxford,

1978); R. J. Knecht, *Francis I* (Cambridge, 1982); Ellery Schalk, *From Valor to Pedigree: Ideas of Nobility in France in the Sixteenth and Seventeenth Centuries* (Princeton, 1986); and Robin Briggs, *Communities of Belief: Cultural and Social Tension in Early Modern France* (Oxford, 1989).

10. Again, for only a few examples from a variety of perspectives, see Schalk, *From Valor to Pedigree;* Beik, *Absolutism and Society;* Richard Bonney, "Absolutism: What's in a Name?" *French History* 1 (1987): 93–117; David Parker, *The Making of French Absolutism* (London, 1983); Sharon Kettering, *Patrons, Brokers, and Clients in Seventeenth-Century France* (New York, 1986); Daniel Hickey, *The Coming of French Absolutism: The Struggle for Tax Reform in the Province of Dauphiné, 1540–1640* (Toronto, 1986); James B. Collins, *Fiscal Limits of Absolutism: Direct Taxation in Early Seventeenth-Century France* (Berkeley, 1988); Albert N. Hamscher, *The Conseil Privé and the Parlements in the Age of Louis XIV: A Study in French Absolutism,* Transactions of the American Philosophical Society, vol. 77, pt. 2 (Philadelphia, 1987); Roger Mettam, *Power and Faction in Louis XIV's France* (Oxford, 1988); and Sarah Hanley, "Engendering the State: Family Formation and State Building in Early Modern France," *French Historical Studies* 16 (1989): 4–27.

11. Major, "Crown and Aristocracy," 631–45.

12. See, for example, William A. Weary, "The House of La Trémoille, Fifteenth Through Eighteenth Centuries: Change and Adaptation in a French Noble Family," *Journal of Modern History* 49 (1977): on-demand supp.; Robert R. Harding, *Anatomy of a Power Elite: The Provincial Governors of Early Modern France* (New Haven, 1978); Jonathan Dewald, *The Formation of a Provincial Nobility: The Magistrates of the Parlement of Rouen, 1499–1610* (Princeton, 1980); James B. Wood, *The Nobility of the Election of Bayeux, 1463–1666: Continuity Through Change* (Princeton, 1980); Denis Crouzet, "Recherches sur la crise de l'aristocratie en France au XVIe siècle: Les dettes de la maison de Nevers," *Histoire, économie, société* 1 (1982): 7–50; Ellery Schalk, "Ennoblement in France from 1350 to 1660," *Journal of Social History* 16 (1982): 101–10; Mack P. Holt, "Patterns of Clientèle and Economic Opportunity at Court During the Wars of Religion: The Household of François, Duke of Anjou," *French Historical Studies* 13 (1984): 305–22; Jonathan Dewald, *Pont-St-Pierre, 1398–1789: Lordship, Community, and Capitalism in Early Modern France* (Berkeley, 1987); and Kristen B. Neuschel, *Word of Honor: Interpreting Noble Culture in Sixteenth-Century France* (Ithaca, N.Y., 1989).

13. See, most recently, J. Russell Major, "Bastard Feudalism and the Kiss: Changing Social Mores in Late Medieval and Early Modern France," *Journal of Interdisciplinary History* 17 (1987): 509–35.

14. See the list of contributors on pp. 231–33 and the list of dissertations directed by Russell Major on pp. 228–29.

15. He has mentioned several book-length projects he hopes to complete upon

his university retirement, including a comparison of the French and English nobility in the early modern period on which he has been working for some time. He also plans work outside the field of early modern France: a book on his native Virginia in the colonial period.

ABBREVIATIONS

AD   Archives départementales
AN   Archives Nationales, Paris
BN   Bibliothèque Nationale, Paris

All translations into English are those of the respective authors.

Society and Institutions

in Early Modern France

1. The Royal Army During

the Early Wars of Religion, 1559–1576

JAMES B. WOOD

INTRODUCTION

The first half of the French Wars of Religion, a period corresponding generally to the reign of the next to the last Valois king, Charles IX
(1560–74), saw a violent and prolonged contest for dominance between the
royal government and Catholic France, on the one hand, and the Huguenots, or French Protestants, on the other. During the first five civil wars
of this period the royal army was the main instrument of coercion used
against the Protestants.[1] But a decisive military defeat of the Huguenots
eluded the royal forces. At the end of every war the crown had to agree to
temporizing and sometimes humiliating interim peace treaties that effectively compromised its authority.[2] Thus the failure of the royal army enabled the Huguenots to continue to survive and even grow stronger in some
localities, a development that was to be a decisive factor in determining
the ultimate outcome of the civil wars.

Why the crown was unable to break the Huguenots militarily is a question historians have not recently been much interested in. There is, for
example, no systematic modern study of the royal army. We know little
about how the royal forces were organized, paid, equipped, or led, how
they fought, thought, saw themselves, or behaved.[3] Yet an understanding of
the military struggle is central to any attempt to comprehend the period as
a whole. And one of the major keys to understanding the military outcome
of the civil wars lies in a detailed study of the royal army. In pursuit of that
goal this essay will show how the nature of the royal armies, their strategic
disposition, and the military situation itself put enormous constraints on
the effective application of force by the crown in its internal war against its

Protestant subjects during the period 1562–76. A fairly fixed sequence of problems was encountered in each war: (1) a lack of initial preparedness; (2) difficulties of mobilization; (3) the large-scale nature of the conflict; (4) an inability to maintain armies in the field; and (5) the nature of demobilization. Over time, an additional factor developed: (6) the effect of cumulative casualties on the army's leadership. By the end of the period the royal army was exhausted and demoralized and in an even less favorable position to obtain a meaningful military decision than it had been in at the beginning of the wars.

LACK OF PREPAREDNESS

In 1957, a young American historian who had himself experienced a war in Europe pointed out that the characterization of Renaissance monarchies as absolutist was hard to reconcile with the small size of their armed forces and the very large areas some of them ruled.[4] These observations certainly apply to France. Many of the solutions to the consequences of the Military Revolution—solutions successfully adopted by Louis XIV's France—had not yet appeared in mid-sixteenth-century France.[5] For example, the idea and reality of a huge standing army simply did not exist. The peacetime army was small and for the most part widely dispersed, and where it was concentrated in any numbers it was tied to the frontier provinces—a strategic disposition of forces based on the assumption and experience that the army was not needed primarily to enforce domestic tranquility but rather was essentially a dynastic instrument to be used in adventures abroad and to defend France from foreign invasion.

The royal army was such an expensive proposition that during peacetime its size was always greatly reduced, both by the elimination of superfluous companies of horse and foot and by reducing the size of the remaining companies. The civil wars did nothing to change this pattern. Even the knowledge that continued warfare was a near certainty could not offset the tremendous expense of keeping an army in the field. Consequently, it was almost impossible for the all but totally demobilized and geographically dispersed army to be prepared for civil war. The crown's forces and military dispositions were simply ill-suited to waging war on its own subjects. As a result, in none of the first five wars were royal forces actually well prepared enough to prevent the Huguenots from concentrating their own forces. The peacetime dispositions of the heavy cavalry and infantry components of the army will clearly demonstrate this lack of preparedness.

Table 1. Peacetime dispersal of gendarme companies, 1559–1574

	1559	1564	1571	1574
Picardy	6	13	8	3
Normandy	8	6	5	5
Ile-de-France	3	8	6	9
Champagne	13	15	11	9
Burgundy	4	5	6	4
Brittany	1	4	2	2
Maine	1	2	3	1
Anjou-Touraine	1	2	2	1
Orleanais	2	3	2	0
Berry	2	2	1	1
Nivernais	0	1	0	1
Bourbonnais	2	3	0	0
Poitou-Saintonge	6	8	5	6
Marche-Limousin	1	1	1	2
Auvergne	0	1	2	1
Lyonnais	2	2	1	0
Dauphiné	1	3	4	3
Provence	1	1	1	2
Piedmont	6	0	1	1
Guyenne and Gascony	4	3	5	7
Languedoc	0	8	3	10
Total	64	91	69	68

Sources: See note 6.

The companies *d'ordonnance,* that is, the gendarmerie, or heavy cavalry, were the heart of the royal army. Though large numbers of lighter cavalry—*chevaux légers* and *arquebusiers à cheval*—were raised during wartime, almost none were supported between wars. The gendarmerie, by contrast, was a permanent force, theoretically paid even in peacetime while rotating through garrison duties.

But between wars the heavy cavalry was widely dispersed, as table 1 illustrates: in 1559, after the treaty of Cateau-Cambresis; in 1564, after the First War of Religion (1562–63); in 1571, after the Third War (1568–70); and in 1574, before the beginning of the Fifth War (1574–76).[6] During peacetime, on the average between 64 and 69 companies of heavy cavalry, amounting to about 6,500 horse, were supported. The only time those numbers were surpassed in peacetime, between the civil wars, was in the aftermath of the First War, owing primarily to an attempt to accommodate both loyal and Huguenot noble commanders in the search for a permanent religious peace. After every civil war the gendarmerie was dispersed throughout the country, and across the whole period the manner of this dispersal remained very stable. About one-third of the companies were based below the Loire, and about one-third concentrated in the three frontier provinces of Picardy, Champagne, and Burgundy. If to the latter are added the companies in Normandy and the Ile-de-France, exactly 52 percent of all gendarme companies (except for 44 percent in 1574) were always divided along a band stretching across northern and eastern France. Within provinces, even on the frontier, companies and parts of companies were also widely dispersed.

The inadequacy of these numbers and placement for fighting a widespread civil war can most easily be grasped by comparing them to the number of companies actually required to fight the wars when they broke out (table 2). In all but one of the first six wars (the Fourth, dominated by the siege of La Rochelle, required fewer cavalry companies) more than 100 companies of gendarmes were utilized. The Second and Fifth wars saw about a doubling and the Third and Sixth wars almost a tripling of the peacetime number of gendarme companies. Full mobilization of peacetime companies, in other words, did not even begin to fulfill the overall requirements for heavy cavalry. In fact, the number of companies assigned to the major field army alone was almost always far more than the total number of peacetime companies. Anjou's army in late 1567, for example, during the Second War, contained 87 gendarme companies, and in the fall of 1568, during the Third War, at least 88 companies.[7]

To sum up, the peacetime number and dispersal all over France of the heavy cavalry companies made it virtually impossible for the crown to achieve easily or quickly any kind of strategic concentration of this most important combat arm. With units scattered all over the map and understrength, with men often actually at their homes rather than in garrison, only rather obvious and lengthy pre-mobilization could concentrate large numbers of gendarmes. Such concentration was impossible to hide from the Huguenots and even if successful could not produce the minimum number of companies thought necessary for a properly outfitted main field army.

When we turn to the infantry, an equally revealing picture of inadequate numbers and inconvenient troop placement emerges. At the beginning of every budgetary year, *états* were drawn up that authorized payment of the

Table 2. Gendarme companies: peak
strengths during the Wars of Religion

War	Year	Companies
1st	1563	103
2d	1568	143
3d	1569	180
4th	1573	87
5th	1576	124
6th	1577	171

Sources: For 1563, Dépôt de la guerre (Service Historique
de l'Armée de Terre, Château de Vincennes), *Ordonnances
militaires,* vol. 10 (hereafter *OM*), no. 48; for 1568, BN,
MSS fr. 4552, fols. 108–10 (also for 1568, companies identified in ibid., 15544, fols. 187–88, and PRO/SP 70/96,
fols. 231–32); for 1569, *OM*, no. 129; for 1573, *OM*, no.
173; for 1576, BN, MSS fr. 3256, fols. 21–22; for 1577,
ibid., 21543, fols. 95–106.
Note: The totals in 1563, 1576, and 1577 are swelled by
the inclusion of a few Protestant companies the crown was
pledged to support.

"gens de guerre a pied tenans garnison pour le service de sa Ma^{te} es villes
chasteaux et places" of the different provinces and governments of the
kingdom.[8] The *états* (one for northern and one for southern France) prepared for Charles IX's approval in January 1572, just half a year before the
Saint Bartholomew's Day massacre, show that the crown planned to maintain during 1572, for the entire country, a grand total of 6,229 infantry-
men, 287 command and staff personnel (provincial lieutenants, captains
and governors of towns and châteaus, regimental officers, engineers, gate-
keepers, and scribes), and an unspecified number of supernumery captains
on small pensions.[9] It is clear from section *A* of table 3, which provides a
proportional breakdown by province of the 6,229 soldiers, how closely infantry garrisons were wedded to a strategic placement inherited from the
wars with France's neighbors in the first half of the century, rather than
being disposed for quick mobilization against an internal enemy. Ten years
after the outbreak of the civil wars, Picardy, the Pays Messin, and what remained of French possessions in Italy (Piedmont) together still contained
62 percent of all the crown's infantry forces. Many provinces contained
no soldiers at all or only a few garrisons. Although more than 80 places
were provided with at least a military captain, only 53 of those places were

Table 3. The infantry establishment, 1572

A. *Location of troops in garrison*

Place or province	Number	% of total
Picardy	1,284	20.6
Champagne	102	1.6
Pays Messin	1,307	21.0
Burgundy	102	1.6
Normandy	233	3.7
Anjou/Touraine	26	.4
Brittany	70	1.2
Paris (Bastille)	20	.3
Suite of King	600	9.6
Guyenne/Poitou	25	.4
Languedoc	360	5.8
Lyonnais	456	7.3
Dauphiné	372	5.8
Piedmont	1,272	20.4
Total:	6,229	100

B. *Size of garrisons*

Troops	Places
965	Metz
600	Calais
456	Lyons
300	Mirandola
212	Verdun
150	Monstreuil
130	Abbeville
100	Havre, Pignerol, Carmaignolles
50–99	Belle-Isle, Aiguesmortes, Rouen, Chalon S.S., Toul, Marsal, Rocroi, Doulans, Rue, Ardres

actually specified by the *états* as having garrisons, though 5 companies stationed in Languedoc and 3 companies in Dauphiné would have increased the number of places in the whole country having garrisons to around 60.

Despite the putative concentration of infantry on the periphery of the kingdom, few of the places that had garrisons contained large numbers of soldiers. Of the 53 garrisons specified by the *états,* only 20, identified in section *B* of table 2, contained 50 or more troops, though the size of the Piedmont garrisons would have been swelled by the presence of Brissac's regiment of 660 men, whose actual assignments to places are not specified. More than half of the total royal infantry was accounted for by the three citadel cities of Calais (600 men), Metz (965), and Lyons (456), and the remaining French possessions in Italy (1,272). Where sizable concentrations were supported, they were thus wedded to the defense of places that (with the partial exception of Lyons, where a citadel had been constructed after the First War) looked outward past the frontiers rather than inward, where the civil wars were fought. Where the crown's garrisons were located away from the frontier they were almost always very small. The only sizable concentration away from the frontiers was the 600 men of Cossein's regiment, assigned to the peripatetic court.

Since the crown refused to denude citadels like Calais and Metz of troops even in a domestic emergency, a large portion of the small peacetime infantry force was unavailable even when civil war came.[10] When war broke out, the number of companies of infantry (about 44 in 1572) had to be increased four- or fivefold simply to supply the main field army (or armies), and all companies (old and new) brought up to full strength. So as in the case of the cavalry, inadequate numbers and a strategic dispersal that made little sense for waging internal war were to handicap the royal army in its struggle with the Huguenots. Furthermore, creating new companies, bringing all companies up to strength, amalgamating scattered companies into regiments, and getting those regiments to the point of assembly of the field army were processes not only made more difficult by peacetime dispositions, but impossible to hide from the crown's internal enemies. To depart from traditional dispositions was to risk war with the Huguenots. The outbreak of the Second and Third wars, in fact, can be directly traced to the two times that the crown tried to break this cycle—by the importation in 1567 of 6,000 Swiss and an increase in the numbers of French infantry, ostensibly to shield the eastern border from the duke of Alva's march to the Low Countries, and by the refusal of the crown in 1568 to disband most of the infantry and cavalry kept under arms after the Peace of Longjumeau under the pretext of escorting the German mercenaries of both sides out of the kingdom.

DIFFICULTIES OF MOBILIZATION

On the outbreak of war the crown had to mobilize its forces, a task immediately complicated and lengthened by the need to get large numbers of troops from the periphery of the country to the main army, and to raise foreign troops and get them into France.[11] The Second Civil War, which broke out late in September 1567 with the Huguenot attempt to seize Charles IX at Meaux, provides a paradigmatic example of the difficulties inherent in mobilization. Only the fortuitous intervention of the 6,000 Swiss (hired to flank the duke of Alva's march to Flanders) who happened to be encamped at nearby Château-Thierry enabled the king to escape to Paris.[12] Summons for help promptly went out, but with the capital threatened by a Protestant blockade, it took six weeks to amass an army of at most 25,000 men, about half of whom were drawn or raised from the north and northeast of the kingdom; the Swiss and a large but militarily dubious Paris militia made up the other half. It was this army that the constable, under intense pressure from the Parisians, led to battle against the Protestants (who were outnumbered seven or eight to one) outside the gates of Saint Denis on 10 November 1567.

The force that defeated the Protestants at Saint Denis, however, was still woefully inadequate for the tasks it faced. Though a battery of cannon had been deployed at the battle, a proper field artillery train still had to be put together. This meant conscripting or hiring hundreds of teamsters with their horses and carts and calling for more than 2,000 pioneers (laborers) from the surrounding *élections*. The first call for these forces went out in October, but it was not until mid-December that all were finally assembled.[13] The cavalry had performed so poorly at the battle that some 50-odd new companies of gendarmes were ordered to be raised, some of which were still understrength at the end of December. Finally, the infantry that had fought at Saint Denis was not numerous enough (once the militia was removed) to support a main field army as well as provide for garrisons around Paris and along the route of the army's march.

The crown, of course, had never intended its full military effort to depend primarily on the resources of only part of the kingdom, in this instance northern France. In all the civil wars gendarme companies had to be siphoned off from all parts of the country and new infantry and light cavalry formations raised in the provinces and sent to the main army. All this, however, took time, and delay often enabled the Protestants to seize the military initiative. In 1567, of course, they mounted a blockade of Paris, but in all the early wars vigorous action was hampered by the necessity of waiting for columns from the periphery (west and south in 1567) to wend their way, or, as was often the case, fight their way, to the main army.

It was also necessary to send abroad for troops. Although their numbers varied, in all the civil wars foreign troops constituted an important part of the royal army (like the Swiss in 1567, who if not already on the spot would have been sent for). But procuring these reinforcements often meant involved and protracted negotiations, long approach marches through difficult country, and as a result, unpredictable delays in arrival. The fact that during the Second War the crown ended up raising about 50,000 French troops for the main army raises the question why these foreign troops were needed at all. The answer, of course, is that the crown's dependence on reinforcements from outside the country was made unavoidable by the dearth of experienced formations at home. A proper field army capable of holding its own in battle with the Protestants required experienced troops. When mobilization began, the experienced pool of French infantry was quickly exhausted (or signed up by the Protestants), and most of the newly raised companies of foot were initially only capable of being trusted with secondary duties like garrisoning towns.[14] For decades the crown had depended, as it would in all of the early wars, on the Swiss cantons for infantry to anchor its line of battle. There was also a limit to the number of heavy cavalry that could be raised on short notice. And when the Protestants, as they did in five of the first six wars, hired large numbers of German cavalry, the crown was likewise forced to do so. So while the recruitment of new companies of horse and foot in the provinces provided additional numbers, it was only from outside the kingdom that large numbers of seasoned or specialized troops could be obtained, despite the delays this inevitably entailed.

At the height of the Second War, the royal army carried on its rolls (i.e., had raised or ordered hired) more than 70,000 troops for the operations of the main field armies around Paris and Champagne. One force, led by the duke of Anjou, moved into Champagne from Paris while a second force under the duke of Aumale was placed on the frontier and a third army led by the duke of Nevers marched northward through Burgundy to join them.

Table 4. The royal army during the Second War of Religion: origins and strength

A. *Major formations in the royal army in December/January, 1567–68*

Formation	Nationality	Companies	Strength	
FOOT				
Swiss, 1st levy	Swiss	20	6,000	
Brissac	French	44	8,969	
Strossi	French	25	4,652	
Martinengo	French	11	2,227	
Foissy	French	6	1,200	
Cerny	French	5	(1,000)	
Monluc	Gascons	12	3,212	
Tilladet	Gascons	10	2,284	
Martigues	Bretons	9	2,100	
Aumale, legionnaires	Champagne	20	(3,600)	
Swiss, 2d levy	Swiss	13	4,000	
Nevers, Piedmont	French	5	900	
Nevers	Italian	21	1,885	
Garrisons Paris region	French	(7)	1,315	
Foot total:		208	43,344	(60%)
HORSE				
Anjou, gendarmes	French	87	(7,830)	
Anjou, *chevaux-légers*	French	15	1,315	
Anjou, *arq. à cheval*	Fr., Gascon	24	1,867	
Martigues, light horse	Breton	9	760	
Arembourg, gendarmes	Flemish	8	1,600	
Nevers/Aumale, gends.	French	34	(3,060)	
Savoyard *chev.-légers*	Savoyard	(15)	1,200	
Baden, *chev.-légers*	German	1	200	
Duke of Saxony, reiters	German	8	2,500	
Rhinegrave/*bassompierre*, reiters	German	11	3,300	
Reiffenberg, reiters	German	9	2,700	
Horse total:		221	26,332	(36%)
ARTILLERY TRAIN				
Teamsters	French	—	275	
Pioneers/Carpenters	French	—	2,100	
Artillerymen	French	—	337	
Artillery train total:		—	2,712	(4%)
Grand total:		429	72,388	(100%)

(continued)

B. *French and foreign components of the royal army by arm, 1567–68*

Arm	French		Foreign		Combined	
	No.	%	No.	%	No.	%
Foot	30,959	71	12,385	29	43,344	100
Horse	14,832	56	11,500	44	26,332	100
Artillery	2,712	100	—	—	2,712	100
Combined	48,503	67	23,885	33	72,388	100

Sources: The most important *états* for the forces with Anjou, Aumale, and Nevers are: for December 1567, BN, MSS fr. 4553, fols. 95–100 (artillery), 101 and 104–7 (summaries of all categories), 112–14 (staff and specialists); for January 1568, ibid., 17870, fol. 294, and PRO/SP 70/96, fols. 114–15, 119–20. There are separate *états* for Martigues's Bretons for November through January, BN, MSS fr. 3898, fols. 227–36, and for the forces with Nevers, ibid., 3240, fols. 70–71, and 4553, fols. 89–90. A preliminary list of Savoyard cavalry is PRO/SP 70/94, fol. 77. There are marching and lodging orders for 6 December in BN, MSS fr. 15543, fols. 60–61, and for an undated time (though clearly later in the campaign in January) in PRO/SP 70/96, fols. 231–32. See also Blaise de Monluc's description of the mobilization of the Gascon forces in *Commentaires de Blaise de Monluc,* ed. Paul Corteault (Paris, 1925), 3:39–47. Figures in parentheses are estimates computed from the number of companies or from strength.

Section *A* of table 4 shows the various formations carried on the army's rolls in December and January of 1567–68. The dependence on troops from the periphery and abroad explains the length of time needed to mobilize. At least a third of the French infantry and cavalry came with reinforcing columns from Brittany and Guyenne or the force led by Nevers, which had begun its journey in French Piedmont. Yet another third of the units on the army rolls (section *B* of table 3) originated outside France—from Flanders, Savoy, Germany, Switzerland, and Italy (including 44 percent of the cavalry). With the exception of the first levy of Swiss, already on the spot, none of these domestic and foreign forces, amounting to more than half of the troops on the army rolls, managed to join the main army before the battle of Saint Denis. Some, as we shall see, arrived too late to be of any operational use at all. And their staggered arrival caused crucial delays and hesitations during the campaign in Champagne.

The first to arrive, in late November, as figure 1 indicates, were a Breton contingent under Martigues and Flemish gendarmes sent by the duke of

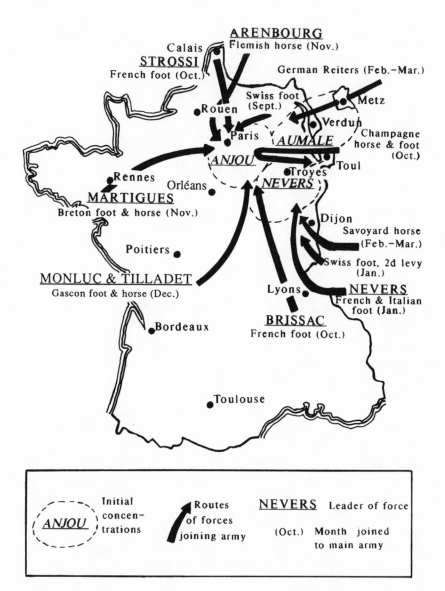

Figure 1. Mobilization of the royal army during the Second Civil War, 1567–1568

Alva. Even with these additions the court was unwilling to authorize a vigorous pursuit of the Huguenot army, which was retreating eastward toward the frontier to join its own large force of mercenary German horse and foot. Great stock was instead put in the anticipated arrival of a large Gascon contingent. But the Gascons fought a pitched battle on their way north and did not reach the area of Montargis until mid-December. The Italian and French troops from Piedmont, led by the duke of Nevers, to whom were joined a second levy of 4,000 Swiss, arrived near Saint Dizier only in early January, after having successfully besieged Macon at the beginning of December. At Saint Dizier they joined the main army, led nominally by the duke of Anjou, which had ineffectually trailed the Protestant army from the time it left Paris until it escaped unharmed into Lorraine, and a sizable force of foot and horse led by Aumale, which had been equally ineffective in preventing the arrival of the Protestants' German mercenaries.[15]

By mid-January, then, the combined royal forces probably amounted to about 60,000 troops, including those detached for garrison duty. This was not deemed sufficient to do battle with the Huguenots and their foreign cavalry until the royal army itself had been reinforced by some 8,500 German cavalry, who were expected at any time. Unfortunately for the crown, none of its Germans arrived in Champagne until late February and some only after the cessation of hostilities in March.[16] A contingent of light horse sent by the duke of Savoy also arrived near Paris only in February, some five months after it had been promised. Lacking cavalry, the army so laboriously and slowly assembled near Saint Dizier by January 1568, instead of fighting, was split up to flank the Huguenots as they marched practically unmolested across France to undertake a siege of the town of Chartres in the center of the country. The bulk of the army under Anjou, wracked by illness and exhaustion, stumbled back into Paris in late February and early March. Unable or unwilling to bring the Protestants to battle, yet equally unable to support what may have been the largest royal field army raised during the wars, the crown concluded the Peace of Longjumeau in March 1568.

From beginning to end the Second War lasted some six months. At the end of the war the army's mobilization was still not complete. The crown's dependence on foreign troops and forces from the periphery of the kingdom forced it into inaction at inopportune times and made concentration of its forces a lengthy and, finally, impossible task. Although the situation of the Second War was not duplicated in any of the other early wars, the types of structural impediments and difficulties the crown encountered in mobilizing its forces were a continuous factor in all of them. In 1562, for example, while the royal army awaited reinforcements at Paris, the Protestants seized Orléans and many other major cities, like Rouen and Lyons. As a result, royal forces initially had to be split up to recover places, a dispersal that allowed the Protestants to gather a strong army at Orléans and actually menace the walls of Paris. In the Fourth War, precipitated by the Saint Bartholomew's Day massacre in 1572, which eliminated much of the general staff and many of the cadres of the Huguenot army, the crown lost almost half a year (including waiting for Swiss reinforcements) before it completed the investment of La Rochelle, allowing that city time to fortify itself sufficiently to withstand a terrible siege in the spring and summer of 1573.

In summary, then, put at a disadvantage by the small size and strategic dispersal of its standing forces, the crown was always forced in raising a proper field army to depend on the arrival of sizable forces from all over the kingdom and outside it. This process took months and allowed the Protestants to seize the initiative. The slowness of this process and its inherent uncertainty added yet another layer of difficulty to the crown's military struggle with the Huguenots.

THE LARGE-SCALE NATURE OF THE CONFLICT

France was, by sixteenth-century standards, a vast country.[17] To march troops unopposed from Calais to Provence took six weeks, and from Gascony to Paris, four weeks. The terrain was often difficult or mountainous, cut up by numerous rivers with few crossings suitable for the movement of large numbers of soldiers and animals. The problems of moving and supplying troops were exacerbated by the fact that water communications across the interior of the country were not easy to use or were nonexistent. The borders of the country ran for hundreds of miles and either were relatively open or stretched over terrain that made it easy for a fast-moving force to elude pursuit. The military struggle, moreover, was spread out over the whole country rather than conveniently concentrated in a single accessible region. At one point or another every part of the country, and usually several regions simultaneously, were in revolt. The geographic focus of campaigns was thus constantly shifting in an unpredictable manner from one part of the country to another, a factor that greatly complicated campaigning.

The enormous military efforts of the Valois in the first half of the century had gone far toward routinizing the waging of war by the French army at or across the frontiers. During its foreign wars the crown rarely had to fight on more than two fronts simultaneously. And whether the fighting was in Lorraine, Picardy, Savoy, or Piedmont, well-established lines of advance and supply had been developed to control and support the movement of forces toward whichever front the fighting was on. The key to the efficient disposition of forces, of course, was that the interior of the country was free of fighting. Encouraging or coercing its subjects to cooperate in supplying and lodging troops was not an easy task, but at least the crown did not have to wage a chronic internal war on them.

The Wars of Religion changed all that. The Huguenots managed to seize towns and cities in many parts of the country as well as raise a large and dangerous field army. They had the advantage over previous rebellions, like the anti-gabelle revolts of the 1540s, of controlling the resources and skills of a number of urban centers, the adherence of large numbers of nobility, and the bankrolls of foreign governments. As a result, the field armies produced by the Huguenots were, in leadership, quality of troops (cavalry and foreign mercenaries), morale, and sometimes even numbers, not hopelessly mismatched against the royal army.[18] Before there was ever a "state within the state" problem during the wars there was a "royal-like army against royal army" problem.

All of these factors combined to confront the royal government during the early wars with perplexing military choices. On the one hand, the crown was institutionally and morally bound to protect its territory and loyal citizenry from attack and occupation by the Huguenots. On the other hand, the crown had to put together a powerful enough army not only to defend the territory it held and reconquer what it had lost, but also to defeat the Protestant army in the field. There was always the temptation and sometimes the duty to pursue multiple objectives. Towns had to be garrisoned and provincial lieutenants allowed to raise substantial forces of their own. The strategic situation sometimes mandated the raising of more than one main army. The consequences of defeat in battle, moreover, were quite sobering. The means to defend the kingdom could be irredeemably lost in a single afternoon of fighting. This meant that very large numbers of troops were needed to meet both local and central contingencies.

For example, in the Second War (1567–68), besides about 70,000 troops raised for the campaign against the Huguenots in the northeast, the garrisons of Picardy, Metz, and Lyons were maintained or even increased. The companies of foot that had been brought to Champagne by Nevers were replaced in Piedmont by newly raised Italian units. At the same time operations in the south and west continued: Blaise de Monluc, for example, was ordered to undertake a full-scale siege of La Rochelle in January of 1568.[19] Though it is impossible to be precise, it seems probable that by January and February of 1568 the crown had authorized the raising of more than 100,000 troops and may have had near that number actually under arms. This was a military effort on a scale worthy of the Army of Flanders in its fight against the Dutch Revolt.[20] And though the size of the army concentrated in Champagne in early 1568 was never surpassed in any of the other early wars, during the Third War (1568–69) a larger total was probably raised overall: first in two large main field armies under Anjou in Poitou-Angoumois and Aumale in Champagne and Burgundy and then in a third army led by Marshal Cossé that had to be raised practically from scratch in 1570, after the combined forces of Anjou and Aumale had been thrown away in the winter sieges undertaken after the royal victory of Moncontour.[21] During the Fourth War, the crown put most of its fast-diminishing resources into the siege of La Rochelle, but serious sieges of Sancerre and Montauban were also mounted.[22]

Some of the difficulties inherent in such a large-scale struggle can be demonstrated by the distances over which men, equipment, and munitions had to be brought in order to mount key operations. Take, for example, the provision of artillery and ammunition for the siege of La Rochelle in 1573. Though the crown possessed hundreds of gun tubes in its various fortresses and arsenals, very few of them were ever actually in any condition to serve. Barrels were burst, ventholes enlarged, carriages and wheels rotted, cables and harnesses old and worn out.[23] For the siege of La Rochelle, the crown managed by a tremendous effort to collect two score or so serviceable guns, mostly from the Arsenal in Paris and other points north. These guns had to be transported laboriously to La Rochelle, using water transportation as much as possible. Several thousand horses and pioneers also had to be mobilized, from as far north as the Pays de Caux, to move the guns and their supplies once they were on land, and hundreds of artillery personnel assembled.[24] But it was the provisioning of the siege train with powder and shot that shows most clearly how it required the resources of practically the entire kingdom to mount a single serious siege.

An *état* of the location of powder reserves drawn up during the planning for the siege illustrates the problem. As is indicated in section *A* of table 5 and the companion figure, 2*A*, twelve localities listed in the *état* contained a total of 385,096 livres (by weight) of large and medium grain powder.

Table 5. Artillery munitions for the siege of La Rochelle, 1573

A. Locations of powder reserves, 1572–73

Place	Grain (in livres, by weight)		Total	%
	Large	Medium		
Paris and hôtel de ville	154,600	23,600	178,200	46.3
Picardy and Normandy				
Amiens	80,000		80,000	20.8
Abbeville	30,000		30,000	7.8
Péronne	12,000		12,000	3.1
Rouen	20,000		20,000	5.2
Loire River				
Tours	10,597	2,299	12,896	3.3
Chinon	2,400	100	2,500	.6
Angers	9,000	1,000	10,000	2.6
Poitou-Saintonge-Angoumois				
Niort	6,600	1,200	7,800	2.0
St.-Jean d'Angély	4,500	300	4,800	1.2
Poitiers	18,800	1,600	20,400	5.3
Angoulême	6,400	100	6,500	1.7
Totals:	354,897	30,199	385,096	99.9

B. Origins of shot at La Rochelle, 1573

Place	Number of balls	%
Paris	660	3.3
Orléans	9,856	49.4
Poitiers	662	3.3
Niort	455	2.3
Melle	240	1.2
St.-Jean d'Angély	1,298	6.5
Angoulême	95	.5
Monberon forges	6,082	30.5
Galleys	600	3.0
Totals:	19,948	100

Source: BN, MSS fr. 3240, fols. 54, 76–78.

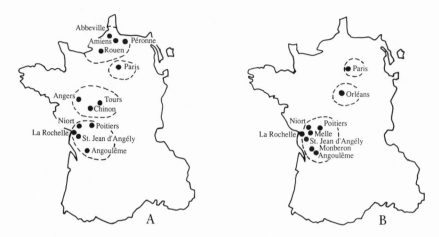

Figure 2. Artillery munitions for the siege of La Rochelle, 1573: A, locations of powder; B, origins of shot

Paris and its hôtel de ville were by far the richest source for powder in the kingdom—178,200 livres, or 46.3 percent of the total. Next in importance were several places in Picardy and the Norman capital of Rouen, which together contained 36.9 percent of reserves. Towns along the Loire had only 6.5 percent of the total. The powder available in the Poitou-Saintonge-Angoumois region closest to La Rochelle (Poitiers, Niort, Saint-Jean d'Angély, and Angoulême) amounted to only 39,500 livres, or 10.2 percent of reserves. Eighty-three percent, in other words, of all available powder reserves was located on or north of the Seine. To prosecute the siege meant gathering more than 350,000 livres of powder from a number of places hundreds of miles away from the site of the siege.

The provision of shot for the siege, as is indicated by section B of table 5 and its companion, figure 2B, was almost as complicated. An inventory of the points of origin of cannonballs in depot at La Rochelle in May 1573 shows that more than half of the 19,948 balls originated as far away as Paris and Orléans (52.7 percent). Another 30.5 percent of the shot was provided by the conveniently located Monberon forges in Angoumois. But a number of other towns in the region managed to provide only about one-fifth of the total. Local resources, therefore, hardly sufficed for a single serious military operation at any distance from Paris. To fight a major siege away from the Paris region required tapping the resources of widely dispersed places hundreds of miles from the scene of action.

The scale of the conflict, in other words, posed tremendous military difficulties. The crown did make great efforts to mobilize forces large enough to enable it to attend to its many military problems. But even when its resources were stretched to the limit there were never enough troops and munitions to meet all its obligations. Considerations of distance, supply, and security complicated campaigns and protracted the time needed to put plans into action. Even worse, at the enormous scale of fighting, the crown simply could not keep its armies in the field for more than a very short time.

INABILITY TO MAINTAIN ARMIES IN THE FIELD

Having overcome its initial unpreparedness and waited the time necessary to gather its forces in numbers large enough for the scale of military problems it faced, the crown was finally in a position in each war to begin its campaign against the Huguenots. At fully mobilized strength the royal army was a formidable military force that even under the trying conditions of the civil wars enjoyed success in most of the battles it fought and many of the sieges in which it engaged.[25] Whether successful or not, however, the forces the crown had assembled and put into motion inexorably began to melt away after only a few months in the field. Normal levels of casualties, sickness, and desertion during the period seem to have steadily reduced the strength of military formations from 2 to 4 percent per month.[26] In addition, battle or siege casualties, or epidemic illness, could result in spectacular levels of attrition. There were also voluntary short-term reductions in strength to be endured: large infantry formations released to recruit themselves back up to strength and garrisons left behind on the march often lessened the strength of the main army. Since horses rapidly wore out, large numbers of cavalrymen had to be periodically released to refresh themselves and their mounts in their home territories. Continual recruiting, the creation of even more new companies, and additional hirings of foreign mercenaries were all used to keep strength from falling. Nevertheless, by the end of a campaign many units were down to half strength or less and armies became shadows of their former selves.

The greatest danger, as a campaign went on, however, was not that an army would disappear, but rather that it would turn into an undisciplined mob, disobeying orders, leaving the camps, and causing disorder everywhere it passed, preying on friend and foe alike. In France during the early wars, the well-organized, large-scale, and formalized strikes by desperate troops so characteristic of the Army of Flanders do not seem to have occurred.[27] But disorder, desertion, and ill-discipline often stalked the royal army.

Most disturbances grew out of similar circumstances: lack of pay and lack of food, and the two were closely related.[28] Soldiers were expected to purchase their own food from the families on whom they were quartered, staging depots set up outside towns, or independent entrepreneurs who contracted to provide standard rations (bread, wine, and beef) at fixed prices. The main army with its camp followers and animals could consume a remarkable amount of food in a short time, more than any urban center in the country except Paris. During the four-week siege of Chartres in February and March of 1568, for example, twenty-five companies of royal troops (only slightly more than 4,000 men) thrown into the city immediately before it was invested by the Huguenots managed to consume 43,515 livres' worth of rations, including over half a million loaves of bread.[29] Chartres was the exception: a well-stocked city in the midst of a region of plenty. The army usually had to stay on the move, for it could strip most areas clean in a matter of days or weeks. In sterile countryside or rough terrain, there was always a real danger that an army could literally starve to death. When sedentary operations were required, the crown had to hire suppliers to deliver enormous amounts of food drawn from entire regions or risk seeing its army vanish. A contract with merchants from Niort for the camp at La Rochelle signed in late 1572, for example, called for the *concessionaire* to furnish *every day,* for a period of six months, 30,000 twelve-ounce loaves of bread, 10,800 *pintes* of wine, and 20,000 livres of beef.[30]

But when pay failed, as it almost always did, or credit from officers or providers dried up, or the crown could not pay its suppliers, only plunder and extortion, or desertion, remained as ways for soldiers to keep themselves alive.[31] Toward the end of a campaign filled with incessant marching often under the most bitter conditions, or the misery of the siege trenches, lack of pay and consequent lack of food (and other necessities, like shoes and clothes) rapidly eroded the army's effectiveness.

The key to maintaining an army in the field, then, was a continual flow of money. Yet pay almost always started failing even before mobilization was complete. Foreign mercenaries were then apt to refuse to march or to fight, and French troops simply disappeared into the countryside. Money was the Achilles heel of the French monarchy, and the cost of maintaining an army on a wartime basis was staggering. Throughout the Wars of Religion the crown simply could not afford to pay the forces it had assembled for more than a few months at a time.

Even in peacetime the cost of the small standing army was formidable. Table 6, drawn from a number of different sources, shows the normal yearly military budget during the 1560s and early 1570s. Total annual costs were in the range of about 4.6 million livres, more than three-quarters of which was spent on the peacetime gendarmerie and infantry companies described in the first section of this essay. Other major expenses were for fortifications and an annual pension for the Swiss cantons. The royal guards, *mortepayes, marine de Ponant,* and galley fleet together accounted for less than 10 percent of the total. The artillery, including procurement of munitions, salaries, and expenditure on the Arsenal in Paris, accounted for a miniscule 3.3 percent of peacetime spending. Even in peacetime, then, around 90 percent of the military budget was spent on salaries rather than capital improvements, equipment, and supplies. This accentuates the overwhelmingly labor-intensive rather than technical or material nature of early modern armies.

It is helpful to remember that during this same period the gross annual revenues of the crown fluctuated between 10 and 13 million livres. An *état* of 1567 analyzed by Roger Doucet, for example, showed revenues of 10,216,194 livres and military expenditures of 4,341,093 livres.[32] Around 40 percent, then, of yearly revenues were normally devoted to current military expenses. This was the basic cost of the peacetime royal army. The cost of this peacetime establishment, of course, hardly corresponded to the true burden on the finances of the monarchy represented by past wars. In 1560 the royal debt, an inheritance of the Hapsburg-Valois Wars, was estimated to be in the neighborhood of 40 million livres. By 1576, the royal debt had climbed to 100 million livres—the difference was almost entirely the legacy of the first five Wars of Religion.[33] Even in a "normal" year, much of the 10–13 million livres collected by the crown had to be spent on the interest and principal repayments of loans specifically floated to finance earlier wars or to try to reduce accumulated arrears in normal military expenditures.

The basic reason why the crown found it impossible to maintain its military effort against the Huguenots can be found in table 7, which estimates the monthly cost of the royal army in December and January of 1567–68. Total charges for the army during the month of December alone came to almost 1 million livres, or almost triple the monthly cost of the ordinary

Table 6. Annual cost of the peacetime royal army, ca. 1560–1574

Type of expense	Amount (livres)	%
Gendarmes	2,300,000	49.6
Infantry	1,247,000	26.9
Artillery	152,000	3.3
Subtotal:	3,699,000	79.8
Royal guards	93,000	2.0
Mortepayes	93,000	2.0
Fortifications	350,000	7.6
Galleys	181,000	3.9
Marine de Ponant	19,000	.4
Swiss pension	200,000	4.3
Subtotal:	936,000	20.2
Total:	4,635,000	100

Sources: Two state budgets from the period were used: that of 1567, in Roger Doucet, *L'état de finances de 1567* (Paris, 1929), and that of 1574, BN, MSS fr. 17870, fols. 278–85. Philip Dur, "Constitutional Rights and Taxation in the Reign of Henry III" (Ph.D. diss., Harvard University, 1941), also contains some useful *états*. Wherever possible summary amounts in the state budgets were compared to individual department budgets, and in some cases the department budgets themselves were used: For example, for the infantry in 1572, the *états* in BN, MSS fr. 3193, fols. 203–10 (for the south), 211–25 (for the north); for the *marine de Ponant* in 1574, ibid., 17870, fols. 287–89; for *mortepayes* in 1571, ibid., fols. 284–85; for galleys in 1560, ibid., 3898, fols. 237–38. For examples of gendarmerie budgets see, for 1559, ibid., 3150, fols. 39–50; for 1560, ibid., 21543, fols. 28–47; for 1567, ibid., 4552, fols. 18–26; for 1574, ibid., 3193, fols. 184–93. From year to year there were small fluctuations in the categories of expenses, but over the whole period, as far as I have been able to determine, annual "normal" military expenses fluctuated by only about plus or minus 5 percent from the yearly total given here.

Table 7. Monthly costs of the royal army,
December 1567 and January 1568

Type of expense	Amount (livres)
DECEMBER	
Gendarmes	(337,396)
French light cavalry	76,794
French infantry	302,517
Foreign infantry	142,265
Artillery train	42,843
Etats and guard	28,454
Vivres	26,610
Miscellaneous	14,913
Treasury costs	10,000
December total:	981,792
ADDITIONS IN JANUARY	
German cavalry	314,000
Foreign light cavalry	32,500 .
Added January expenses:	346,500
January total:	1,328,292

Sources: These expenses have had to be compiled from
a number of sources. See especially the *état abrégé* of
December 1567, BN, MSS fr. 4553, fol. 101. Other *états*
in ibid. are artillery, fols. 95–100, *vivres,* fol. 102, and
staff, fols. 112–14. Nevers and Aumale are included with
Anjou's *états.* There is a separate *état* for Martigues's
Bretons, who were paid through January by the Estates
of Brittany, ibid., 3898, fols. 227–36. Monluc's Gascons
were paid by the province for their first month but were
then on the king's payroll. The Flemish gendarmes, who
were being paid by Spain, are not counted. The expense
of the French gendarmerie, which was paid by the quarter, is estimated for a force level of 143 companies pro-
rated for one month. For the January figures for the army,
see the *abrégé,* ibid., 17870, fol. 294; and PRO/SP 70/96,
fols. 114–15, 119–20.

military budget. But these expenses were increased by more than an additional 300,000 livres in January 1568, when pay for German mercenary cavalry and Savoyard light cavalry were added to the war's cost. Expenses in January therefore were running around 1,328,000 livres per month, or an annual rate of almost 16 million livres. Even this enormous sum does not represent total expenses: the cost of remaining garrisons in Picardy, Metz, Lyons, Piedmont, and all infantry and light cavalry companies raised for operations outside the northeast are not included (a guess of at least another 100,000 livres per month for those expenses would probably be conservative), nor are such regular items as fortifications and the galleys.

The level to which royal military expenditures mounted in January 1568 implied an annual level of spending of about 18 million livres, or much more than the whole of royal revenues (more than half of which were normally committed to nonmilitary expenses). Revenues could never be raised high enough (especially since much of the country escaped from taxes during civil disorder) even to begin to cover such large wartime obligations. As a short-term measure, of course, the government could adopt all kinds of fiscal expedients. Mostly, however, under Catherine de Medici's influence, the government borrowed money from anyone it could persuade or coerce, often at ruinous interest rates. During the Second War, for example, enough was raised and borrowed to pay the field army for the first two or three months in the field—that is, enough to get it assembled. But by February 1568, bankruptcy stared the government in the face. Thus, financial problems dictated military policy, and this, the shortest of the wars, was brought to a negotiated end in March of the same year.[34]

Such ruinous levels of expenditure were the norm rather than the exception during the wars. During the Fourth War, for example, the armies assembled for the sieges of La Rochelle, Sancerre, and other places also were well on their way to costing a million livres per month.[35] Such financial burdens could only be sustained for a few months or, in the Third War, heroically, for a single year. In all the wars, the crown ran out of money before it could achieve any type of decisive military decision over the Huguenots. Once the money ran out it was only a short time before the royal armies lost their effectiveness and began to disintegrate. At that point the crown had no choice but to enter into premature, and usually unfavorable, peace negotiations. The cost of fighting had outrun both the ability and the will of the monarchy to sustain its military effort.

THE NATURE OF DEMOBILIZATION

Once peace was declared the army had to be demobilized both for financial reasons and to reassure the Huguenots that the crown was serious about the peace. Foreign mercenaries posed special problems because the sums of money that they frequently were owed were impossible to raise. Because they were both numerous and unified—the German mercenaries were considered especially dangerous—priority had to be given to getting them out of the country as soon as possible. Usually some combination of a cash down payment and letters of credit drawn on foreign financial centers persuaded them to leave, but it was always a scramble to pay them at the end of each war because their contracts specified that they would continue to be paid until they had returned home.[36]

French troops were often simply dismissed to make their way home however they could. The gendarme companies would be promised a general muster within a few months as they were sent back to their home provinces, at which time extra companies were dismissed and remaining companies reduced in strength.[37] The infantry and light cavalry companies raised at the beginning of the war were more often simply broken, whereas the infantry companies that had existed before the war were reduced in strength and again scattered in garrisons.[38] All need for suppliers, pioneers, and horses for the artillery train ended immediately with the peace. Demobilized soldiers caused disorders, looting and pillaging their way home, often in bands too strong for local officials to handle. The small number of commissars and military police (who also more than likely had not been paid) were, of course, helpless once the army had broken into hundreds of little bands.

Demobilization, then, was quite simply a product of exhaustion and neglect rather than planning. The same problems repeated themselves at the end of each war. The circumstances of demobilization, however, are less important than its result for our understanding of the cycle of events that underlay all the wars and give them what little continuity they possessed. The simple fact was that wars were so expensive that the crown had to demobilize right back to the status quo antebellum—the unpreparedness that had marked its armed forces before each war.

And so the cycle remained ready to repeat itself, with each of the five factors discussed so far developing sequentially out of the preceding factors and interconnecting with them in a fashion that made the chances of a clear and decisive military decision over the Huguenots impossible. Unpreparedness and small numbers contributed to the difficulties of a long mobilization process made even longer by the very scale of forces and military operations that were necessary. The scale of the conflict in its turn led to operational and logistical problems and above all financial problems that made a long-term maintenance of military effort impossible. The financial problems associated with scale and maintenance of effort in their turn led to chaotic demobilizations that left the army in the same state of unpreparedness that it had been in at the beginning of the cycle. Over time, moreover, this repeating cycle began to have an independent, long-term effect—the progressive exhaustion and debasement of army cadres—that increasingly contributed to the difficulty of achieving a military decision.

EFFECT OF CUMULATIVE CASUALTIES ON THE ARMY'S LEADERSHIP

Before 1576 there were only tentative signs of the deleterious effect of war casualties on the armed forces. France was a demographically robust country, after all, and at least at the beginning of each war recruiting soldiers does not seem to have been as big a problem as paying them, though the enthusiastic Catholic response of the first two wars faded quickly after the particularly grueling Third War. Even the crown's chronic financial problems did not fatally interfere with the raising of substantial numbers of soldiers. In a short-term sense, indeed, the problem was not that wars were too expensive but that they were not expensive enough. The crown always managed to scrape together enough money and men to put its armies in the field—but lacked the financial resources to maintain them there. Nevertheless, the royal army was in the field during half of the fourteen years between 1562 and 1576. And while we will never know precisely what total army casualties reached, it would not be surprising if they were approaching the six-figure level by 1576. The effect of cumulative casualties on the army's leadership, however, is the most important area in which an exhaustion of human resources and change of what can only be called moral and political horizons can with some certainty be assumed.

During the Wars of Religion leaders of all grades literally *led* their men, and though we do not have the kind of detailed casualty lists of later wars there is much evidence of an extremely high wastage of leaders. Table 8 presents two examples of high rates of infantry leadership casualties: one from the siege of Rouen in 1562 and the other from the siege of La Rochelle

Table 8. Casualty rates

A. *Casualties among officers and sergeants at the siege of Rouen, 1562*

Paper strength by rank	Number wounded	% of that rank
17 captains	8	47
17 lieutenants	3	18
17 ensigns	9	52
34 sergeants	18	53
85 all ranks	38	45

B. *Leader casualties at the siege of La Rochelle, 1573*

Individual outcome	Number	%
Unharmed	42	27.1
Wounded	47	30.3
Killed or died of wounds	66	42.6
Totals:	155	100

Sources: For Rouen, BN, MSS fr. 15877, fols. 347–49, which also contains fascinating information on types of wounds and the weapons that caused them; for La Rochelle, PRO/ SP 70/125, fols. 122–45. See also ibid., 70/127, fols. 225– 26; and Simon Goulart, *Mémoires de l'estat de France sous Charles IX* (Meidelbourg, 1578), 1:291–93, for other casualty lists. Brantôme claimed to have seen at La Rochelle a casualty list kept by Philippe Strossi, the colonel general of French infantry, which listed 266 officers killed. He estimated total royal casualties at the siege at 22,000 troops. Pierre de Bourdeille, seigneur de Brantôme, *Oeuvres complètes*, ed. Ludovic Ladanne (Paris, 1868), 4:90.

in 1573. In 1562, after Rouen had fallen to a siege by the royal army, the duke of Guise ordered a list made of the officers and sergeants of the seventeen French infantry companies at the siege who had been wounded. This list, intended to be used as a guide to distribution of combat bonuses, suggests a strikingly high casualty rate for officers and sergeants. Out of the seventeen companies' total maximum paper strength of 85 cadre, 38 had been wounded, or 45 percent of all officers and sergeants. But if we keep in mind the fact that Guise's list did not identify those officers who had been killed, and the seventeen companies were almost certainly not at full strength (since the campaign was already entering its eighth month), this 45 percent wounded rate can only be considered a *minimum* total casualty rate. If any appreciable number of officers and sergeants had been killed at the siege (which certainly seems to have been the case, though no exact numbers are known), the total casualty rate would have quickly climbed to more than half of the cadre.

Another glimpse of how high total casualties among cadre could climb can be gleaned from a list of prominent persons killed or wounded at the siege of La Rochelle in 1573. The list contains the names of 155 French leaders at the siege—great noblemen, regimental officers, and company captains. As the siege progressed, when officers on the list were wounded or killed, the anonymous compiler noted that fact next to their names. By the end of the siege, of the 155 men on the list, only 42, or 27.1 percent, had received no entry by their names—that is, had escaped injury (though 3 had been captured in sorties). Sixty-six men, or 42.6 percent of the total, were noted as killed in action, and 47 men, or 30.3 percent, were wounded, a total casualty rate within the leadership at the siege of 73 percent.

Such casualty rates among officers inevitably led, over time, to diminished effectiveness and war weariness among the army's leadership. The Rouen and La Rochelle examples, of course, are primarily examples of infantry officer casualties. Although it is impossible to discover the fate of all cavalry captains, comparisons of lists of gendarme captains at various times with the biographical data given in Vindry's *Etat-major* show, for example, that at least 21.4 percent of the 112 men who held captaincies during the 1562–63 period (the original cohort of gendarme captains, as it were) were killed in action or assassinated during the course of the wars.[39] Many others suffered crippling wounds or died of accidents or illnesses contracted in camp.

There are clear signs of exhaustion among cavalry captains by the time of the Fifth War, when gendarme captains often simply failed to show up at assembly points with their units. Henry III, for example, issued orders in August 1575 to assemble all gendarme companies, promising that they would be paid for the first quarter of that year. The promise that arrears would be made up apparently did not convince all captains to bring their companies to the assembly points. The earlier order had to be repeated in

Table 9. Chronological origins of gendarme
captaincies, 1564–1578

Made captain in:	Number of captains in:				
	1564	1571	1574	1576	1578
1559 or before	40	23	13	16	12
1560–64	51	34	29	31	29
1565–71		11	15	31	43
1572–74			11	15	16
1575–76				31	28
1577–78					43
Totals:	91	68	68	124	171

Sources: For the 1564 (1563), 1571, 1574, and 1576 gendarmes,
see the note to table 1. For 1578, BN, MSS fr. 21543, fols. 95–106.

October, and again in December, accompanied by complaints that many
companies ordered to the assembly points had still not arrived. A further
order issued in February 1576 repeated the same complaint.[40]

It may not be an exaggeration to claim that over the course of the first
five wars the leadership of the army had been decimated. The first casualties (to desertion) had been those noblemen who had converted to Protestantism, and this included some of the best officers in the army, including
Coligny, Andelot, and Condé. Then the casualties of battle and siege line
and the dangers generally present in such a fratricidal conflict began to
mount. By 1576 most of the great nobles who had led the army before the
civil wars were dead or retired. Antoine de Bourbon, the constable Montmorency, Guise, Aumale, Monluc, Tavannes, the Brissacs, Martigues—all
had departed from the scene. Even those of lesser rank were fast disap-
pearing. Table 9, for example, shows the chronological origin of gendarme
captaincies at various points of demobilization from 1564 to 1578 (the end
of the First War to the end of the Sixth War). As early as 1564, only 40 of 91
captains of gendarme companies (or 44 percent) had commanded companies in or before 1559. By 1574, in the aftermath of the Saint Bartholomew's
Day massacre and the Fourth War, the figure was only 13 of 68 captains
(19 percent), and in 1578 it was only 12 of 171 (7 percent). By 1578 a majority of gendarme captains had first become captains *after* the massacre.

At that time 93 percent of the heavy cavalry captains had never led their gendarme companies against a foreign foe—their military horizons had come to consist exclusively of the experience of fighting fellow Frenchmen.

By the late 1570s, then, a whole generation of officers had been initiated into command positions who knew little except an environment of an increasingly unsuccessful series of civil wars. The First and Third Wars, at least, had included some great victories. But the Fourth War ended with the frustrated siege of La Rochelle and the Fifth War with a combined Huguenot and German mercenary army encamped in the center of France dictating peace terms. Habits of bad behavior, ill-discipline, disobedience, and venality—the warlordism that was to plague national and local politics until the end of the civil wars—were already well under way. The officer corps for all practical purposes had been purged of elements who could remember a unified country and wars against foreign foes. In the late 1570s the royal army's officers, knowing for the most part nothing except increasingly aimless civil war, stood ready to contribute in even greater measure to the agonies France was to suffer during the 1580s and 1590s.

CONCLUSION

In 1576 France faced two more decades of civil war. Some aspects of the wars changed: As they continued after the mid-1570s they seem, at the local level, to have been fought without the confessional passion of earlier years, and at the national level, to have been primarily a product of the court intrigues of great nobles. Even the Catholic League uprisings of 1588–89, which reintroduced an element of religious passion at the local and provincial level, took on less the aspect of a crusade against Protestantism than that of a struggle between ultra-Catholic France and the crown for control of the royal succession and the kingdom.

The basic military problems facing the crown, however, did not change. The cycle of difficulties I have identified—unpreparedness, difficulties in mobilization, the scale of the conflict, the impossibility of maintaining forces in the field for long, and chaotic demobilization—continued, while exhaustion owing to the cumulative impact of chronic warfare deepened.

Such structural, strategic, and operational factors provide an underlying continuity to the wars that makes their overall indecisiveness comprehensible. Many of these factors, after all, also affected the Huguenot military efforts, and their construction of a "state within a state" was in many respects an attempt to overcome many of the same problems. As in most wars before modern times, a political solution that permitted exit from the cycle was needed, and in the end Henry IV's creative conversion and massive bribery played a more critical role than military victories in bringing the wars to an end.

That the Wars of Religion were militarily indecisive is, in retrospect, not surprising. Many of the problems that plagued the army during its campaigns had been prefigured in the Hapsburg-Valois Wars, which were often similarly militarily indecisive. At first glance many of the elements I have identified seem part and parcel of the changes that were leading to the Military Revolution: fairly large armies, widespread use of individual firearms and artillery, use of professional mercenaries, the introduction of more efficient fortifications, chronic or lengthy campaigns dominated more by sieges than battles, and tremendous levels of expenditure.[41] Yet in mid-sixteenth-century France these elements were not so much leading to military innovation as retarding it. They were problems rather than solutions. The standing army was still very small, the field armies were over-dependent on foreigners, and the state was not yet adequately organized to tap enough national resources to avoid the near complete dissolution of its armies after only a few months in the field.

We are, it seems, a long way from Louvois. Yet here is perhaps one of the most historically significant aspects of the Wars of Religion: not only were the difficulties inherent in the level of warfare practiced in France formidable, but warfare was not yet the technical and financial monopoly of the state. Perhaps the same may be said of the early Dutch Revolt and even the English Civil War. By recentering war inside the kingdom, the civil wars increased the difficulties the crown had to face and over time inexorably reduced its chance to fight an effective or decisive internal war. Military innovations of some magnitude were needed before solutions to the problems of the inadequate nature of existing standing armies, large-scale, long-term warfare, and fiscal and organizational inefficiency were to be found. In France internal war had the effect of postponing rather than abetting the most significant changes, which were eventually to solve the problems the Military Revolution posed. The Military Revolution required internal peace, and such peace would be found in France only after the Fronde. Only then would the seemingly insoluble problems of the cycle of military insufficiency be solved in a manner that simultaneously enabled France to dominate Europe militarily and made successful military defiance of the French monarchy by its own subjects an impossibility.

NOTES

1. Dates for the first five wars are: First, March 1562–March 1563; Second, September 1567–March 1568; Third, August 1568–August 1570; Fourth, August 1572–June 1573; and Fifth, February 1574–May 1576. There is really no adequate history of the wars, but James Westfall Thompson, *The Wars of Religion in France, 1559–1576* (New York, 1909), while outdated, is probably the best. Mack Holt of George Mason University is now writing an up-to-date history of the period of the wars. For the general history of France in the sixteenth century see J. H. M. Salmon, *Society in Crisis: France in the Sixteenth Century* (New York, 1975). The most convincing summary of developments during the period of the first five wars is the conclusion to Philip Benedict's *Rouen During the Wars of Religion* (New York, 1981), 233–50. For another view of the impact on France of the first two decades of the wars see James B. Wood, "The Impact of the Wars of Religion: A View of France in 1581," *Sixteenth Century Journal* 15, no. 2 (1984): 131–68.

2. For the peace treaties see N. M. Sutherland, *The Huguenot Struggle for Recognition* (New Haven, 1980).

3. The most useful introduction to the nature of the royal army on the eve of the wars is Ferdinand Lot, *Recherches sur les effectifs des armées françaises des Guerres d'Italie aux Guerres de Religion, 1494–1562* (Paris, 1962). On the artillery, see the useful article by Philippe Contamine, "Les industries de guerre dans la France de la Renaissance: L'exemple de l'artillerie," *Revue historique* 271 (1984): 249–80. John A. Lynn's "Tactical Evolution in the French Army, 1560–1660," *French Historical Studies* 14 (1985): 176–91, while interesting, is based too narrowly on secondary sources.

4. J. Russell Major, "The Renaissance Monarchy: A Contribution to the Periodization of History," *Emory University Quarterly* 13 (1957): 112–24.

5. The best guide to the literature on the Military Revolution is the work of Geoffrey Parker, especially *The Military Revolution: Military Innovation and the Rise of the West, 1500–1800* (Cambridge, 1988).

6. Scores of *états* and *départements* for the gendarmerie have survived. Lack of space precludes listing all of them in this essay or even distinguishing in a systematic way the different types of documents they represent. But for 1559 see BN, MSS fr. 3150, fols. 39–50; for 1564, Le Général Suzanne, *Histoire de la Cavalerie françoise* (Paris, 1874), 1:62–66; for 1571, Dépôt de la guerre (Service Historique de l'Armée de Terre, Château de Vincennes), *Ordonnances militaires*, vol. 10, no. 153 (vol. 10 is hereafter abbreviated simply as *OM*); for 1574, *OM*, no. 178, and for a little earlier in 1574, BN, MSS fr. 3193, fols. 184–93, which identifies companies that were to be reduced to partial pay.

7. For 1567 see the army's order of march, PRO/SP 70/96, fols. 231–32. For the roster of forces with Anjou in late 1568, BN, MSS fr. 17528, fols. 119–25 (misdated

but from internal evidence clearly from late 1568), supplemented by ibid., 3193, fols. 195–201.

8. BN, MSS fr. 3193, fols. 203–10 (for the south, quotation from 203r), 211–25 (for the north).

9. Only 75 of the 6,229 soldiers were cavalrymen. Some of the command and staff personnel drew pay as rankers as well as pay for their higher position. The number of supernumery captains was probably less than 100 (a handful appointed by the colonel general of infantry, 20 or so on the king's pension list, and a couple of score Italian captains appointed by the commander of French Piedmont)—it is impossible to be more exact.

10. BN, MSS fr. 3216, fols. 17–18, is an example of mobilization of troops in Picardy in the fall of 1567 or 1568 that shows the division of troops between garrison and main army.

11. For a good example of the concerns that mobilization entailed, see Antoine de Navarre's June 1562 memo to the queen mother, with her responses: ibid., 15877, fols. 84–85.

12. For a lively account of the attempted coup according to Michel de Castelnau, who claimed to have tried to warn the court beforehand, see *Les mémoires de Messire Michel de Castelnau, seigneur de Mauvissière*, 3d ed. (Brussels, 1731), 1:194–201.

13. See the detailed November 1567 *assignation* for the artillery, BN, MSS fr. 4554, fols. 9–14, which can be contrasted to that of the following December, ibid., 4553, fols. 95–100.

14. The soldiers' habit of joining whichever side could pay them is illustrated by a comment of the duke of Etampes during the First War. He had been ordered by the queen mother in July 1562, for economy reasons, to let go some of the soldiers he had assembled in Brittany. "Remonstrera aussi que," he explained, "licentiant ledict duc d'Estempes ses gens, il y a grand dangier qu'il s'affoibiera et renforcera ses ennemys, car telles gen suivant l'escu." A. Lublinskaya, *Documents pour servir à l'histoire des guerres civiles en France (1561–65)* (Moscow, 1962), 97.

15. The Second War's fall and winter campaign can be followed in some detail through the daybook of the duke of Anjou's council, which notes important events and decisions and abstracts dispatches sent and received by Anjou. The daybook begins in late November 1567, when the main army left Paris, and ends in early March 1568, when it regained Paris. The daily summaries, which are interspersed with copies of correspondence, are in BN, MSS fr. 15543, 15544, and 15545. Two other important sources for the Second War are *Lettres de Henri III, Roi de France*, ed. Michel François (Paris, 1959), 1:11–78; and *Lettres de Catherine de Médicis*, ed. Hector de la Ferrière (Paris, 1880), 3:59–140.

16. See Castelnau's description of the reception given him and the reiters of William of Saxony who arrived too late to be of any service, *Mémoires* 1:214–18.

17. The military problems posed by the civil wars in France can be profitably compared to those involved in the Dutch Revolt. For the Dutch Revolt, see Geoffrey Parker, *The Army of Flanders and the Spanish Road, 1567–1659* (Cambridge, 1972).

18. The Huguenot forces are as little studied as the royal army and deserve a history of their own. In the course of research for this essay I came across a number of useful *états* that could be used to reconstruct the composition of Huguenot forces—most in the PRO/SP series.

19. The detailed royal instructions to Monluc are in BN, MSS fr. 15544, fols. 187–88. This document is an interesting example of a proposed mobilization of forces from all over the west and southwest. For Monluc's description of the preparations for the siege see his *Commentaires de Blaise de Monluc,* ed. Paul Corteault (Paris, 1925), 3:68–82.

20. Between 1567 and 1665 the number of troops in the army of Flanders rarely exceeded 80,000 men. Parker, *Army of Flanders,* 28.

21. Anjou had ignored Tavannes's shrewd advice immediately after Moncontour: "Nous les avons bien frottez, ast'heure faictes la paix." Pierre de Bourdeille, seigneur de Brantôme, *Oeuvres complètes,* ed. Ludovic Ladanne (Paris, 1868), 4:50.

22. For Jean de Lery's eyewitness account of the siege of Sancerre, with its famous episodes of cannibalism, see the excellent edition and commentary of Geralde Nakam, *Au lendemain de la Saint Barthélemy: Guerre civile et famine: Histoire mémorable du Siège de Sancerre (1573) de Jean de Lery* (Paris, 1975).

23. Several inventories for arsenals from this period have survived. For Rouen in 1568–69, BN, MSS fr. 3217, fols. 50–55. Among many for Piedmont, the December 1573 inventory, ibid., 4554, fols. 112–17. For Marseilles in 1571, ibid., fols. 33–37. For Narbonne in 1572, C. Douais, "Les guerres de religion en Languedoc," *Annales du Midi* 4 (1892): 65–67, 331–42.

24. For the February 1573 roll of artillery personnel at La Rochelle, BN, MSS fr. 3240, fols. 86–88 (bread rations), 100–106 (payroll).

25. A mark of the royal army's success in battle is the quip reportedly made by the king of Navarre (later Henry IV) after his victory at the battle of Coutras in 1587, that from then on at least, no one would be able to say that the Huguenots had *never* won a battle (my emphasis). Garrett Mattingly, *The Armada* (Boston, 1959), 157.

26. See Parker, *Military Revolution,* 46–61.

27. Parker, *Army of Flanders,* 185–206.

28. As the count de Salm (the count Rheingrave), pleading with Catherine de Medici from the camp before Le Havre in June 1563 to have his men paid, expressed it: ". . . car le soldat ne peult vivre de l'air, et ordonner pour nostre payement. Car la ou la fain est et necessite, il advient desordre, le dommaige tumbera pour le service du roy et de vous, madame." Lublinskaya, *Documents,* 264.

29. "Etat des dépenses faires par la ville de Chartres, pendant les troubles et pendant le siège de ladite ville (ler Octobre 1567–18 Avril 1568)," ed. Lucien Merlet, *Bulletin historique et philologique du comité des travaux historiques et scientifiques*, 1840:394–438.

30. BN, MSS fr. 4554, fols. 102–4.

31. For an example of the endemic banditry war could lead to, see J. H. M. Salmon, "Peasant Revolt in Vivarais, 1575–1580," *French Historical Studies* 11 (1979–80): 1–28.

32. Roger Doucet, *L'état de finances de 1567* (Paris, 1929), 3–6; Martin Wolfe, *The Fiscal System of Renaissance France* (New Haven, 1972), 106, 205–6.

33. Doucet, *L'état*, 8, 10; Wolfe, *Fiscal System*, 113, 159.

34. See Wolfe, *Fiscal System*, chaps. 5–7, pp. 137–213.

35. BN, MSS fr. 4554, fols. 78–81, 92, 98–100. Also ibid., 15556, fols. 1–2.

36. For the efforts taken to pay and to get the German mercenaries of both sides out of the kingdom, see the extensive and interesting correspondence in ibid., 15608.

37. See the preamble statement in *OM*, no. 117, for an example of the crown's regrets and promises of pay.

38. The 1572 infantry *états*, again, showed only seventy-five light horse for the whole kingdom. Cf. notes 8 and 9 above.

39. Fleury Vindry, *Dictionnaire de l'état major françois au XVIe siècle* (Paris, 1901), 2 vols. Sources for the cohort of gendarme captains from 1562–63, including a few Protestants like Coligny and Condé, are PRO/SP 70/48, fols. 184–87; *OM*, no. 48; Lancelot la Popelinière, *L'histoire de France* (La Rochelle, 1581), vol. 1, fol. 349; A. Communay, "Les Gascons de l'armée francaise," *Revue de l'Agenais* 21 (1894): 384–86; and Lot, *Effectifs*, 190–91.

40. *OM*, nos. 199, 205, 206, 208, 212.

41. Parker, *Military Revolution*, passim.

2. The French Constitution Revised:

Representative Assemblies and Resistance

Right in the Sixteenth Century

SARAH HANLEY

In sixteenth-century France the scholars, legists, and political pamphleteers who were educated in the *mos gallicus* method of historical and legal research debated the origins of French institutions and French public law, or the ancient constitution.[1] During the religious wars, when the stakes were very high,[2] some of the antiwar *politiques* among them attempted to bridge the gaps that polarized the whole society. One anonymous *politique* writer produced in the erudite *Discours politiques des diverses puissances* (1574) a secular vision of a French polity that represented the interests of all citizens.[3] When the activist writer and publisher Simon Goulart read the *Discours politiques,* he applauded the good fortune that brought it to his attention and promptly published the treatise in his expanded edition of the *Mémoires de l'estat de France, sous Charles Neufiesme* (1578 and 1579).[4] Thoroughly educated in history and law and conversant with the tenets of civic humanism, the author of the *Discours politiques* linked the political platform of the *politiques* and the political theories of the *monarchomaques* and offered a revision of the French constitution fit for the temper of the times.[5] A reading of the text of the *Discours* in context thus casts light on the constitutional notions that competed for place during the last half of the sixteenth century.

The *Discours politiques* blends the Ciceronian notion of *communication,* or association, which holds human societies together, with the rhetoric of civic humanism, which stresses the uniqueness of the civic polity, and characterizes the French state as a *communion politique,* the only human association capable of uniting all persons for the common good.[6] In that polity all corporate bodies including religious ones are subordinated to the transcendant political state, so religious toleration by necessity prevails.[7] The tie that binds all persons in the *communion politique* is law, and kings are the intermediaries who must act as judges and priests of the law.[8] In tones that openly disdain the bleak Augustinian notion of a human body politic doomed to corruption and decay, the *Discours* promotes a human civic polity invested with infinite promise.

The *Discours* focuses on one polity, the state of France, which subscribes to an ancient constitution and stands on a bedrock of law. The constitutional precepts of juristic ideology (legal-hereditary succession, separation of public office from individual incumbents), which were dramatized in civic rituals by symbolic reference to "the king's two bodies" (the office is immortal; kings are not),[9] are restated by the *Discours* in more precise terms: the civic polity (or the state of France) over generations is immortal; its individual citizens are not. In time, therefore, the citizens of a state thus reproduced over time must maintain the state by following the active, not the contemplative, life; by heeding legists who practice law, not philosophers and theologians who merely speculate about it;[10] and by defending the French state as did the renowned patriot Brutus, who killed the tyrant Caesar to save the Roman republic.[11]

This juristic interpretation of the French constitution is supported by critical readings of Roman and canon law and classical texts, standard biblical citations, and references to Christian tradition.[12] The *Discours* makes ample use of Roman law precepts, including tutorship, not to commend unbridled political power but to develop constitutional restraints on such authority. The argument develops constitutional principles in three ways: first, by proposing the idea of a sovereign community defining the king's relationship to the community; second, by identifying a viable agency, or institution, to represent the community; and third, by designating legal procedures to depose a king-turned-tyrant from public office.

SOVEREIGN COMMUNITY

The *Discours politiques* locates sovereign authority in the whole community, which invests that authority in the king not as an individual but as an officeholder. In the long discussion about "public administration" and the nature of male officeholding,[13] familial metaphors underscore the distinction between public and private interests.

> The sovereign community (*le peuple*) is superior to him [the king], and the prince recognizes that [superiority] when he tenders the oath to the community, [swearing] to maintain its liberties and to guarantee it from oppression. . . . The king cannot exist without the people, but the people can exist without the king, who is the child of the country in respect to his [biological] generation and is made father of the country through his [public] office.[14]

By birth into the royal family, successors to kings are only candidates for the royal office; but by the legal assumption of office, they are actually created kings and remain forever beholden to the community.

Concentrating on the tenets of juristic ideology, the *Discours* makes a distinction between legal-hereditary succession and dynastic, or blood, succession. The royal office does not devolve from father to son by virtue of personal blood inheritance; it passes through a male lineage in accordance with French public law.[15] Referring to Roman law, the treatise argues that the principles of *saisine* and *prescription* protect the innocent son of a tyrant from being divested of the legal right to royal office.[16] But it also warns that neither kings nor their successors can allege those legal precepts to remain in office if they do not fulfill the charge for the public welfare (*utilité publique*).[17] The treatise defines the proper exercise of office in terms of tutorship,[18] stating that the very "structure of our state of France," which is analogous to the kingdom of Israel (governed by kings and elders) and the republic of Rome (governed by caesars and senators), requires that French kings submit to the counsel of like ministers, or co-tutors.[19]

Alleging proofs from Roman and canon law to argue the case for popular sovereignty, the *Discours* maintains that sovereignty belongs to the community, which grants it to the king conditionally, and that the grant can be revoked if abused.

> The community (*le peuple*) gave [public] power to the prince. . . . If he abuses it they [the community] can invoke the law which holds that the thing [public power] given can be revoked due to culpability of the one to whom it was rendered. . . . [In this discussion] I refer always to public power [invested in the king as holder of the royal office] as opposed to that of the prince himself [as a private individual] which is quite a different matter.[20]

Refuting conservative arguments that support unlimited royal power, the *Discours* makes allusions to Roman law precepts, *Lex Regia* and *Lex digna vox*, but interprets them in a manner that deflates the claims of tyrants to sole control of public authority.[21] Readers are reminded that kings do not hold their power from god and the sword,[22] that rulers do not have unlimited power (*merium imperium*) over life and death,[23] and that "what pleases the prince" does not necessarily have "the force of law."[24] The treatise selects another set of Roman law proofs to support arguments that limit royal power. The proper interpretation of the law is made through natural reason and equity, not through arbitrary royal command.[25] Having demonstrated that sovereignty resides in the community, that the community legally vests it in a succession of officeholders, and that kings as officeholders must exercise the charge properly or forfeit it, the *Discours* identifies the governmental agency (of co-tutors) that represents the sovereign community in public affairs.

REPRESENTATIVE INSTITUTIONS

At the outset the *Discours politiques* mentions the representative capacity of the estates but dismisses the clergy from membership;[26] in further discussion the treatise effectively bypasses the estates, at least in the form of an estates general.[27] The *Discours* specifies a representative agency that is comprised of three groups of nobles and officeholders charged with the exercise of public power: (1) princes, peers, and officers of the crown, (2) inferior magistrates, and (3) *parlementaires* (officeholders in the parlements). The *Discours* deliberately refrains from giving this assembly a name but ascribes to its members representative functions as "assessors for the people who collectively wield more power than the prince," as "attorneys" for the multitude, and even as the "estates," and treats them as co-tutors with the king in public administration.[28] For purposes of this study I have entitled that assembly the "Assembly of Public Assessors."

The composition of the Assembly of Public Assessors warrants attention. The *Discours* considers the assembly, functionally at least, to contain the estates, because it includes royal officeholders from two estates, excludes the clergy, and invites into the body the *parlementaires*, a very judicious move. Adopting a Roman law rationale, the *Discours* notes that the Assembly of Public Assessors is composed of the "saner and major part" of the community,[29] holds the ultimate power of the sword, *merum imperium,* [30] and has the authority to reprimand and punish a king in the face of notorious and manifest tyranny.[31] Finally, the *Discours* deftly twists the meaning of the medieval Romano-canonical maxim *quod omnes tangit* (which expressed a limited notion of representation) to signify a natural law precept that makes representation obligatory. "Nature teaches that what touches all [i.e., the community] must be approved of by all [i.e., the Assembly of Public Assessors]." [32] Here the *Discours* does not simply name an agency empowered to resist a tyrant but designates one that is ideally representative within the context of the times. This designation of the Assembly of Assessors to represent the sovereign community is followed by a challenging discussion of the right to resist royal authority.

RESISTANCE RIGHT

The *Discours* moves beyond other theorists of the time, because the author not only designates the Assembly of Assessors to investigate the case of a king-turned-tyrant but also obliges the assessors to take legal action following an indictment and designates legal procedures to implement the action. The treatise first provides legal grounds for the indictment, then outlines the judicial procedure for a trial.

Boldly adapting Roman private law to the service of French public law, the *Discours* cites the capital crime of *plagium,* a tenet of the *Lex Fabia,* as grounds upon which to indict a culpable king.

> It is said that those who [illegally] buy, sell, or place a free person [in servitude], as well as those who receive, detain, imprison, or otherwise abuse [a free person], are indicted with the crime of *plagium.* . . . The same can be said of those who weaken a community (*le peuple*) in order to lead it [the community] into the webs of tyrants who draw it into servitude.[33]

If the crime of *plagium* can be imputed to a private person who enslaves an individual, then that crime can also be imputed to a public person (i.e., an officeholder) who seeks to subject a whole community. Furthermore, the crime of *plagium* indicted not only the person who enslaved a free individual but also that person's accomplices.[34] By inference, then, the members of the Assembly of Assessors, who are co-tutors with the king in public administration, are warned that failure to indict a tyrant with the crime of tyranny (akin to *plagium*) marks them as accomplices who are equally guilty and justiciable before the law. Armed with the legal grounds on which to indict a king and his accomplices for tyranny, the *Discours* turns to the problem of adjudication.

The *Discours* outlines judicial procedures for instigating legal action against the indicted monarch. The Assembly of Public Assessors must hold a trial (with or without the king in attendance) to hear the charges. If found guilty, the king is deprived of his office and reduced to the status of a private person; then he may be sentenced by the assessors.[35] According to this radical plan, the assembly can indict the king with the capital crime of tyranny (abuse or neglect of the obligations of royal office), try him before the Assembly of Assessors, depose a convicted king from royal office, and sentence him in court as a common criminal. The *Discours* also allows a court of last resort, tyrannicide, but only if the king sets himself above the law and prevents convocation of the assembly or refuses to stand trial.[36] Should the king obstruct the procedure, the Assembly of Assessors tacitly presumes his guilt and automatically deposes him from office. Once reduced to the status of a private person by such tacit agreement, the tyrant is legally declared an outlaw and is subject to the hand of a patriotic citizen-assassin acting with immunity to defend the state of France.[37] Readers who might question the radical act of tyrannicide are reminded that Brutus accomplished such a patriotic deed in Rome and that an ancient Scottish compact recorded by the chronicler Hector Boethius in the early sixteenth century allowed tyrannicide under similar circumstances.[38]

The resistance plan set forth by the *Discours* is both constitutional and radical.[39] First, the composition of the Assembly of Public Assessors includes male individuals from the Second Estate (princes, peers, and officers of the crown) and the Third Estate (inferior magistrates, probably the provost of Paris, provincial governors, etc.) but excludes individuals from the First Estate (clergy). Second, the assembly includes the *parlementaires,* presumably from the Parisian court (perhaps joined by provincial cohorts), who were reputed by some at the time to be a "Fourth Estate" and to represent all the orders of the kingdom.[40] And third, the Assembly of Public Assessors possesses the legal authority to convene judicial proceedings in order to hear charges against a king charged with tyranny and to depose him in due course. The astute inclusion of the *parlementaires* in the Assembly of Assessors doubly invested that public forum with constitutional authority: first, because the Parlement of Paris, as a standing body, claimed to represent the estates of the kingdom when they were not assembled; and second, because the presence of the *parlementaires* provided the legal expertise necessary for the indictment of the king and the adjudication of the case. As stated by the *Discours*, the Assembly of Public Assessors is obliged to instigate this constitutional procedure against a tyrant in order to bring to judgment a king who was originally "the child of the country" (by lineage and birth), became the "father of the country" (by assumption of public office), and degenerated into the "parricide of the country" (by defaulting on constitutional obligations).[41] As in many political arguments set forth in early modern France, the constitutional lesson was taught through an extended family metaphor.

The *Discours politiques des diverses puissances*, both *politique* and *monarchomaque* in conception, presented a revised constitution for the French polity that included a standing representative assembly and a workable plan for resistance. The revised constitution was all the more subversive for being potentially realizable in the 1570s and 1580s. In these times the proposed convocation of a so-called Assembly of Public Assessors would not have strained credulity. In fact, the composition and role of the Assembly of Assessors remarkably resembled the *Lit de Justice* assemblies first convoked to address constitutional issues by Francis I in 1527 and 1537, historically legitimized as ancient French practice during the 1540s and 1550s, and convoked for constitutional purposes again by Charles IX in 1563, 1565, and 1573.[42] In all of those *Lit de Justice* assemblies the king, princes and peers, officers of the crown, *parlementaires* (Parisian and provincial), and other officeholders articulated publicly the constitutional precepts of juristic ideology that the *Discours politiques* would reiterate later. At *Lits de Justice* from 1527 through the 1560s constitutional discourse also revealed differences of opinion about whether the Parlement of Paris served as co-tutor with the king in governance and represented all the estates of the kingdom,[43] important points that the *Discours* picked up and pronounced upon affirmatively. Two *Lits de Justice* in 1527 and 1537 were trials held to judge the public defaults of Charles (II), duke of Bourbon, greatest of the French nobles, who was deprived of office and sentenced posthumously; and the emperor, Charles V, who was sentenced in absentia after being deprived of offices held under French auspices.[44] Legal minds might well have presumed that a French assembly that represented all the estates and was convened by the French king in the Parlement of Paris to try the Holy Roman Emperor, deprive him of office, and sentence him in absentia could likewise be convened in an emergency by the Assembly of Assessors to bring an incumbent French king to trial, present or not.

It is significant that the *Discours politiques* did not give a precise name to the representative assembly it set forth. The silence may have reflected the cautious stance of a *parlementaire* who trusted that informed readers would know what assemblage fit the bill. In any case, the subversive potential of such a convocation during the 1570s and 1580s, whether called an Assembly of Assessors or a *Lit de Justice* assembly, may help to explain why Charles IX, after convoking three *Lits de Justice* (one in 1563 and two in 1565), convoked only one more in 1573, when he was constrained to affirm his brother Henry's French succession rights once the latter became king in Poland.[45] The subversive potential may also account for the fact that Henry III held several royal *Séances* in the Parlement of Paris but did not convoke a *Lit de Justice* assembly during his entire reign.[46] The nature of attendant political crises tends to favor this explanation.

Looking at the French political crises of the 1570s, one can surmise how some readers might have thought that the *Discours politiques* offered suggestions worth pondering. During the 1570s Francis, duke of Alençon and Anjou (unmarried and the brother of three kings without progeny: Francis II, Charles IX, and Henry III), attracted a military cadre of nobles and Huguenots outside the royal aegis.[47] Because he was the last Valois always waiting in the wings, the duke of Anjou's perennial familial disaffection proved dangerous. Suspected of complicity in a plot to murder Charles IX and steal the crown while the successor, Henry (future Henry III), was in Poland (1573–74), the duke of Anjou and Henry of Navarre (future Bourbon king Henry IV) were confined in Paris by royal order while cohorts went on trial. Even so, when Anjou escaped to his own appanage in Angers (joined later by Navarre), Henry III (who became king of France in 1574) could not find nobles willing to retrieve him. Playing king in his own realm, the duke of Anjou issued declarations on public affairs, advocated religious tolerance, and called for a meeting of the Estates General, thereby linking himself, rhetorically at least, with the antiwar *politique* party and the *monarchomaque* resistance theorists. Amid all these pressures Henry III issued the interim pacification Edict of Beaulieu (1576), which contained articles favorable to the Protestants, and convened the Estates General at Blois. At this point the *politiques* (noble and bourgeois) counted on the duke of Anjou to help them defuse the war plans of the Catholic League. They were sorely disappointed. At the Estates meeting Anjou defected from the peace party and supported the royal party, which promptly rescinded the pacification edict and demanded a uniformly Catholic state.

In these times speculation no doubt ran rampant. Was Charles IX the quintessential king-turned-tyrant in the wake of the Saint Bartholomew's Day massacres; upon his death should the duke of Anjou succeed in place of Henry (king in Poland), or did Anjou forfeit that right in the face of his alleged treachery? Once king of France, did Henry III default on constitutional obligations by allowing the Catholic party to kindle war plans at the Estates General, by declaring in the Edict of Union that Henry of Navarre (a Protestant) was not crown-worthy, and by taking counsel from social "minions" rather than political co-tutors? Whether or not such speculation occurred, the author of the *Discours politiques* allowed for such contingencies. The author stressed the constitutional obligations of kingship and the legal charge of tyranny entailed in default, legally justified a change in the line of succession for cause, set aside the Estates General as a representative agency in favor of an Assembly of Public Assessors that could claim to represent all the estates, and devised judicial procedures to accomplish the deposition of a tyrant in that standing body. Set in historical perspective, the bold revision of the French constitution imagined by the *Discours* provided an alternative interpretation that made resistance to royal authority patriotic, legal, and possible.

On one front this revised constitution must have seemed admirably fit to address vexing constitutional and political problems. On another front, however, the constitutional scheme outlined by the *Discours politiques* contained the seeds of bitter fruit. The *Discours* presented a tightly argued plan that justified the right to resist and provided legitimate means to accomplish the deposition of a tyrant; therefore, the final daring resort to tyrannicide was unnecessary in the French context. Yet steeped in the heady rhetoric of civic humanism, the author, it is clear, could not refrain from employing the ringing exhortations and famous examples from historical memory that allowed such learned play with political eloquence on the contemporary scene. When the *Discours* admitted tyrannicide as a last resort to save the *communion politique,* rhetoric and history called to mind patriotic citizens likened to a Brutus or a Cassius in the Roman republic of another time. But the French assassins of the Valois Henry III in 1589 and the Bourbon Henry IV in 1610, standing in the wings and apprised of the lesson, were religious zealots whose limited conceptions about civic polities drastically undermined the French constitution as imagined some decades before by the author of the *Discours politiques.*

NOTES

I wish to thank colleagues at the Shelby Cullom Davis Center for Historical Studies, Princeton University, for provocative discussions about ideology and politics, most especially, Lawrence Stone, Gerald M. Sider, and Baruch Knei-Paz; and I am grateful to the National Endowment for the Humanities for a summer stipend to complete this work.

1. See William F. Church, *Constitutional Thought in Sixteenth-Century France* (New York, 1969), for the theories of the legists; Donald R. Kelley, *Foundations of Modern Historical Scholarship: Language, Law, and History in the French Renaissance* (New York, 1977), for the confluence of law and history and the *mos gallicus* method; and Sarah Hanley, *The Lit de Justice of the Kings of France: Constitutional Ideology in Legend, Ritual, and Discourse* (Princeton, 1983; French ed., Editions Aubier Montaigne, Paris, 1991), for the manner in which constitutional precepts were propagated and amended.

2. For a sense of the tensions, consult Donald R. Kelley, *The Beginning of Ideology: Consciousness and Society in the French Reformation* (Cambridge, 1981); Robert M. Kingdon, *Myths About the St. Bartholomew's Day Massacres, 1572–1576* (Cambridge, Mass., 1988); Michel Pernot, *Les guerres de religion en France, 1559–1598* (Paris, 1987); and J. H. M. Salmon, *Society in Crisis: France in the Sixteenth Century* (New York, 1975).

3. *Discours politiques des diverses puissances establies de Dieu au monde, du gouvernement legitime d'icelles, & du devoir de ceux qui y sont assujettis; nécessaires & pleins d'excellentes instructions à toutes sortes de personnes* (1574). For a preliminary paper given at the University of Perugia, see Sarah Hanley, "The Discours Politiques in Monarchomaque Ideology: Resistance Right in Sixteenth-century France," in *Assemblee di stati e istituzioni rappresentative nella storia del pensiero politico moderno* (Perugia, 1982), 121–34; and for further discussion, see Kingdon, *Myths*, chap. 11.

4. [Simon Goulart, ed.], *Mémoires de l'estat de France, sous Charles neufiesme: Contenans les choses plus notables, faites et publiées tant par les Catholiques que par ceux de la Religion, depuis le troisiesme édit de pacification fait au mois d'aoust 1570, jusques au regne de Henry troisiesme, & reduits en trois volumes, chascun desquels a un indice des principales matieres y contenues . . . à Meidelbourg* ([Geneva], 1579), vol. 3, fols. 147v–213r (the edition used here is the second printing of the 3d ed. of 1578). The 1st ed. of Goulart's three-volume *Mémoires* (1576, reprinted 1577) does not contain the *Discours*. See Leonard Chester Jones, *Simon Goulart, 1543–1628: Etude biographique et bibliographique* (Geneva, 1917), 11, 14, 18, 20, 297–98, 302, 475–79, 560–63, on Goulart and the *Discours;* and Goulart, *Mémoires,* vol. 3, fol. 147r, on the *Discours,* whose author, he stated,

was an important, intelligent, and erudite person. Probably the author was a legist, perhaps a *parlementaire*.

5. For three *monarchomaque* treatises, see François Hotman, *Francogallia*, ed. Ralph E. Giesey and J. H. M. Salmon (Cambridge, 1972); Théodore de Bèze, *Du droit des magistrats sur les subjets* . . . , ed. Robert M. Kingdon (Geneva, 1971); and Etienne Junius Brutus [pseud.], *Vindiciae contra tyrannos* . . . , ed. A. Jouanna, J. Perrin, M. Soulié, A. Tournon, and H. Weber (Geneva, 1979). For a comparative analysis of these three treatises, consult the introductions to the scholarly editions above; and see Ralph E. Giesey, "The Monarchomach Triumvirs: Hotman, Beza, and Mornay," *Bibliothèque d'humanisme et Renaissance* 32, no. 1 (1970): 41–56; and William F. Freegard, *Roman Law and Resistance Right: A Study of Question Three of the Vindiciae contra tyrannos* (Ann Arbor: University Microfilms, 1971).

6. *Discours*, fols. 173r–74r, 181r, 202r, 211v. Accordingly, "All forms of association (*communication*) reside in the political (*communion politique*). It is to that [the *communion politique*] which all men must hold [allegiance] . . .": fol. 174v. The idea of the *communion* of political interests (i.e., the state of France) derives from notions in Plato, *Republic* 5, Aristotle, *Politics* 3, and especially Cicero, *Offices* [1.16.50 (incorrectly cited in the margin as *De Finibus*) and 2.12.42.43]. Note: the *Discours* in marginal citations often fails to cite sources and leaves many only partially identified; therefore, the sources, or parts of them, that I have located are placed here *in brackets* (as above) when they do not appear in the treatise.

7. *Discours*, fols. 106v, 206r; and on religious toleration, see fols. 178r–v; on the relativity of religious differences, fols. 212v–13v; and on the subordination of religion to politics, fols. 173v–74r.

8. *Discours*, fols. 198v, 200v, 202v. The allusion is unusual for the time and echoes the jurist Ulpian's contention that jurists may be called priests, as they worship justice [Roman law, *Digest* 1.1.1, marginal gloss], quoted in Ernst H. Kantorowicz, *The King's Two Bodies: A Study in Medieval Political Theology* (Princeton, 1957), 139–43 and n. 162.

9. For the ways the funeral, entry, and *Lit de Justice* rituals in the sixteenth century represented the "king's two bodies" by focusing on the office of kingship, rather than its incumbents, consult Ralph E. Giesey, *The Royal Funeral Ceremony in Renaissance France* (Geneva, 1960); Lawrence M. Bryant, *The King and the City in the Parisian Royal Entry Ceremony: Politics, Ritual, and Art in the Renaissance* (Geneva, 1986); and Hanley, *Lit de Justice;* and for the legal antecedents of the notion, see Kantorowicz, *King's Two Bodies.*

10. *Discours*, fols. 166v, 193v, 197v, suggesting that the author finds medieval political theorists, who did not specify any agency or procedure to accomplish deposition of a tyrant, much too conservative. Quentin Skinner, *Foundations of Modern Political Thought* (Cambridge, 1978), vol. 1, chaps. 1–6; vol. 2, chaps. 4–6, summarizes medieval views.

11. *Discours,* fol. 177v, following Cicero, *Philippics* [2.13.33]. This view echoes the Florentine chancellor Leonardo Bruni, who made Brutus an immortal patriot

for the good deed. See Hans Baron, *The Crisis of the Early Italian Renaissance* (Princeton, 1966), on the phenomenon of civic humanism; and Jerrold Seigel, *Rhetoric and Philosophy in Renaissance Humanism* (Princeton, 1967), for the Renaissance transformation of Cicero from a medieval monk to a civic activist.

12. For the number of citations: Roman law, *Corpus Juris Civilis* 76, *Libri Feudorum* 2; canon law, *Corpus Juris Canonici* 27; classical works, Aristotle 26, Plato 14, Cicero 60; biblical sources, Old Testament 60, New Testament 22. Other citations include Boethius, Demosthenes, Diogenes, Horace, Ovid, Sallust, Seutonious, Seneca, Tacitus, Virgil, and Xenophon.

13. *Discours*, fols. 153v, 158r, 162v–66v, 170v, 172v, 175v–79r, 180v–82v, 198v, 201v, 206r, 210r–v. *Administration publique* (or *civile*) is a male endeavor. Women are forbidden to hold office owing to character defects and "seminal" incapacity, and they are accused of repeated attempts to turn public office into family property; see fols. 149r–52v, 170r–71v. In fact, officeholding was a family affair, and male officeholders continually pressured the government to obtain inheritance rights to office and secured such rights with the *paulette* in 1604; consult Sarah Hanley, "Engendering the State: Family Formation and State Building in Early Modern France," *French Historical Studies* 16, no. 1 (1989): 4–27; and idem, *Lit de Justice*, chaps. 10–12. For a discussion of "seminal theory" in politics, see idem, "The Engendered State: Society, Gender, and Politics in Early Modern France" (in progress).

14. *Discours*, fol. 194v; also fol. 155v, following Old Testament, *Deuteronomy* [17]; and fol. 159v.

15. *Discours*, fols. 160r, 203r, where the legal component in legal-hereditary succession is emphasized. These juristic precepts were demonstrated in ritual and discourse from 1527 and were spelled out in the Majority *Lit de Justice* assembly of Charles IX in 1563; see Hanley, *Lit de Justice*, chaps. 2–7.

16. *Discours*, fols. 199r, 200r [Roman law, *Digest* 36.1.13].

17. *Discours*, fols. 198v, 201v–3v [Roman law, *Digest* 44.3.11 and *Codex* 1.30.2]. All public power must be exercised for the public welfare (*utilité publique*): fols. 157r–v, 176v, 181r, 189v, 193r, 196v, 207r, 208r, 210r–11v.

18. *Discours*, fol. 181r [reminiscent of the jurist Labeo, Roman law, *Digest* 4.6.22.2].

19. *Discours*, fol. 185r.

20. *Discours*, fol. 208v, following Roman law [*Codex* 8.56.10] in consort with canon law [*Decretum* C.23, q.2, c.1].

21. *Discours*, fol. 165r. The famous Roman law maxims and sources are not named or cited, but the passage clearly recalls [*Digest* 1.4.1 and *Codex* 1.14.4].

22. *Discours*, fol. 189r, recalling the Roman law maxim *Rex emperator suo regno* ("The king is emperor in his own realm . . . and holds the crown from god and the sword"), which was popular in the sixteenth century; see Hanley, *Lit de Justice*, chap. 6 and n. 7.

23. *Discours,* fol. 204v, following Roman law [*Digest* 2.1.3]; and see also fol. 182r for the same allusion.

24. *Discours,* fol. 165r, unidentified reference to *quod principi placuit* from Roman law [*Digest* 1.4.1].

25. *Discours,* fol. 197v–98r, following Roman law [*Digest* 1.1.9; Gaius on equity]; fol. 202r, following *Codex* 1.8.

26. *Discours,* fol. 188r, charging that the Catholic clergy would sell the kingdom to the pope; fols. 182r–v, 209v–10v, where the term "estates," now minus the clergy, does not refer to a meeting of the Estates General or provincial estates but to a standing assembly.

27. *Discours,* fols. 210v–11r. J. Russell Major has argued that the practice of representation entailed in convocations of Estates General and provincial estates produced a more decentralized and consensual monarchy in the sixteenth century; see *Representative Institutions in Renaissance France, 1421–1559* (Madison, 1960); and *Representative Government in Early Modern France* (New Haven, 1980). The scholarly essays collected in idem, *The Monarchy, the Estates, and the Aristocracy in Renaissance France* (London, 1988), chaps. 4–10, point to different types of meetings that alleged representation. The *Discours* transfers the notion of representation to a different assembly.

28. The composition of this assembly, which wields more power than the king, is drawn from *Discours,* fols. 181v–82r. The key terms used to describe the assembly, which represents the *peuple* or *multitude générale,* are *assesseurs, procureurs, honorable compagnie,* and *estats.* Members are drawn from an elect group of male nobles and officeholders, not from the populace (or multitude) or women, who are never trusted to rule, and not from the clergy, whose allegiance is to Rome.

29. *Discours,* fol. 163v, unidentified source [Roman law, *Digest* 50.1.19], the *sanior et maior pars.*

30. *Discours,* fol. 204v, following [Roman law, *Digest* 2.1.3].

31. *Discours,* fols. 209v–11r.

32. *Discours,* fol. 181v, unidentified but clearly transposed from [Roman law, *Codex* 5.59.5.2]; also found in [*Digest* 42.1.7]. For the sixteenth-century use of this concept in league with Parlement's insistence on a co-tutorship role from 1527 through the 1560s and after, see Hanley, *Lit de Justice,* chaps. 2, 6–8. The medieval origins of this procedural maxim, *quod omnes tangit ab omnibus comprobetur,* which entailed advice but not consent and was often tied to co-tutorship, are discussed in Gaines Post, *Studies in Medieval Legal Thought* (Princeton, 1964), chaps. 3–4.

33. *Discours,* fol. 186v, following the notion of *plagium* in *Digest* 1.1.3. For other references, consult [*Digest* 48.15; 1.1.11] and also [*Codex* 9.20]. The *Discours,* fol. 194v, adds related biblical passages on *plagium* from *Jeremiah* [34:27] and *Exodus* [21:16].

34. Consult Adolf Berger, *Encyclopedic Dictionary of Roman Law,* Trans-

actions of the American Philosophical Society, vol. 43, pt. 2 (Philadelphia, 1953), 552, 632.

35. *Discours*, fol. 209v, following Roman law [*Codex* 1.1.12]; see, in addition, fols. 208v–12v. By means of an allusion to conciliar theory, readers are reminded that a pope charged with heresy or some other scandalous crime could be tried by a church council, deposed, and judged as a private person: fols. 209r–10r. On medieval conciliar theory, see Brian Tierney, *Foundations of Conciliar Theory* (Cambridge, 1955).

36. The *Vindiciae* allowed tyrannicide, but it is a random act taken without benefit of judicial hearing; see Freegard, *Roman Law and Resistance Right,* 348–60; and Giesey, *Monarchomach Triumvirs,* 47–53.

37. *Discours*, fols. 212r–13r, where the assassin, transformed into a civic hero, merits "glorious renown for having exterminated the tyrant," following a citation from Cicero, *Philippics* [2.13.33].

38. *Discours*, fol. 212r. This so-called compact ("conventions" kept in the "Cartipholace des roys"), supposedly mentioned by Hector Boethius (1485–1536), is not contained in Hector Boece, *Chronicles of Scotland*, Bellenden trans. (1685), vols. 1–2, ed. Edith C. Batho and R. W. Chambers (London, 1938). But there are several passages from which the notion might have been extracted; see ibid. 1:69, 102, 194–95; 2:51, 60, 99, 101, recounting how kings of Scotland were condemned and executed by public assemblies.

39. Skinner, *Foundations* 1:305, considers resistance theory in the *Discours* to be anarchic, whereas the findings here suggest that the treatise surely is radical but follows an innovative constitutional scheme.

40. For the malleable way in which the function of the estates was conceived in concert with the Parlement of Paris, see the references of Francis I and Henry II to the *parlementaires* as a "Fourth Estate" in 1527, 1552, and 1558; and the description accorded the Parlement of Paris as an "abridged form of the three estates, the image and replica of all orders of the kingdom" in 1563: Hanley, *Lit de Justice,* chaps. 2, 3, 6–8, and a summary, pp. 274–77.

41. *Discours*, fols. 176v–77v, citing Cicero, *Philippics* [2.13.31].

42. See Hanley, *Lit de Justice,* chaps. 2–9.

43. See n. 40 on Parlement and representation.

44. See Hanley, *Lit de Justice,* chaps. 2–3.

45. Ibid., chap. 9.

46. Ibid., especially pp. 212–17. The argument has been made that Henry III did hold *Lits de Justice* because the journals of Pierre de l'Estoile and Jacques-Auguste de Thou refer to them, and that clerks in Parlement might have failed to record the assemblies because of religious tensions: Mack P. Holt, "The King in Parlement: The Problem of the *Lit de Justice* in Sixteenth-Century France," *Historical Journal* 31, no. 3 (1988): 507–23. Holt admirably reconstructs religious tensions in that period, but his hypothesis about *Lit de Justice* convocations somehow held but

never recorded is not supported by the evidence. The most reliable sources (which provide corroboration) do not record *Lits de Justice* between 1574 and 1589: the registers of Parlement (the best source); the scholarly treatises of Bernard de La Roche-Flavin, Pierre Dupuy, Théodore Godefroy, etc. (who read the registers); and the records of masters of ceremonies (who notified participants and planned elaborate rituals). The most unreliable sources (which fail to provide corroboration) do mention *Lits de Justice* in those years: the journals and memoires of L'Estoile and de Thou, which are full of errors. L'Estoile misdates events and gathers differently dated entries under one year, mixes together chronicles of events and anecdotes, and contains passages worded almost exactly like passages in de Thou, which suggests that one copied the other; see Henri Hauser, *Les sources de l'histoire de France au XVIe siècle (1494–1610)* (Paris, 1906), vol. 3, nos. 1420, 1478; vol. 4, no. 2585. De Thou began to write his entries only in 1593, then researched, wrote, and revised 138 books at the rate of one and a half a month. When the manuscript went to press in 1604, it consisted of fragments and texts written at different times and in different hands. Even worse, after 1609, when the work was placed on the Catholic church Index, de Thou altered some of his original text; and later on, his cohorts, Rigault and Dupuy, admittedly altered more passages: see Samuel Kinser, *The Works of Jacques-Auguste de Thou* (The Hague, 1966). Forced to choose on the weight of the evidence, I rejected the accounts of L'Estoile and de Thou in favor of the other, more reliable sources, as set forth in Hanley, *Lit de Justice*.

47. For the following account, consult Mack P. Holt, *The Duke of Anjou and the Politique Struggle During the Wars of Religion* (Cambridge, 1986), chaps. 2, 9.

3. The Sword as the Robe in

Seventeenth-Century Provence and Brittany

DONNA BOHANAN

Since World War II the historiography of early modern France has produced substantial debate and revision in institutional and social history. Among the most important changes in interpretation has been J. Russell Major's definition of the Renaissance monarchy, which sees this institution as limited in its authority by several innate characteristics and by external factors, not the least of which was an aristocracy that continued to play a vigorous and determining role in the political life of the realm.[1] Major is highly critical of the older, traditional assumption that absolutism occurred in France as early as the reign of Francis I and that this trend was accommodated by a general crisis and decline of the French aristocracy.[2] For Major this seems incompatible with the political and social realities that he has observed in studying the sixteenth and early seventeenth centuries.

Further, the "crisis" interpretation of the aristocracy posited the notion of a functional division within the nobility, or the famous partition of sword and robe, which allegedly created sufficient internal strife and conflict to undermine the class as a whole and thereby permitted the expansion of royal authority with little effective noble opposition. This division refers to the gulf between descendants of the medieval warrior aristocracy and the families who had only recently joined the ranks of the nobility by virtue of officeholding or letters of ennoblement. It entails much more than differences in antiquity and origin, because the sword nobility persisted in a military role and a rural way of life while the robe devoted themselves to government offices and were more urban in their orientation. Such discrepancies were reinforced by exclusive marriage patterns, as each group supposedly refused to marry with the other and thereby perpetuated their very separate existences and their often hostile relationship. Of this sword-robe conflict, Major is similarly skeptical. What he and others have recognized is that the traditional interpretation of the French nobility consists largely of generalizations based on a contemporary literature that was distinctly anti-noble, if not contemptuous of the perceived decrepit moral, economic, and political state of the nobility; moreover, it lacked any real underpinning in detailed archival evidence.[3]

Such notions of aristocratic division and crisis are also flawed by their exclusive consideration of the northern aristocracy, a group whose lives and culture shaped the image of the feudal nobility so familiar to us today. Yet as far back as the Roman Empire the aristocracy of much of southern France had evolved in a rather different way and in a considerably different cultural environment. Among their distinguishing traits, many southern nobles lived primarily in town and participated as a privileged elite in their urban community. Seventeenth-century Aix-en-Provence, for example, was home to a sizable noble population, which was enlarged by the presence of *anoblis* who had purchased offices, but which also included many older noble families whose ancestors had lived there for centuries. This older nobility was typically southern in that it was not simply a by-product of feudalism. Because southern elites were originally based on wealth and antiquity rather than valor, fiefs remained superfluous to nobility in the Midi. Though many nobles sought their additional prestige, ennoblement occurred in the Midi without infeudation, a fact that alone raises questions about the sword-robe construct, because it reduces the descriptive value of the term "sword" as applied to the south of France.[4]

Beyond the issue of the origins of nobility, the activities and investments of noble families in Aix contradict assumptions about sword-robe conflict and portray a native nobility considerably more fluid than that traditionally described by historians. Although the antiquity of these families ranged widely, differences in origin were rarely reflected in their occupations. Older families, together with *anoblis*, purchased positions in the courts almost immediately after their creation in the early sixteenth century, and it was the availability of venal offices that subsequently facilitated the assimilation of old and new families into essentially one urban nobility. Moreover, these trends were not confined to the Midi. In comparing Brittany, also a unique part of the realm, one observes important parallels. Specifically, an analysis of the composition of the Parlement of Brittany reveals that the judicial activities undertaken by the older Provençal families did not result solely from their urban orientation, for families in Brittany, legitimately described as sword nobility, had similarly directed their investments and activities. And this too contradicts the idea of conflict between two opposing categories of elites.

The local nobility of Aix-en-Provence consisted of 81 extended families in the seventeenth century; that is, 81 extended noble families who lived there can be classified as native Aixois. Among these 81 families, 38 were old and 43 new, and a majority (68 families) of both groups occupied offices in the Parlement of Provence and the Cour des Comptes during the seventeenth century.[5] Of these 68, almost half, or 31, were old families, a fact that obviously confirms occupational similarities between the two groups. Old houses were not unlike *anoblis* in that they routinely invested in offices and bequeathed them to the principal heirs along with the family titles and landed property. The Coriolis family, whose nobility dated at least to 1450 and who figured prominently in local attempts to prevent the intrusion of royal authority, saw four successive generations of eldest sons occupy the office of president in Parlement during the century.[6] Admittedly, their line of succession in this office was interrupted for more than a decade as punishment for Laurent de Coriolis's complicity in the 1630 Revolt of the Cascaveoux, but otherwise the Corioliscs were not unusual in this pattern of investment and devolution. Many old families appear to have carefully guarded offices across generations as one of their most precious investments.

Yet it is important to note that royal offices were not the most lucrative of financial investments open to nobles in Aix. In fact, when compared to the returns on landed property and commercial investment (a financial opportunity that southern nobles appear to have enjoyed with impunity), the income from an office paled significantly. A salary (gages) for an office in the courts consisted of interest on the sum originally paid for the office, and this ranged generally from 1 to 4.5 percent.[7] According to Sharon Kettering's calculations, in 1647 the incomes for various offices in Parlement were as follows: the first president received 2,062 livres; the other presidents made 1,650 livres; and councillors earned 1,225 livres. Other benefits of office included exemption from the gabelle, the *ban* and *arrière-ban*, and the right to collect fees for general legal services. Even taken together these rewards constituted only a limited return on the investment. And frequently payment was not forthcoming or increases in salary were accompanied by forced loans to the crown, events that made offices even less attractive as an economic investment.[8]

Nevertheless, the demand for offices increased tremendously and drove their prices to unprecedented levels in the seventeenth century. Early in the period the office of councillor in Parlement sold for between 3,000 livres and 6,000 livres. Before long its cost had increased dramatically, so that by 1633 the same office of councillor sold routinely for 50,000 to 60,000 livres. Factoring a 60 percent devaluation of the livres *tournois*, Kettering has figured this to be a 400 percent increase in the cost of the same office over a relatively brief period of time. By the end of the century prices had generally stabilized at a high level: the office of president *à mortier* selling for 120,000 livres and that of councillor for 64,000 livres.[9]

This substantial increase in the cost of judicial offices was not the result of an inflationary trend in the regional economy, because other prices in Aix rose only very slightly during the century.[10] More to the point, Kettering found that when the prices of offices reached their highest point the volume of sales did also,[11] so it is clear that it was demand for offices that raised their costs to such elevated levels. Demand of this magnitude could only have been generated by the competition of both old and new families for positions in the sovereign courts. New families sought offices for the reasons traditionally ascribed to them; old families did so because of a tradition of service to the urban community, because of political opportunism, and because they recognized in officeholding a new *marque de noblesse*.

Such parallels between old and new in Aix also extended to education. Yet here the crisis historians have argued a gross deficiency among the sword nobility, one that increased the disparity between sword and robe and that saw members of the old nobility lose out on political opportunities simply because they lacked the educational background to perform in a judicial or financial capacity.[12] Although historians have argued that ignorance contributed to the political demise of the sword and created an educational and cultural gap between old and new, this does not appear to have been the case in Aix. As old families began to move into the courts, they also began to send their sons to the university for the necessary legal education. During the seventeenth century 30 of the 38 old noble families had members who graduated from the University of Aix. These families earned a total of 141 terminal degrees, 94 of which were doctorates in law and theology.[13] Significantly, these figures are not unlike those for the *anoblis* within this native nobility. The university register indicates that 37 of the 43 new families had members matriculate, for a total of 119 terminal degrees. A shared interest in education is also evident in the contents of noble libraries, inventories of which reveal remarkably similar intellectual interests among the two groups. The libraries of old and new alike were dominated by legal, historical, and classical literature.[14]

There is, nevertheless, a body of literature, largely pamphlets and treatises, from the sixteenth and early seventeenth centuries that is highly critical of the traditional nobility because of its ignorance and general antipathy toward letters. Seizing this literature, the crisis historians have summarily condemned the realm of the traditional nobility as a vast cultural wasteland. But Ellery Schalk would suggest that many of these authors might be read with a different emphasis; that is, while pointing out the shortcomings of the French aristocracy, they wrote also to propose a program for their rehabilitation. In fact, Schalk has brought to our attention the extent and the full social and cultural significance of this literature. He considers it part of a noble *prise de conscience* that took place in the late sixteenth century and that transformed ideas of nobility.[15] He believes that as nobles sought the education prescribed by their critics the very meaning of nobility shifted from a medieval one of function to a modern one of birth and culture, so that by the second half of the seventeenth century the most widely held image of nobility was one that associated it with letters and a certain degree of cultivation. This appears to have been the case in Aix. To avoid disqualification and exclusion from politics, the old nobility of Aix adapted to changing circumstances by embracing institutional education.

Nor were these old families in Aix unusual in their ability to function in modern political and bureaucratic circumstances. To the north and in an area perhaps as peculiar as Provence, the composition of the Parlement of Brittany reveals a similar kind of adaptation by old noble houses. Brittany offers a particularly instructive comparison with Aix and Provence because it is well documented that substantial numbers of sword families lived there in the seventeenth century. In his impressive study of the eighteenth-century Breton nobility, Jean Meyer acknowledges the preponderance of sword families, and he divides this elite by antiquity and origin into three large groups.

The oldest group, those ennobled by the early fifteenth century, constituted 28 percent (577 families) of the Breton nobility. Included were 410 families whose origins were chivalric but whose antiquity could not be precisely dated. What is certain is that they presented at the first reformations of nobility in the early fifteenth century and emerged with their status upheld. They ranged from the very ancient to a larger group ennobled in the fourteenth century prior to the Breton Civil War. These and the 167 families able to document their antiquity precisely were the oldest sword families.[16]

The second group consisted of more recently ennobled sword families, dating at least to the first half of the sixteenth century and described by Meyer as "écuyers d'extraction." They constituted 55 percent of the provincial nobility.[17] Their numbers, particularly those ennobled by 1500, may be explained in part by a renewal of the sword during the fourteenth and fifteenth centuries. Thus, one finds emerging in Brittany at this time a new sword nobility that families could enter rapidly through military service and the acquisition of fiefs.[18] There also appears to have been a sort of ducal robe nobility surfacing in the fifteenth century that exhibited sword characteristics and that was sometimes related to the older provincial aristocracy. Michael Jones writes, "A number of ducal secretaries, forefathers of the *noblesse de robe,* may have come from ancient noble families."[19] This phenomenon of fifteenth-century upward mobility is one that needs more systematic study by social historians. Upward mobility and ennoblement occurred frequently in both Brittany and Provence well before the introduction of royal courts and the wholesale purchase of government offices, which worked as agents of ennoblement in the sixteenth century and were responsible for the creation of the new robe nobility traditionally and thoroughly examined by historians. The *anoblis* of the fifteenth century constituted a vital element of both provincial nobilities, and, according to Meyer, were an important part of the late medieval nobility. As such, they should be considered separately from the new robe nobility or the third stratum. This third group, ennobled by office or letter after 1550, constituted a mere 17 percent of Brittany's nobility.[20]

The structure of the Breton nobility, specifically the size of the sword component, is remarkable and undoubtedly unusual. Meyer would agree and, in fact, has offered some explanations. He writes that the Breton nobility did not experience the most tragic effects of the crisis of the late Middle Ages. Although affected by the first part of the Hundred Years' War and the Breton Civil War, this region did not endure the widespread destruction and loss of life that prevailed in other French provinces. The relative peace of the fifteenth century and the prosperity that Brittany experienced through the sixteenth century preserved a robust sword nobility. Also, Brittany's geographical isolation within the kingdom and its limited urban development meant that its nobility was cut off from many of the trends that affected the greater French nobility. Isolation may have shielded its sword families from the menacing economic and political developments of the early modern period and contributed to their preservation in such amazing abundance.[21]

Here also existed (as in Provence) a level of sword involvement in judicial politics that indicates much more mobility or flexibility than has been traditionally associated with the sword. In fact, the sword's presence in the Parlement of Brittany is so overwhelming that Meyer has suggested that the distinction between robe and sword was less pronounced in Brittany than elsewhere, even though the sword was so numerically evident in the region.[22] Almost equal numbers of sword and robe families occupied offices in the Parlement of Brittany during the seventeenth century. Old families numbered 144 and new families 143. The number of individuals from old families who entered the Parlement during this hundred-year period was 283, actually more than the figure of 245 for new families. There was, it should be noted, a slight tendency for new families to precede the older families in obtaining offices, and in the second half of the sixteenth century one finds more new families entering the court than old. But by the 1630s their numbers were approximately the same, and the sword had clearly shifted into robe activities.[23]

How does one explain the extent of this sword participation in the Parlement? In part the answer has to do with the sword nobility's participation in the ducal Parlement and the Estates of Brittany during the Middle Ages. The histories of these two institutions are intertwined so that they were virtually inseparable during the fourteenth and fifteenth centuries. In describing the birth and evolution of the Breton Estates, P. S. Lewis explains that until the end of the fifteenth century this political assembly was entangled in the local judicial assembly or Parlement.[24] The Estates emerged from the Parlement, "itself a more or less narrow enlargement of the *curia ducis*."[25] As such, the Parlement assumed the judicial functions of the curia and more. It also consented to taxation, thereby acquiring the function of the Estates, and the terms "Parlement," *Parlement général,* and "Estates" appear to have been used interchangeably without distinction as to the agenda and content of individual meetings. The bourgeoisie entered this assembly only in the fourteenth century (the first documented instance occurring in 1352),[26] and failed to play an effective role in its meetings until the early fifteenth century, so that it remained a distinctly feudal institution for most of the Middle Ages.[27]

Lewis argues that, owing to the late inclusion of the Third Estate, taxation and finance did not figure prominently in the deliberations of the

Breton Estates; rather, it was the judicial realm that occupied participants until the end of the fifteenth century when a Court of Parlement seceded from the Breton Estates. This institution evolved from the 1390s as a judicial committee within the Estates and was attended by civil servants from the ducal council.[28] Members of the Estates who did not sit in meetings of this court did not act as judges, but they did concern themselves with the administration of justice as a component of their prerogative to discuss political and administrative issues. It is Lewis's belief that the "regularity of their appearances was occasioned by the judicial necessities of a court with which they had little directly to deal but which they were pleased to think derived its authority solely from the larger body of which they were members."[29] It would appear that their association with justice, judicial politics, and the ducal Parlement/Estates prepared sword families to enter the royal Parlement in the early modern period. Justice was part of the sword families' traditional role in Breton politics, and they were therefore altogether familiar with and comfortable in the capacity of magistrates by the sixteenth century.

In response to appeals from the Breton Estates and the provincial governors, Henry II in 1553 created a royal parlement for Brittany. Concerned that this action might encourage independence in a province that continued to exhibit considerable autonomy and localism, the king was also determined to circumscribe the power of this institution. To this end, he restricted Breton participation in the court to only half of the councillors (*originaires*). The remaining councillors (*non-originaires*) were to come from other provinces.[30] In reality, however, this fifty-fifty rule was not strictly applied. When *originaire* positions were unavailable it was not uncommon for native families to enter the court through positions reserved for nonnatives. One such case involved René de Beauce, who entered the royal Parlement as a councillor in 1609. He acquired a *non-originaire* office whose former occupant, a non-Breton, had recently died—this in spite of the fact that Beauce came from a local noble family whose antiquity dated to the thirteenth century. In 1638 Beauce resigned his position in favor of his son, Joachim, but the *non-originaire* classification of the office did not change.[31] When Joachim died in 1653 the family sold the office to Amaury-Charles de la Moussaye, another Breton from a family dating to the feudal nobility of the thirteenth century. And yet this position was still designated for the occupancy of a non-Breton.[32] Over the course of the seventeenth century, the old native families of Brittany had 228 members occupying offices, 47 of which were theoretically reserved for outsiders.

By their acquisition of *non-originaire* positions, sword families revealed the extent to which they valued judicial offices.

Among the older Breton houses that served in the Parlement of Brittany, one finds houses of very ancient lineage and chivalric origins. In 1696 Jacques-Gilles de Kersauzon became the first member of his family to serve in the Parlement. His house was a very old one that had participated in the crusade of 1248.[33] The family Andigné, whose nobility dated from the twelfth century, was represented in the Parlement by three members who occupied in succession the office of councillor.[34] And in 1650 the Bourdonnaye family, whose antiquity is documented as far back as 1208, founded a veritable dynasty in the Parlement when Louis de la Bourdonnaye, viscount de Coetion, entered the court as a councillor. In 1677 his son, Yves Marie de la Bourdonnaye, also became a councillor, occupying this office until 1687 when he resigned it in favor of his brother, Jacques Renaud. The latter served as councillor until he became president *à mortier* in 1711, a position that he held until 1722, when he resigned it in favor of his eldest son.[35] The eighteenth century saw similar activity in the Parlement among this family. Of all the sword families, the Kersauzon, Andigné, and Bourdonnaye were among the oldest to move into the court, and by their participation they in particular demonstrated the ease with which old families moved from sword to robe occupations.

Overall, 144 old noble houses served in the Parlement, and only 27 of these families were not originally from Brittany. Among the remaining 117 Breton families, 71 were classified in the reformation of 1668 as being of *ancienne d'extraction de chevalerie,* and 46 were families ennobled in the fourteenth or fifteenth centuries as part of the aristocratic renewal of the late Middle Ages.[36]

The prevalence of this kind of functional mobility challenges the idea of sword-robe division and strife, one of the most widely held assumptions about the early modern nobility. In Brittany, as in Aix, the older families were well represented in judicial politics. The concept of a robe nobility is inappropriate for Aix, and much of southern France, for the reason that the term "sword" is largely inappropriate. As used by the crisis historians, the existence of one implies the existence of the other. The old nobility, with its urban and civic orientation, moved easily and automatically into what historians have designated the realm of the robe. But the same thing was also true of Brittany, where, in fact, a genuine sword nobility did exist, or had at some point existed, a case that is perhaps even more interesting and revealing. Jonathan Dewald has suggested that we would do better to think in terms of sword and robe as components of a reasonably cohesive group, rather than viewing France "as dominated by a pair of fundamentally hostile elites."[37] For much of France this is clearly a more realistic perspective, but for the south we might proceed a step further to suggest that sword and robe were never really identifiable components.

NOTES

1. J. Russell Major, "The Crown and the Aristocracy in Renaissance France," *American Historical Review* 69 (1964): 631–45; idem, "Noble Income, Inflation, and the Wars of Religion in France," *American Historical Review* 86 (1981): 21–48; idem, *Representative Government in Early Modern France* (New Haven: 1980).

2. This interpretation of the nobility and the monarchy of early modern France comes most notably from Lucien Romier, *Le royaume de Catherine de Médicis*, 2 vols. (Paris, 1922); and Pierre de Vaissière, *Gentilshommes compagnards de l'ancienne France* (Paris: 1901). More recently these ideas have been propounded by Roland Mousnier in his introduction to Roland Mousnier, J. P. Labatut, and Y. Durand, *Problèmes de stratifications sociale: Deux cahiers de la noblesse pour les Etats Généraux de 1649–1651* (Paris, 1965); and in Mousnier, *La vénalité des offices sous Henri IV and Louis XIII*, 2d ed. (Paris, 1971). The idea of a separate robe nobility is an underlying assumption in Mousnier's description of French institutions and society, *Les institutions de la France sous la monarchie absolue, vol. 1, 1589–1789* (Paris, 1974). It is equally important in Davis Bitton's concise treatment of the decline of the aristocracy, *The French Nobility in Crisis, 1560–1640* (Stanford, 1969). For an excellent summary of this debate and a survey of its main participants, see J. H. M. Salmon, "Storm over the *Noblesse*," *Journal of Modern History* 53 (1981): 242–57.

3. Recent attempts to remedy this state of historical scholarship include James B. Wood, *The Nobility of the Election of Bayeux, 1463–1666: Continuity Through Change* (Princeton: 1980); and Jonathan Dewald, *The Formation of a Provincial Nobility: The Magistrates of the Parlement of Rouen, 1499–1610* (Princeton, 1980).

4. The material concerning the nobility of Aix is treated at much greater length in my forthcoming book, *The Nobility of Seventeenth-Century Aix-en-Provence: A Privileged Elite in Urban Society* (Louisiana State University Press). See in particular chap. 1, "Urbanism and Nobility in the Midi."

5. The list of noble families considered Aixois was compiled from material included in the following sources: "Jugement de la noblesse de Provence, 1667," Bibliothèque Méjanes, MS 1133, "Répertoire des jugements de noblesse en l'année 1667 . . . ," MS 1134; Artefueil, *Histoire héroique et universelle de la noblesse de*

Provence (Avignon, 1757), passim; François-Paul Blanc, *Origines des familles provençales maintenues dans le second ordre sous le règne de Louis XIV: Dictionnaire généalogique* (Aix, 1971), passim. I have classified a family as old if its nobility was certain before 1500, which is just prior to the arrival of the sovereign courts in Aix and the period of wholesale ennoblement aided by the purchase of office. Information on officeholding may be found in Balthasar de Clapiers-Collonques, *Chronologie des officiers des cours souverains de Provence*, 2d ed. (Aix, 1904).

6. Bohanan, *Nobility*, chap. 2, "Structure and Wealth."

7. Sharon Kettering, *Judicial Politics and Urban Revolt in Seventeenth-Century France: The Parlement of Aix, 1629–1659* (Princeton, 1978), 225.

8. Ibid., 225–31.

9. Ibid., 221–24.

10. During the seventeenth century the price of wheat in Aix fluctuated dramatically, but the general long-term trend was one of very slow inflation, if not stagnation. "Rapport de Grains, 1570 jusques à 1670," AD, Aix, B3709; "Rapport sur les Grains, 1626–1681," B3710.

11. Kettering, *Judicial Politics*, 225.

12. Bitton, *French Nobility*, 46–48, 62–63.

13. "Répertoire alphabétique des gradués de l'Université d'Aix, 1531–1791," AD, Aix, I–V. Also see Donna Bohanan, "The Education of Nobles in Seventeenth-Century Aix-en-Provence," *Journal of Social History* 20 (1987): 757–64; idem, *Nobility of Seventeenth-Century Aix-en-Provence*, chap. 7, "Education and Letters."

14. Bohanan, "Education of Nobles"; idem, *Nobility*, chap. 7.

15. Ellery Schalk, *From Valor to Pedigree: Ideas of Nobility in France in the Sixteenth and Seventeenth Centuries* (Princeton, 1986), 175–76.

16. Jean Meyer, *La noblesse bretonne au XVIII siecle* (Paris, 1966), 1:57.

17. Ibid.

18. Michael Jones, *The Creation of Brittany: A Late Medieval State* (London, 1988), 228–29.

19. Ibid., 230.

20. Meyer, *Noblesse bretonne* 1:57.

21. Ibid., 58–59.

22. Ibid. 2:929.

23. These figures have been compiled from the material in Frédéric Saulnier, *Le Parlement de Bretagne, 1554–1790: Répertoire alphabétique et biographique de tous les membres de la cour* (Rennes, 1909). For consistency, I classified the *parlementaires* of Brittany as I classified the native nobility of Aix; that is, I considered a family old if its nobility was firmly established by the year 1500. This date is well in advance of the creation of the Parlement in Brittany. It is also a slightly more conservative system of classification than that used by Jean Meyer. Again, Meyer considered families ennobled in the early sixteenth century as part of the

late medieval nobility, whereas I have, for the sake of consistency with Aix, included them with the new nobility. Meyer's figures therefore differ slightly from mine. In analyzing the composition of the Parlement through the major reformation of 1668–72, Meyer determined that 63 percent of the families that had entered the Parlement by 1668 were part of the medieval nobility. Another 20 percent were ennobled later in the sixteenth century, and 17.5 percent entered the rank in the seventeenth century.

24. P. S. Lewis, "Breton Estates," in his *Essays in Later Medieval French History* (London, 1985), 134.

25. Ibid., 128.

26. Major, *Representative Government*, 93–94.

27. Lewis, "Breton Estates," 129.

28. Ibid., 133.

29. Ibid., 134.

30. John J. Hurt, "The Parlement of Brittany and the Crown: 1665–1675," in *State and Society in Seventeenth-Century France*, ed. Raymond F. Kierstead (New York, 1975), 47.

31. Saulnier, *Parlement de Bretagne* 1:65.

32. Ibid. 1:66, 2:662.

33. Ibid. 2:553–54.

34. Ibid. 1:30–31.

35. Ibid., 131–35.

36. Ibid., passim.

37. Dewald, *Formation of a Provincial Nobility*, 309.

4. Narrowing Horizons:

Commerce and Derogation in Normandy

GAYLE K. BRUNELLE

In 1627 Cardinal Richelieu created a company of commerce and colonization called the Compagnie de Canada. Article 16 of the company's charter stated, "It will be permitted to all persons of any quality whatsoever, whether ecclesiastics, nobles, officers or others, to enter into the said company without for this reason suffering derogation of the privileges accorded to their orders."[1] Twelve short years prior to that date, in 1615, Jacques Sonning had a curious Latin document notarized in Rouen. Sonning was a scion of a prominent Rouennais family that had given the city many merchants and municipal officials during the sixteenth century. Evidently feeling insecure about his family's status, Sonning requested and received from King James of England a letter stating that the family was descended from a line of English nobles called Sunninghill. Notwithstanding the family's mercantile activities since its arrival in France, Louis XIII and the Rouennais Cour des Aides accepted the document as proof of nobility and sustained Jacques Sonning's claim to noble rank.[2]

Half a century earlier still, Gabriel de Bures, sieur de Bethencourt, a prominent citizen of the port city of Dieppe, also went before the Rouennais Cour des Aides to defend his nobility. Unlike Sonning, Bures did not wish to discontinue his lucrative but questionable activities, probably consisting of the combination of piracy and commerce that typically attracted nobles from ports such as Dieppe. Rather, he sought from the king permission to engage freely in maritime ventures without fear of accusations of derogation and lengthy court cases over whether he should pay the taille. Bures was given what he demanded by the king in letters patent delivered at Troyes in 1563. The letters stated that the king "ordained again that the said de Bures was a noble person extracted of noble race even though he has and nevertheless may continue to take charge of vessels and voyage by sea without anyone being able to say or pretend that he has in any manner derogated from his state of nobility."[3] It took him two years, but in 1565 Bures was finally able to get his royal letter registered by the Cour des Aides.

Finally, another fifty years before Bures's case, the Rouennais brothers Jehan and Guillaume Blondel were accused of derogation in the Rouennais Cour des Aides by the parish of Aumenesches in the *élection* of Alençon, where the brothers owned two *seigneuries*. The parish accused the two of directly farming their lands and engaging in commerce (probably by selling their produce in the town), both activities that were widely considered to constitute derogation. The town wanted the brothers either to cease their activities, which put them in direct competition with the local farmers and merchants, or to pay the taille. The brothers' defense was simple. They admitted to the practices with which they were charged but stated that the nobles of Normandy were "permez de pouvoir marchander tenir terres à ferme ne faire aucune desrogeance" and that they could thus continue to live nobly without any infringement of their noble privileges.[4] The court agreed and the brothers were sustained in their case and omitted from the tax rolls.

These four examples demonstrate graphically that the definition and enforcement of derogation changed in France from the early sixteenth century to the early seventeenth. In 1500 a noble could openly engage in practices that sixty-five years later would have brought him under charges of derogation. A noble in 1565 required royal permission for activities that his ancestors would have considered a right, or at least an infraction of little consequence, and these royal mandates often were registered by the Cour des Aides only reluctantly and after repeated directives from the crown. The Sonnings in 1613 believed that they needed a letter from the king of England to uphold their claims to nobility in the face of the mercantile past from which they had already ostensibly broken. By 1627 Richelieu felt constrained to announce that nobles could invest in a royal company engaged in overseas commerce and colonization even though royal edicts had already stated that maritime commerce was open to nobles.[5]

Derogation poses a difficult problem for modern historians and as a result tends to be ignored or viewed as an inconsequential holdover from the feudal age that eventually disappeared in the eighteenth century when nobles finally won the right to engage in commerce.[6] Moreover, historians generally assume that derogation became an issue for debate in the seventeenth century only because of a "crisis of the nobility" that began in the latter half of the sixteenth century. Nobles found themselves squeezed financially and socially by the rising bourgeoisie that bought power and prestige through royal offices. Mounting prices and stable rents diminished their income and forced nobles to overcome their traditional pride and resort to commerce, tax farming, and direct cultivation of their lands in order to avoid economic ruin. Thus the traditional prohibition against nobles engaging in commerce became a law only "at a moment when one began to have reason to fear that the rule was not observed."[7] Before that time, nobles' own sense of honor prevented them from derogating often.[8]

The first part of this theory is probably correct. Even the term *dérogeance* is absent from law codes, royal edicts, cahiers of the provincial estates, and works of legal theorists until the early sixteenth century. The legal definition appears to have evolved through cases brought before the Parisian and provincial Cours des Aides during the late fifteenth and sixteenth centuries. The number of trials mounted steadily after 1560 as royal edicts and legal theorists began to address the issue and formulate a theory of derogation. The laws concerning derogation were highly unstable because they evolved not only according to changing legal opinion but also in line with royal expediency. Both law and theory were poorly synchronized with the public conception of derogation and, more important, with noble practices.[9]

Before it is possible to examine how noble behavior differed from theory, however, it is advisable first to define the meaning of derogation. Probably the best legal definition of derogation was provided by Marcel de la Bigne de Villeneuve in a law dissertation for the University of Rennes. According to Villeneuve, derogation was in essence a voluntary and temporary suspension of noble privileges by a noble who chose to engage repeatedly in activities not in keeping with noble status. The penalty was not derogation itself, but its consequences, the most severe of which was inscription on the tax rolls. It was not necessarily hereditary and could be relieved either by simple suspension of the derogatory activity or, more often after 1600, by letters of relief issued for a price by the crown. A single act could not cause derogation; a pattern, or life-style, of ignoble activity was required.[10]

Behavior liable to derogation fell into three main categories. Direct farming of land and practice of skilled trades were considered ignoble because they were means of earning a living through manual labor. Commerce was also forbidden to nobles, although exceptions were often made for overseas commerce or large-scale wholesale commerce, provided that the noble invested only, or captained his ship, and was not engaged in buying or selling. Finally, tax farming and possession of many lower-echelon municipal and royal offices constituted the third category of behavior disallowed for nobles.[11]

Of the three, commerce was the subject of greatest public debate for a variety of reasons. Commerce probably generated more wealth for nobles than the other two categories, particularly as most nobles who farmed their lands themselves or entered trades did so out of poverty, not choice. Moreover, the numbers, practices, and legalities of nobles engaged in commerce varied widely throughout France. Regions where commerce traditionally was more lucrative than agriculture, such as Brittany and Provence, had a long tradition of merchant nobility. Some cities, for example Marseilles and Lyons, specifically exempted nobles pursuing mercantile careers from derogation. These places tended to ignore or vehemently oppose any incursions from Paris on their local nobility's right to partake in trade. Normandy also had a long tradition of gentlemen glassmakers and merchants and it was not until 1560, in accord with the Estates General of Orléans, that the Rouennais Cour des Aides began to insist regularly that nobles engaged in commerce be inscribed on the tax rolls.[12]

It was no accident that theories of taxation and of derogation were developed simultaneously in the late fifteenth and sixteenth centuries. The most feared penalty for derogation was subjection to the taille, and this tax became a permanent French institution only after the Hundred Years' War. Cases of derogation were tried before the Cour des Aides because towns or government fiscal agents wanted to force nobles profiting from commerce, tax farming, or other "nonnoble" activities to pay taxes equally with their counterparts in the Third Estate.[13] Thus the increasing numbers of judgments against the defendants in derogation suits in the sixteenth and seventeenth centuries do not necessarily indicate growing commercial activity among nobles or expanded efforts by parishes to prosecute them. Rather, the rise in litigation resulted from the swelling fiscal needs of the crown, which made it more willing to support and even instigate prosecutions of nobles for derogation. By the same token, the new stringent enforcement of derogation very likely tended to force nobles to curtail their suspect behavior, or at least to hide it more carefully, and the numbers of nobles engaging in commerce probably shrank rather than grew after 1560. The possibilities for nobles to profit from commerce in particular diminished considerably during the latter half of the sixteenth century because an active commercial career was more difficult to conceal than speculation in taxes or offices. This must have worsened nobles' already difficult adjustment to the volatile economic environment of the late sixteenth century, since it limited their ability to compensate for declining rents through nonagricultural revenues.

An examination of the cases of derogation tried before the Rouennais Cour des Aides supports these assertions. These cases appear not only in the subseries "Noblesse," devoted specifically to derogation and ennoblement, but also in the "Expeditions" and "Mandements." The "Noblesse" preserves the most complete documentation of the cases, but unfortunately too few of the verdicts of these trials were recorded with the testimony to found a solid quantitative analysis. More verdicts survive in the other two subseries, but details of the arguments are too often woefully inadequate. Even so, the cases that have been preserved from all three subseries, some of them with full trial records extant, illuminate the changes in both the theory and practice of derogation from the fifteenth to the seventeenth centuries.

Relatively few cases of derogation were tried before the Rouennais Cour des Aides in the late fifteenth century, perhaps between ten and fifteen per year. Created only in 1450, the court required time to establish itself and delineate its jurisdiction. Moreover, the taille and many of the *aides* were relatively new, and legal precedents pertaining to them had to be laboriously developed through court cases.[14] By the same token, the fifteenth- and early sixteenth-century disputes are distinguished from later trials by several features. The earlier cases seem to have been brought most often by parishes independently, with little or only belated involvement by royal officials such as the *procureur général du roi,* who played such a prominent role in later prosecutions. The parishes, not the procureur, aggressively presented their own arguments and did not shrink from accumulating written testimony and challenging the veracity of nobles in court.[15] By contrast, later records often specifically designated the procureur as instigator of the process, although parishes were still usually mentioned as co-plaintiffs.[16]

Given the growing numbers of ennoblements and the concomitant mounting concern about usurpation of nobility, not to mention the insatiable fiscal appetite of the crown, it is not surprising that the courts had become much more rigorous in their prosecution of derogation by the late sixteenth and the seventeenth centuries. They tended to be quite lenient, on the other hand, in their verdicts before 1560, both because derogation was not yet regarded with the sense of urgency that the issue would later acquire and because a legal definition of behavior liable to derogation had not yet been devised. Thus, well into the sixteenth century, litigants and judges alike were still quite unclear about which types of noble activities were tolerable and which constituted derogation. Parishes and the courts, for example, tended to view past inscription on taille rolls as tacit admission of membership in the Third Estate and were reluctant, even in the face of royal letters of relief, to accept the concept that derogation was a temporary and reversible condition.[17]

The accused were often equally confused about the legalities of derogation. Marin de Boisbunoult in 1583 seemed well informed about the intricate theories of derogation. He claimed in response to his parish's charges of derogation that his father had not been a roturier and that the alleged marriages of some of his relatives to commoners, even if they had taken place, were inconsequential because any resulting derogation was temporary and did not pass to his branch of the family. Furthermore, Boisbunoult insisted, marriage to commoners caused derogation only if the noble woman married a commoner, since "l'homme annoblit la femme et non par la femme l'homme." Yet evidently he remained unsure whether his legal ground was solid, since he had still gone ahead and obtained the extra security of letters of relief from the crown.[18]

Poor Jehan Billeheust in 1488 was far less well informed than Boisbunoult. Billeheust did not even know if he was a noble, much less whether he had derogated. He testified that his family was from Vire, where his father had been a merchant and his grandfather a tabellion. Evidently the family's nobility had never before been questioned by his parish, and Billeheust had no idea if his father's trade made him liable to the taille or not. The witnesses were of little assistance, since they could not even agree whether his father had been a merchant. Regrettably, the verdict is missing from this case.[19] Thomas de Lespine in 1477 and the Rouennais Blondel brothers in 1513 were quite certain that their commercial and agricultural activities in no way threatened their noble status.[20]

In these earlier cases the Cour des Aides seems to have ruled most often in favor of the accused noble, even in the face of openly admitted nonnoble pursuits that fifty or a hundred years later would very likely have been condemned. Further, it tolerated improper and explicitly forbidden activities if the accused could demonstrate mitigating circumstances, such as financial constraint. Frequently before 1560 nobles blamed their own or their ancestors' derogation on the unusual circumstances of the Hundred Years' War. Guillaume Meslet dit de Roncherolle explained that his father had been imprisoned by the English and forced to enter commerce in order to raise the ransom money for his release. Meslet of course assured the court that he had ended his commercial career once the ransom had been paid. Evidently the court believed Meslet, since he seems to have been maintained in his exemption from the taille. The four Dabouville brothers made a similar and equally successful argument in 1482. Probably the most interesting version of this defense was Richart Gourmont's statement in 1489 that "his father Pierre had contributed to the taille in the said parish of Varreville owing to the wars and hostilities of the period of the English occupation, during which time he was a merchant and did not wish to remain a noble because he would have been forced to go to war with the said English" against the French.[21] Of course, these arguments were plausible only in the generations immediately following the war, although they were used again with success after the Wars of Religion.[22]

Letters of relief of derogation were normally obtained from the king with equal ease and used to force the Cour des Aides to acquit when it was reluctant to maintain nobility in the face of manifestly nonnoble behavior. Gabriel de Bures's case was only one in a long line of such instances. Charles VIII allowed Jehan de la Perelle to retain his noble rank despite his mercantile career because the family had suffered financially during the Hundred Years' War. Richard Gourmont also received a royal letter excusing his father's behavior during the war. At the end of the sixteenth century the Cour des Aides maintained the nobility of the Bazire family because they presented a 1481 royal letter giving the family the right to continue as "monnaiers en la monnoye de Saint Lô," a position that the family had held for several generations.[23]

On other occasions, judging from those cases where the details of the trials have been preserved, the trials and the verdicts were simply quite idiosyncratic, with little rationale given for maintaining the nobility of an individual who openly admitted behavior incompatible with noble status. The Cour des Aides sustained Jehan de Caudecoste's evident usurpation of noble rank because "his father inherited money from his uncle Henry and with this had the means to live nobly and have himself ennobled." Thomas de Lespine won a favorable verdict because his ancestors had been noble and even though he was accused of having trafficked "tant par mer que par terre" and of running a public hotel and tavern, not activities easily mistaken or overlooked.[24]

Clearly the accused nobles were given the benefit of doubt in these early cases. The courts and crown seem to have been reluctant before the mid-sixteenth century to support the efforts of parishes to submit nobles or nonnoble rural elites to taxation even when the evidence was overwhelmingly in support of the parishes' position. Official opinion appeared to agree with defiant assertions such as that of Thomas de Lespine that the king had given nobles the right to engage in commerce without loss of their noble privileges. Although some defendants lost their cases when there was blatant evidence of nonnoble behavior or usurpation of nobility before 1560, most seem to have been acquitted and actually were allowed to continue their suspect activities, while towns observed with growing anxiety their shrinking tax rolls and the ever-increasing fiscal demands of the crown. This was the reason why it was the Third Estate, much more than the nobility, that grew alarmed about usurpation of nobility, ennoblements, and derogation in the sixteenth century.

This concern is evident in the cahiers of the Estates Generals held during the sixteenth and seventeenth centuries. Repeatedly the representatives of the Second and Third estates demanded an end to ennoblements and usurpations that threatened to dilute the nobility and cheapen its value. Merchants and nobles alike were jealous of their privileges and continuously requested that they be reconfirmed unchanged. Both groups asked, though for different reasons, that the crown refuse to create more ennobling offices and buy back many of those already sold. But the Third Estate went further, insisting also that nobles keep to their proper pursuit, warfare, and leave to the Third Estate its means of survival, commerce. Their opposition to any new taxes or infringement of free trade, even when the results might benefit them, was uncompromising. Whereas nobles in some years asked to be allowed to enter in commerce, nonnobles petitioned that commerce be reserved to the Third Estate.[25]

The motivation for merchants' intransigence on this issue is obvious. If nobles had been permitted to enter commerce without paying taxes, they would have had a distinct economic advantage over ordinary merchants because their tax exemptions lowered the cost of their capital and swelled their profits. A noble selling his own agricultural produce or other products could undercut the prices of competing merchants whose profits were diminished by the taille and the many *aides* levied on commerce. If enough nobles had chosen a commercial profession, or even dabbled in trade, nonnobles would have lost much of their share of the markets and been driven to bankruptcy. The only alternative would have been to ennoble all merchants, a step that would have drastically cut municipal and royal revenues.

Merchants discerned a similar danger in the royal monopolies on overseas commerce granted by Henry IV and Louis XIII, and in Richelieu's companies of commerce and colonization. Monopoly holders had in effect a legal right to control a particular source of supply. By controlling the products, they necessarily dominated the markets as well. Moreover, since they were exempt from many or all taxes, they could also wrest markets from suppliers of products that were similar to their own but obtained outside the monopoly—fish and furs, for example. Merchants would thus be forced into either bankruptcy or accommodation with the monopoly. Either way, they would as a result lose control over their own commercial operations. This prospect was intolerable to most merchants, and that is why only a small percentage of the total merchant population allowed itself to be coaxed by Richelieu's offers of nobility into joining the royal companies. By contrast, numerous officeholders and robe nobles were persuaded to invest in the companies by Richelieu's assurances of immunity from derogation of their usually recently acquired noble status.[26]

Fortunately for the merchants, the constant penury of the crown doomed the efforts of those who sought to draw the nobility into commerce in the sixteenth and seventeenth centuries. One of the prime attractions of officeholding was the ennoblement, immediate or gradual, that the purchaser of an office could expect. As ennoblement, through offices or royal grant, became increasingly venal, the crown strove to eliminate competing means of obtaining nobility and to establish itself as the sole source of ennoblement. Royal officials mounted growing efforts to ferret out usurpers and force them either to pay taxes or pay for the privilege of tax-exempt noble status. Even those who had legally acquired ennobling offices were often required to pay surtaxes—in effect, to repurchase their nobility.[27] Caught between its desire to preserve the concept of the nobility's privileged status and its need to extract revenue from the nobility, the crown found itself supporting the Third Estate's demands that the nobility be either forbidden to trespass into nonnoble economic pursuits or forced to pay taxes along with nonnobles.

During the second half of the sixteenth century derogation theories were formulated and laws created, but it was not until the reign of Louis XIII that successful prosecutions became frequent. This development is strikingly illustrated in the "Mandements" of the Rouennais Cour des Aides. After 1615 the volume of derogation cases exploded. There were more letters relieving derogation registered in the "Mandements" during the year 1624–25 (twenty-five) than in the entire period 1554–1615 (twenty-four). The high numbers of letters of relief did not slacken throughout the reign of Louis XIII.[28] Most of these letters did not, to be sure, concern commercial derogation. The majority were granted to noble widows of roturiers who wished to regain their noble status. But all types of derogation also continued to be prosecuted, and it is clear that a more strict derogation policy was being enforced.

Many of those found guilty of derogation were not ultimately inscribed on the tax rolls, however. Rather, they were often obliged to repurchase offices and letters of nobility in order to maintain their tax immunity. Likewise, many were forced to acquire a series of letters of relief from the king and wage a persistent and costly battle to have them registered in the face of the mounting skepticism of the Cour des Aides. Pierre de Bellemare's nobility was challenged simply because his guarantor in the farming of an abbey's revenues was his nonnoble son-in-law. In order to escape derogation, he obtained a letter from Henry IV that described Bellemare's accuser as an "homme de peu" and instructed the court to maintain his nobility.[29]

Because the total quantity of nobles engaging in commerce and tax farming is unknown, it is difficult to determine whether the threat of derogation effectively reduced their numbers. That nobles had pursued mercantile careers in the fifteenth and sixteenth centuries and that some persisted throughout the seventeenth is evidenced by the many cases of commercial derogation that were tried. Moreover, the king was still willing to give relief for commerce and tax farming for a variety of extenuating circumstances. Paris Le Coq, sieur de la Saussaye, was relieved in 1641 of derogation caused by his ownership of tax farms because his father had been forced to acquire the farms to recoup his financial losses suffered during the religious wars. Le Coq claimed that he had only inherited them and had sold them as soon as decently possible. As for those nonnoble lands he farmed, well, he had inherited the lands of his wife, the daughter of a hotelkeeper.[30]

Fernande de Palme-Carrillo was ennobled in 1644 despite his lifelong commercial career because he was descended from a Spanish noble family. Nobles in Spain were allowed to engage in commerce, and Palme-Carrillo claimed to have been ignorant of French rules of derogation. The king accepted his argument and allowed him to receive French letters of nobility.[31] This document is interesting because it alludes to the commonly accepted difference between wholesale and retail commerce. Generally, the former was tolerated if practiced on a large scale or by means of overseas voyages, whereas the latter was unanimously condemned. The letter of relief stated that Fernande was eligible for ennoblement only because he never had "mesles du detail."

Similarly, it was the manner in which he trafficked that saved Jean Baptiste Chaslon, *écuyer* and gentleman of the king's chamber, from derogation in 1645. Chaslon was given royal permission to import and sell wheat because he had "intelligences" in countries that supplied commodities needed by the king, such as grain.[32] Faced with many similar royal exemptions, the Cour des Aides seems to have strengthened its resistance to registering such letters of relief. Judic Boivin, separated from her roturier husband, failed to persuade the court to accept the letters of relief that she had obtained from the crown. The court did not deny their validity, but simply ruled that despite the letters she had failed to provide convincing evidence that she had in fact been noble before her marriage.[33]

The crown also tightened its policy regarding letters of relief during the seventeenth century. Although it continued to grant them, after about 1640 some letters, while lifting derogation, still required the offending noble to pay the taille for a specified period of time. Jean Ferreur, sieur des Brosses et de Mortefontaines, received a royal letter of relief that required the court to maintain the defendant's noble privileges despite the fact that his grandfather had been a merchant and that his father, before becoming a royal counselor and secretary of Navarre, had begun his career as a procureur of the *présidial* of Alençon. Still, the letter also mandated that the defendant had to pay the taille imposed upon him for derogation "pendant que la guerre durera."[34] Thomas Bréard, sieur de Terrefoute, received a similar "penance" in his 1679 letter of relief.[35]

The changes in royal policy regarding letters of relief are only part of a much more important shift in royal attitudes toward derogation. During the sixteenth century, individuals usually sought and obtained such letters as insurance before a court process over derogation. The letters were often unnecessary because the court ruled in favor of the accused anyway. Even when the letters did help to nudge the court against a verdict of derogation, they did not in any manner imply guilt. By the same token, it was not unusual for the king to write directly to the court, as in the case of Gabriel de Bures, stating that no relief was necessary because no derogation had taken place. The court frequently came to a similar decision on its own.

By the seventeenth century a technical but crucial change had taken place. Far fewer individuals seem to have been simply acquitted of derogation. Many suspects never even resorted to the courts. Rather, most nobles accused of derogation went ahead and obtained relief directly through royal letters before their cases were tried. This system was more expedient and sure for the noble and more profitable for the king. However, it forced most nobles suspected of derogation to admit their guilt. Gone were most defiant assertions such as that of the Blondel brothers that nobles had the right to engage in commerce. Nobles had been forced to accept the concept that activities such as commerce and tax farming were forbidden to them, and that their descendants down even to the third generation could suffer for their misbehavior.

Nobles found themselves condemned increasingly for minor infractions or the sins of their fathers. Pierre Dodenon was forced to obtain relief simply because he was guaranteed in a loan by a tax farmer; Jean Danmesnil, because his father had purchased the offices of notary and tabellion; and Thomas Le Vailliant, because his father forty years earlier had acquired an office in the bailliage of the *vicomté* of Bayeux. Gilles Canyvet, a Catholic, had been thrown out of his Protestant father's home. He derogated when poverty forced him to take to farming.[36] Jean Baptiste Chaslon was constrained to acquire letters of relief even though he had previous royal permission to engage in commerce, and in a type of overseas wholesale commerce that should have been exempt according to previous royal edicts. Thus many nobles were unwittingly caught in changing standards of derogation.

This trend culminated in the clauses included in the articles of association of the seventeenth-century royal companies of commerce. The turning point seems to have come in the mid-sixteenth century with the 1560 Estates General of Orléans. The earlier edicts of Louis XI encouraging nobles to engage in commerce were here overturned, and royal policy, in accord with the wishes of the Third Estate especially, opposed nobles' entry into commerce from this time until the mid-seventeenth century.[37] Although nobles appear to have publicly supported this policy in the cause of purifying their order, some still persisted in investing in commerce, tax farms, and nonnoble offices, since the crown continued to grant letters of relief for these activities. In 1584 Charles de Cossé, comte de Brissac, invested in a commercial fishing voyage to Newfoundland organized by three prominent Rouennais merchants.[38]

Nobles became more cautious in their commercial investments, however, and more selective in the types of commerce with which they would become involved. Many engaged merchants as secretaries and receivers, and it is likely that some invested in the commercial ventures of these

trusted employees. The Rouennais merchant Eustace Trevache was a financial adviser to the duc d'Elbeuf, and another Rouennais merchant, Guillaume Bosquet, worked in a similar capacity for the cardinal de Bourbon,
who supported commercial and colonial ventures in the New World.[39]
During the sixteenth and early seventeenth centuries nobles were drawn
to the New World trade, where their participation was allowed and
even encouraged. The Montmorency family obtained control of an early
seventeenth-century New World commercial monopoly, and numerous
lesser nobles captained expeditions that had commercial as well as colonial goals.[40] Richelieu lamented the reluctance of the majority of nobles to
invest in his commercial companies, but their hesitation is understandable
given the taint that by then had become attached to any type of commercial
activity. Even in the New World trade, nobles' scope for involvement was
reduced by the royal companies of Richelieu and Colbert because crown
officials, rather than the noble owners of the monopolies, now controlled
the affairs of the companies. Nobles, like nonnoble merchants, found that
the crown desired to restrict their participation in New World trade to
passive shareholding. Furthermore, unlike the merchants, nobles could not
compensate through other types of commercial ventures.

The changes in the meaning and enforcement of derogation between the
late fifteenth and early seventeenth centuries were of great consequence to
nobles. They were not the result of behavior changes among the nobility or
the Third Estate, but rather caused those alterations. Evidence exists from
the fourteenth century forward that nobles regularly invested in and directed commercial ventures.[41] The stream of commercial derogation cases
tried before the Cours des Aides in Rouen, Paris, and elsewhere, and the
many letters relieving derogation granted by the crown, demonstrate that
throughout the early modern period nobles persisted in engaging in commerce, tax farming, and other suspect behavior in order to enhance their
revenues. These cases also indicate that nonnobles' desire to prosecute
nobles for these activities remained fairly constant throughout the late
Middle Ages and early modern period. Despite the increasing disdain with
which such activities were regarded by some theorists of the Second Estate,
in Normandy at least there remained a core of nobles willing or constrained to risk derogation by pursuing commercial interests. Even so, the
new rigor with which derogation was defined and condemned must have
discouraged many nobles from venturing outside their traditional military
and political functions.[42]

Equally important, the vicissitudes of the crown's attitude toward dero-

gation are a useful indicator of its relationship to the Second and Third
estates. Contrary to widely held views, the end of the prohibition against
nobles engaging in commerce did not signify a triumph of the Third Estate
and the bourgeois capitalist world view over the aristocracy. Nobles had
long desired to enhance their revenues through commerce, tax farming,
and other nonmilitary pursuits. It was nonnoble merchants who sought
with equal persistence to force them to sacrifice either commerce or their
tax-exempt status. During those periods when the crown chose to ignore
derogation and allow nobles in commerce, most of the late Middle Ages
and Renaissance as well as the eighteenth century, it was in fact signifying
its support of the nobility and of the concept of a privileged aristocracy.
Kings such as Louis XI who had been tolerant of derogation and increased
ennoblements hoped to strengthen the aristocracy by infusing into it new
blood and new revenues from commerce.[43]

By the same token, kings who enforced strict derogation laws, such as
Louis XIII and Louis XIV, were in fact restricting the financial resources
of the nobles in accordance with the desire of the Third Estate, which
feared competition from the tax-exempt and therefore cheaper noble capital. Such rulers may not have consciously sought to harm the nobility by
their derogation policies, but their intentions did not alter the effects of
those policies. Unwittingly or not, rulers who upheld rigorous interpretations of derogation were placing themselves in the role of protectors of
the Third Estate against encroachment on its privileges by the nobility.
When the crown finally acquiesced in the eighteenth century to demands
that nobles be allowed to engage in commerce, it was forsaking its defense
of the Third Estate in favor of the interests of the Second. This change,
which enlarged the economic horizons of the nobility after their temporary
constriction during the fifteenth and sixteenth centuries, demonstrated the
strength, not the weakness, of the eighteenth-century French nobility and
its close relationship with the crown.

NOTES

1. *Collection de manuscrits contenant lettres, mémoires, et autres documents
historiques relatifs à la Nouvelle-France,* 2 vols. (Quebec, 1883), 1: 70. Article 12
of the 1626 Company of Morbihan contained similar assurances to nobles. "Edicts
du roy pour l'établissement du commerce au Havre de Morbihan," Archives Municipales de Nantes, CC 82.

2. AD, Seine-Maritime (hereafter ADSM), Cour des Aides, "Noblesse," 3 BP 0018, 17 March 1615.

3. Ibid., "Expeditions," 3 BP 287, 30 June 1565, fols. 213v–14.

4. Ibid., "Noblesse," 3 BP 7119, Blondel, 1513.

5. Louis XI, Charles IX, and Louis XIII during their reigns issued edicts allowing nobles to engage in maritime and some wholesale commerce without endangering their noble status. It should be noted, however, that nobles were justifiably distrustful of the force of these edicts, since the crown was not steadfast in its position on derogation and the Third Estate tended to pressure the crown and sovereign courts to take a harsher stance on the issue. "Protocole de Louis XI," BN, MSS fr. 5727, fol. 56; René Gandilhon, *Politique économique de Louis XI* (Rennes, 1940), 115ff.; Hervé Du Halgouët, "Gentilshommes commerçants et commerçants nobles au XVIIe et XVIIIe siècles," *Mémoires de la Société d'Histoire et d'Archéologie de Bretagne* (Rennes) 16, no. 1 (1936): 146–88; Marcel de la Bigne de Villeneuve, *Essai sur la théorie de la dérogeance de la noblesse* (Rennes, 1918), 63–64; Gaston Zeller, "Louis XI, la noblesse et la marchandise," *Annales E.S.C.* 18(1946): 331–41.

6. Beginning in the seventeenth century a polemic was carried on in the popular press between opponents and supporters of eliminating the penalties of derogation for nobles engaging in commerce. L'Abbé Coyer, *La noblesse commerçante* (Paris, 1756); Jean Eon, *Le commerce honnorable* (Nantes, 1646); Henri Lévy-Bruhl, "La noblesse de France et le commerce à la fin de l'Ancien Régime," *Revue d'histoire moderne*, n.s., 8(1933): 209–35; La Bigne de Villeneuve, *Essai*, 147ff.; Gaston Zeller, "Une notion de caractère historico-sociale: La dérogeance," *Cahiers internationaux de sociologie*, n.s., 22(1957): 40–74.

7. Lévy-Bruhl, "Noblesse de France," 210.

8. For a classic description of the crisis of the sixteenth century, see Davis Bitton, *The French Nobility in Crisis, 1560–1640* (Stanford, 1969); also J. H. M. Salmon, *Society in Crisis: France in the Sixteenth Century* (New York, 1975); Etienne Dravasa, *"Vivre noblement": Recherches sur la dérogeance de noblesse du XIVe au XVIe siècles* (Bordeaux, 1965), 42ff.; and Zeller, "Caractère historico-sociale," 44–45.

9. Dravasa, *"Vivre noblement,"* 13, 72ff.; Georges Picot, *Histoire des Etats Généraux*, 5 vols. (Paris, 1872), 2: 276, 294; Paul Viard, *La dîme écclesiastique au XVIe siècle* (Paris, 1914), 104; Zeller, "Caractère historico-sociale," 42ff.

10. La Bigne de Villeneuve, *Essai*, 65–66.

11. Ibid., 78ff.

12. Edmond Esmonin, *La taille en Normandie au temps de Colbert* (Paris, 1913; reprint, Geneva, 1978), 224ff.; Du Halgouët, "Gentilshommes commerçants"; François Marchetti, *Discours sur le négoce des gentilshommes de la ville de Marseille et sur la qualité de nobles marchands qu'ils prenoient il-y-a cent ans . . .* (Paris, 1671); François Olivier-Martin, *L'organisation corporative de la France*

d'Ancien Régime (Paris, 1938), 119–20; M. Planiol, *La très ancienne coutume: Assises, constitutions de Parlement et ordonnances ducales* (Plihon, 1896), 405ff.; Zeller, "Caractère historico-sociale," 42ff.

13. Dravasa, *"Vivre noblement,"* 94ff.

14. Dravasa found fourteen cases brought before the Rouennais Cour des Aides in 1486–87, eleven in 1493–94, and eight in 1497–98. Ibid., 90–92. In general, before 1500 the Rouennais Cour des Aides appears to have tried fewer than fifteen cases of derogation per year.

15. ADSM, Cour des Aides, "Noblesse," 3 BP 7119, Benard, 1475; Bellemare, 1482[3]; Boisleveque, 1482; Belleheust, 1488; Blondel, 1513; Blancivillain, 1520; 3 BP 7128, Lespine, 1476[7].

16. One of the earliest cases that names the procureur as primary prosecutor dates from 1536. Ibid., 3 BP 7119, Pierre Berthelot versus the *procureur général du roy*. See also ibid., 3 BP 7113, Constant, Jacques et Jean le Gentil versus the *procureur du roy*, 1580; and 3 BP 7119, Charles de Boisguyon versus the *procureur général du roy*, 1624.

17. Ibid., 3 BP 7123, Boisbunoult, 1583; 3 BP 7119, Boivin, 1671.

18. Ibid., 3 BP 7123, Boisbunoult, 1583.

19. Ibid., 3 BP 7119, Billeheust, 1488.

20. Lespine insisted that the king had given nobles the right to engage in commerce without losing their nobility. Ibid., 3 BP 7128, 1477 (a.p.); 3 BP 7119, Blondel, 1513.

21. Ibid., 3 BP 7119, Dabouville, 1482; 3 BP 7125, Gourmont, 1489; 3 BP 7100, Meslet, 1491.

22. Ibid., "Mandements," 3 BP 20, 10 April 1617; 3 BP 31, 29 July 1641.

23. Ibid., "Noblesse," 3 BP 7126, Jehan de la Perelle, fifteenth century; 3 BP 7125, Gourmont, 1489; 3 BP 7113, Bazire, late sixteenth century.

24. Ibid., 3 BP 7122, Caudecoste, 1482; 3 BP 7128, Lespine, 1477.

25. Charles de Robillard de Beaurepaire, ed., *Cahiers des Etats de Normandie sous le règne de Charles IX* (Rouen, 1891), 8ff.; idem, *Cahiers . . . sous le règne de Henri III,* 2 vols. (Rouen, 1891), 222–29; idem, *Cahiers . . . Henri IV,* 2 vols. (Rouen, 1891), 1:55, 71; idem, *Cahiers . . . Louis XIII et Louis XIV,* 3 vols. (Rouen, 1891), 1:130, 2:325, 3:51, 206–9; Dravasa, *"Vivre noblement,"* 119ff.; Jeanne Petit, *L'assemblée des notables de 1626–1627* (Paris, 1936), 175ff.; Picot, *Histoire des Etats Généraux* 2:276.

26. Of the 106 associates of the Company of New France in 1629, 26 were listed as either merchants or bourgeois, 10 have no occupation listed, one was a sea captain, and one a medical doctor. The remaining 68 were predominantly royal officials, with a few municipal officials mixed in. *Collection de manuscrits,* 80–85.

27. Roland Mousnier, *La vénalité des offices sous Henri IV et Louis XIII,* 2d ed. (Paris, 1971), 26ff., 330–31.

28. ADSM, Cour des Aides, "Mandements," 3 BP 4–32.

29. Ibid., "Noblesse," 3 BP 7113, Bellemare, 1605.

30. Ibid., "Mandements," 3 BP 31, 29 July 1641.

31. Ibid., 3 BP 32, 30 January 1644.

32. Ibid., 3 BP 32, 20 June 1645.

33. Ibid., "Noblesse," 3 BP 7119, Boivin, 1671.

34. Ibid., 3 BP 7113, Ferreur, 1643.

35. Ibid., Bréard, 1679.

36. Ibid., "Mandements," 3 BP 23, 19 January 1612, 13 March 1625, and 30 August 1625; 3 BP 25, 20 July 1628.

37. Picot, *Histoire des Etats Généraux* 2:276.

38. ADSM, Tabellionage de Rouen, 2ème série heritages, 17 January 1584.

39. Both Bosquet and Trevache invested in commerce with the New World, and both of their noble patrons or members of their families also had interests in the New World. Ibid., 1 meubles, 9 February and 20 June 1559, 6 December 1560, 11 January and 1 and 8 February 1561, 1 December 1565, 7 and 23 February and 10 May 1566; 2 EP 1/332, 12 June 1566; 2 meubles, 20 February 1576; 2 EP 1/362, 5 May 1581 (four contracts of this date); 2 EP 1/365, 14 February and 27 May 1582; 2 EP 1/360, 13 June 1584.

40. Henry P. Biggar, *The Early Trading Companies of New France* (Toronto, 1901), 94ff., 112, 137, 185.

41. Dravasa, "*Vivre noblement,*" 21ff.

42. Ibid., 159ff.

43. Gandilhon, *Politique économique de Louis XI*, 115ff.; Zeller, "Louis XI . . . et la marchandise," 333ff.

5. Absolutism and Municipal Autonomy:

Henry IV and the 1602 Pancarte

Revolt in Limoges

ANNETTE FINLEY-CROSWHITE

Historians have often described Henry IV's handling of municipal issues as spontaneous and motivated by urban strife. This argument emphasizes that Henry sought to solve pertinent problems, but that he did so with little insight into town matters and certainly with no clearly defined municipal policy. Rather than taking any real initiative, he merely reacted to circumstances that forced his hand as a means of maintaining order.[1]

Deeper analysis into crown-town affairs, however, reveals a more complex situation. Henry IV had a long and varied history of interaction with the towns. When he first became king in 1589, for example, the majority of his country's people, including some of the largest and wealthiest towns of the realm, were united against him in the Catholic League. Defeating the league resulted as much from a systematic application of diplomatic maneuvers as from military genius. Henry lured rebellious towns to his side by offering to forgive the municipalities for their disloyalty, and by promising comprehensive recognition and maintenance of municipal liberties, privileges, constitutions, and charters as rewards for accepting his kingship.[2] Royal administration of municipal issues changed almost immediately, however, after the flood of capitulations that occurred in 1594, a fact which suggests that Henry regarded as suspect urban tradition, privilege, and autonomy. The king knew that a definitive victory over the league could be achieved only through the establishment of a strong monarchy. To this end, he implemented strict measures designed to regularize municipalities and bring them under stronger crown supervision. Henry intervened in local politics and manipulated the outcome of elections; he reduced the size of some municipal governments and ordered that no one was to be elected to magisterial office without his consent; he interfered when necessary to avert scandals and corruption within town governments and to determine more fairly the outcome of municipal elections.[3] Impositions of the royal will in urban politics can be found in numerous instances in all of the major league towns, and these assaults upon municipal independence lend validity to the hypothesis that Henry IV possessed a municipal policy that was not merely reactive. When possible he tried to subjugate municipal autonomy to royal authority.

In summarizing Henry's relationship with urban governments, historians have often referred to his exertion of royal authority in the town of Limoges.[4] In 1602 a revolt occurred there against the hated municipal tax, the *pancarte,* and Henry IV conveniently used this event to restrict the town's liberties and exert the power of the crown. David Buisseret believes that the riot in Limoges was just the kind of civil disorder that forced Henry into action.[5] J. Russell Major speculates that the disturbance provided the king with a sought-after excuse to curtail municipal privilege.[6] In no case, however, has analysis of the outbreak of violence in Limoges and the aftermath been very thorough. Thus, the revolt will be examined here as a means of discerning the "limits" of the king's municipal policy by answering the question, Was Henry IV an archaic ruler content to forget about the towns unless they provoked his attention or a reform-minded monarch intent on strengthening royal authority at the expense of municipal freedoms?[7]

THE RIOT

The riot that occurred in Limoges between 20 and 22 April 1602 arose out of opposition to a 5 percent sales tax on merchandise sold in towns. Known as the *sol pour livre* and vulgarly called the *pancarte,* the imposition had been promulgated in May 1597 after the Assembly of Notables (1596–97) approved its use as an aid to balancing the royal budget and as a means of shifting some of the tax burden from the countryside to the urban centers.[8] When it was renewed in 1601, an *arrêt* specified that all towns without exception would be liable for the tax and Henry and Sully began efforts to oversee its collection.[9] The towns, however, were reluctant to accept the tax, and favored towns won the right to pay a one-time subvention in place of the imposition.[10] Riots against the *pancarte* took place in Poitiers and in Limoges before the tax was finally suppressed on 10 November 1602.[11]

The tumult set off in Limoges on 20 April 1602 began when a chevalier of the *guet* from Orléans named Lambert, under orders to publish the *pancarte* and announce its collection in all public squares, arrived in the town with a company of archers. Trouble brewed as Lambert began his mission. Murmurs and cries denouncing the *pancarte* arose from an anxious crowd until Lambert could no longer hear his own voice over the noise. When a group of angry women sparked off an attack from the agitators and wounded two of the archers with rocks, the officer and his men retreated to their hotel, bolting the doors behind them.[12] Afterward and for the rest of the day "a deafening ferment" hung in the air.[13] Instead of dwindling during the night, moreover, the number of protesters grew so that by the next day they occupied all the main avenues in Limoges. In the morning they assaulted the house of a *trésorier de France,* Jehan du Verdier d'Orfeuille, who had signed the *pancarte* and was thus blamed for it. The windows of his house were broken, but no attempt was made to penetrate the interior. Before noon the crowd dispersed and d'Orfeuille was able to leave his dwelling and go to dine with the bishop, Henri de la Martonie. He was spotted, however, passing by the town's fish market, and the riot recommenced. A group of rock-throwing women chased him to the bishop's residence. The treasurer was so shaken he remained there for several days.[14]

The following morning, all the boutiques in Limoges were closed. Troops of agitators formed and marched on the *maison de ville,* where they yelled for the consuls to chase Lambert and his archers from town. At this point, for the first time since the trouble began, the municipal magistrates took some initiative. They spoke to the people and attempted to quiet them. The rioters left the *maison de ville* in an excited state, however, and proceeded to the Place Saint-Michael of the Lions before the hotel Breuil, where Lambert was in conference with the governor of Limoges, the baron of Châteauneuf. Four to five thousand protesters were said to have gathered in the place and begun hurling insults at Lambert. They attacked the hotel, but were repelled by a strong defense from within. The town magistrates, thinking their warning sufficient, had failed to follow the crowd to the Breuil. They arrived there only much later, after the riot had long since got out of control. One of them, Jacques Martin, a president at the *siège présidial* of Limoges and former consul, persuaded the people that he would negotiate with the king to suppress the hated tax. His influence calmed the rioters, and they allowed the consuls to enter the hotel. That evening Lambert was given safe-conduct from Limoges, and peace was restored.[15]

THE AFTERMATH

To punish the town for its disobedience, Henry IV dispatched Anthoine Le Camus, sieur de Jambeville, the president of his Grand Conseil, with a special commission to restore order and render justice. Jambeville arrived on 19 May and immediately held a session with the municipal government. He informed its members that the king considered the riot "a pure rebellion and disobedience against the authority of the crown." [16] The king understood that not all of the townspeople had participated in the disturbance, and he decreed that only the guilty would be punished. Jambeville then addressed the town magistrates directly. The individuals the king perceived as most responsible for the sedition, he announced, were the consuls who had failed to act properly to prevent and/or dispel the riot. For this reason the king called for the resignation of all twelve ruling consuls, and Jambeville asked them to take off their consular capes and put them on a table before him. In their place the king chose directly, with no recommendation from the townspeople, six new consuls to serve out the rest of the term. These six were Jean de Mauple, *trésorier général de France;* Jean Bonin, *procureur du roi au siège présidial;* Gaspard Benoist, *élu de l'élection;* Joseph de Petiot, *juge de la ville;* Durand-Brugière, bourgeois; and Pierre DuBois, bourgeois-merchant. All six protested, but in the end they had no choice but to follow the king's command, take the consular oath, and be inducted into office.[17] Henry IV's punishment did not stop there. His reduction in the size of the consular government in Limoges from twelve to six was made permanent, and he diminished the size of the electorate from an indeterminate number of citizens who held suffrage rights to only one hundred bourgeois, who were to be elected in groups of ten from each of the ten *quartiers* of Limoges before the consular elections each year. In this way the incumbent consuls would choose the one hundred bourgeois the day before the actual consular elections, and these one hundred would in turn elect the six new consuls. In addition, for the first election held under this new system, in December 1602, Henry declared that he would himself choose the one hundred bourgeois.[18]

Jambeville remained in Limoges throughout June dispensing justice in the name of the king. Most of the people connected with the riot were among the poorer inhabitants of the town, and in a letter to the chancellor Bellièvre, Jambeville wrote that he was "losing his mind" trying to separate the truth from the lies in all of the conflicting stories he had heard.[19] Many of the protesters had fled the town after Jambeville's arrival, but two were caught in Bergerac and returned to Limoges. They were broken on the wheel in the Place Saint-Michael of the Lions, the scene of much of the riot.[20]

THE OUTCOME

It might appear that Henry IV's decision to revise election procedures in Limoges was the direct result of the *pancarte* riot and the king's wish to punish individual errant magistrates. In this sense the riot has always been viewed as the sole stimulus for his interaction with Limoges, and the conclusion is thus drawn that he responded to municipal situations only when civil strife forced his attention.[21] No doubt Henry used the opportunity of the riot to strengthen the crown's authority in the town, but closer examination of the local history reveals that Limoges was a troubled place during his reign and inclined to minor disturbances and riots.[22] Municipal elections before 1602 often brought on problems between leaguers, Protestants, and royalists, to the extent that Henry was forced to intervene frequently in the municipal government. In this light, the *pancarte* riot seems not to have been the catalyst that sparked the king's action, but rather the climax of many years of urban conflict that he decided to settle once and for all. Henry condemned the twelve consuls of 1602 for failing to suppress the riot, but in reality he was blaming the institution of the consulate itself, which had caused him too many problems and no longer functioned to maintain peace.

More than just the riot, therefore, influenced Henry IV's design for Limoges. His anxieties were revealed in a speech Jambeville delivered to the consulate during that councillor's stay in the town. He told the town government that in Henry's judgment the traditional election procedure (before 1602) had brought about nothing more than "intrigues, seditions, and tumults."[23] Their king believed, furthermore, that the riot in Limoges had been preceded by a takeover of magisterial posts by people of low quality. "A government so insolent and disordered," Jambeville warned the consuls, "can only await some terrible accident that will cause the ruin and desolation of the town in the future."[24] For this reason, he said, Henry had interceded and altered the process of the consular elections: he acted in the best interest of the town. Henry wrote to the duke of Montmorency shortly after the revolt took place: "I will take resolution with my council of the order that I wish to establish in Limoges to break the partiality that exists there, and also of the example I wish to make for the punishment of the bad and for the containment of the just in the affection they have to the good of my service."[25]

The "partiality" to which Henry alluded referred to the complicated history of election tumults in Limoges, which he was tired of confronting by 1602. Part of the problem stemmed from a rift within the community between various interest groups that periodically tried to gain control of the municipal consulate. Old hostilities generated by the Catholic League lingered for most of Henry's reign, even though the townspeople were by and large loyal to the king.

Tensions were high between Catholics and Protestants in Limoges, and this fact contributed greatly to the election disputes that occurred frequently in the town. The viscounty of Limoges belonged to the Albret family, until it was finally united with the kingdom of France in 1606 by the last king-viscount, Henry IV.[26] Before Henry's reign, however, his mother, Jeanne d'Albret, as viscountess of Limoges had encouraged the spread of Protestantism in the region. To counteract the Huguenot strength, Catholic confraternities sprang up and incited hostilities by acting like vigilante groups and using murder and pillage to forestall the spread of the new religion.[27] The Huguenots were far from idle victims, even so, for in the city of Limoges the clergy regularly had to pay companies of armed guards to keep their churches from being pilfered or ransacked.[28] Evidence that some of the more influential bourgeois had become Protestants exists for the 1563 elections. In that year Charles IX made an unprecedented move and manipulated the elections so that only Catholics won places on the consulate.[29]

The history of the Catholic League in Limoges is also of particular interest. The league was never completely successful in taking over the town, although throughout the period 1589 to 1594 many important citizens openly belonged to the league, and conflict always existed between this group and the consulate, which was controlled by an alliance of royalists and Protestants. In 1589, after the death of Henry III, the bishop Henry de la Martonie, leader of the league in Limoges, attempted to overthrow the municipal government in the city.[30] Yet the events that occurred between 15 and 17 October 1589 reveal a complex situation in which leaguers, royalists, and Protestants were all forced to defend themselves in an environment in which anarchy reigned for several days.[31]

No one was safe as the various factions vented their hostilities on their enemies. This danger is aptly illustrated by a skirmish that occurred between a group of leaguers and members of the consulate on the first day of the coup. When four royalist consuls and the king's intendant, Mery de Vic, tried to persuade a group of league guards to release several recently captured Huguenot hostages, they were met by rock-throwing street fighters who yelled: "Death to the Huguenots, Kill, Kill, Long live the Cross!"[32] The consuls attempted to calm their assailants, but began to retreat when a leader of the league movement, the judge and fellow consul Martial de Petiot, arrived with his troops and fighting broke out. The situation was quite hopeless, because most of the consuls were unarmed. They held their consular capes over their heads and waved them wildly as a sign to the mob to remember their distinguished place in the society. Oddly, the leader of the aggressors was their peer and colleague in the municipal government. Gunfire erupted, and when the smoke cleared the consul Etienne Pinchaud lay dead in the street, his ineffective cape draped uselessly across his chest. Another consul, Thomas Durand-Brugière, was wounded.[33]

By the second day of the coup most of the consuls had locked themselves in the château and the town was riddled with barricades. The leaguers occupied the churches of the town, and from a central command in the church of Saint-Michael, they organized forays to murder Huguenots and pillage the houses of both Protestants and royalists. The leaguer movement had no cohesion, however, and after two days of terrible violence the participants began to abandon the cause. Control was regained by the royalists on the third day, and four leaders of the coup were executed on the site of Pinchaud's murder. The viscount de Pompadour had originally given aid to the league attempt in Limoges, but he left the city when he heard that the duke of Epernon was on his way to relieve the royalists. Epernon arrived on the nineteenth of October with two thousand men in arms and five hundred cavalry. His troops pillaged the town the following day. Great excesses were committed against the leaguers under the pretext of serving the king. The homes of the compromised were ransacked, and the leaguers themselves were either fined or exiled.[34]

This kind of violence and destruction produced bitterness among the consuls and the townspeople, and since nothing was really resolved by the coup of 1589, Limoges remained divided between leaguers and royalists for years to come. Problems began to arise in earnest when exiled leaguers returned and settled in Limoges, after letters patent were issued to that effect in February 1596. Their reinstatement was met with great rejoicing by the townspeople, and a Te Deum was sung to celebrate the reconciliation.[35] Thereafter factions quickly formed. Disturbances and tumults between the groups became common.[36] Le Camus de Jambeville even expressed frustration over this problem in a letter he wrote to Bellièvre during his investigation of the *pancarte* riot. Lamenting over the difficulties he faced in settling the affair, Henry's officer stated: "But I assure you with truth, Monsieur, that it will take a more able man than myself because each person has his interest and so great recommendation that those whom I hope to relieve search me out so that I am constrained to unravel testimonies by short means."[37]

Political and religious passions, moreover, seemed to erupt each year around election time. In December 1591, for example, the *maison de ville* was mobbed during the consular elections by a group of royalists who demanded that neither a leaguer nor a Huguenot be allowed in the municipal government. Although the agitators were mostly laborers and merchants, the instigators of the disturbance were actually two very influential persons in Limoges, Jacques Martin, a president at the *siège présidial*, and his brother, the *lieutenant criminel*. The consuls quickly fled from the scene of the incident and the town militia dispelled the tumult. Subsequently, Martin and his brother were exiled, along with other participants, for their involvement.[38]

The election of 1593 took place in the presence of the governor of Limoges, and in 1594 a member of the king's Conseil Privé observed the event. In 1596 (after the return of exiled leaguers) and for the succeeding three years, however, tensions were so high that Henry IV was forced to intervene each year and directly select ten of the twelve municipal magistrates. Fraud was revealed in the election process in 1600 when it became known that the Huguenots had brought a number of artisans to the *maison de ville* and paid them each ten sous to vote for Huguenot candidates. The governor of the province, the duke of Epernon, informed the king of the circumstances, and Henry decided to choose the twelve consuls from a list of thirty notables.[39] In 1601 Henry IV sent a list of thirty names to Limoges, from which he allowed a regular election of ten consuls. The newly elected ten in turn chose the final two consuls to make up the normal pre-1602 twelve-member municipal government.[40] Finally, in May 1602, following the *pancarte* riot, Henry established his six appointees in municipal office. In December of that same year, when new elections were to be held and the king had decided that for the first election observed under the new system he would choose the one hundred bourgeois himself, he wrote instead to the town saying that he did not have the time to select the electorate and so maintained the six consuls from 1602 in office for the year 1603.[41] The first time incumbent consuls were allowed to name one hundred bourgeois did not occur until December 1604, because the king made the selection in December 1603. Except, then, for the 1601 election, Henry IV controlled most of the appointments to consular offices in Limoges between 1596 and 1603.[42]

Annual elections in Limoges clearly provided the setting in which popular violence was not necessarily inevitable, but at least probable. The crowding together of people from all strata of the city produced a volatile situation. Often the municipal authorities could not maintain control and hostilities exploded. Whether consuls were Catholic or Protestant, ex-leaguer or royalist, was a matter of sufficient concern to the voting populace to engender the threat of suspicion, fraud, bribery, and/or riot in every election from 1591 to 1600. These disturbances subsequently forced Henry IV to intervene to maintain order. His action following the *pancarte* riot was thus made as a bold attempt to quell recurring trouble in Limoges, trouble that too often caused unruly elections. He did not make strictly retaliatory responses to punish the town for the disturbance. In the king's edict announcing the restructuring of the municipal government in Limoges, he pointed not to the *pancarte* riot as the reason behind his decision, but to the divisions within the society that existed and provoked disorder. Henry stated: "The long duration of civil wars and troubles of our realm have greatly debased the morals so that good regulations that were instituted in our towns to prevent disagreements among the inhabitants have served to separate and divide them as so often occurs to our very great regret in our town of Limoges, capital of Limousin."[43] It should not be construed that Henry IV did not use the opportunity of the *pancarte* riot to exert greater control by the crown over the municipal government, nor that his actions were not in part punitive. Undeniably, however, his decisions were aimed at resolving more enduring issues than the riot itself.[44]

This point is made clear by examining the transformation Henry IV's legislation wrought on the composition of Limoges's consulate. On the one hand, reducing the sheer number of municipal magistrates elected each year from twelve to six made the town government smaller and more easily

Table 1. Number of consular positions, family names, and percentage of recurring family names in Limoges's municipal government (1592–1610)

Years	1592–1602 (Excluding 1599)	1602–10
Total consular positions	112	48
Family names appearing in consulate	80 (71%)	26 (54%)
Rate of repetition of family names in consulate	29%	46%

Sources: Archives Municipales, Limoges, BB2 (elections held 7 December each year), fols. 3–138; Louis Guibert, ed., *Registres consulaires de la ville de Limoges, second registre (1592– 1662)* (Limoges, 1884), 1–2, 20–22, 31–34, 39–47, 57–59, 73, 79, 113, 115, 117, 129, 133.

observable by the crown. On the other hand, the king's decision to decrease the size of the electorate from a vast body of all those heads of households considered "citizens" to only one hundred bourgeois, who were themselves chosen by incumbent consuls, recast a loosely oligarchical town government into a tighter oligarchical structure, and one that was commanded by only a handful of the city's most influential robe and bourgeois families. The post-1602 electoral system thus functioned to virtually guarantee that the same elite families would dominate the town council. For example, between 1592 and 1602 (excluding the year 1599), elections were held for 112 consular positions, and, of this number, 92 individuals filled the offices (several persons were elected more than once) (see table 1). Within the group of 92, there are 80 different family names. These 80 family names represent 71 percent of the total 112, a 29 percent rate of repetition of family names in the town government. In contrast, during the latter period, 1602–10, although the number of available offices shrank to only 48, filled by 41 individuals, a disproportionately smaller number of family names are represented: only 26 names, or 54 percent of the total 48. This is a 46 percent rate of repetition, an increase over the first rate of repetition of more than one-third.

It is also interesting to note that of Henry IV's original 6 consuls from 1602–3, 4 were royal officeholders, 1 was listed as a bourgeois, and the last was a bourgeois-merchant. Theoretically, by the act of 1602, the 6 consuls chosen each year were to be selected from citizens on the taille roles.[45] This change should have barred royal officeholders exempt from the tax from municipal office.[46] But Henry IV ignored the stipulation when he named 4 royal officeholders in 1602–3. Not surprisingly, royal office-

Table 2. Social composition of municipal
officeholders in Limoges (1602–1610)

Category	Number	Percentage
Royal officials	19	47
Listed only as "sieur de"	4	10
Bourgeois	17	41
Merchant	1	2
Total	41	100

Sources: See table 1.

Table 3. Actual breakdown of positions listed
in election returns for forty-six consuls
(1602–1610)

Position	Number	Percentage
Trésorier général	4	10
Lieutenant-général	1	2
Conseiller siège présidial	2	5
Procureur du roi	3	8
Avocat du roi	2	5
Médecin du roi	1	2
Receveur général	1	2
Juge	3	8
Elu	2	5
Sieur de	4	10
Bourgeois	17	41
Marchand	1	2
Total	41	100

Sources: See table 1.

holders continued to share importance with the commercial bourgeois (as
they had done in the late sixteenth century) in Limoges's municipal government well into the mid-1650s.[47] Tables 2 and 3 reveal the social position
of the 41 different consuls who held municipal office between 1602 and
1610. Although 6 consuls were elected each year, 7 persons held the office
on two occasions between 1602 and 1610. Unfortunately, it is not known

if the magistrates listed on the election returns as "bourgeois" were prac-
ticing commerce or simply drawing income from their investments. Since
many of the well-known wealthiest merchants in Limoges were listed only
as "bourgeois," however, it is assumed that a strong link was maintained
between the consular magistrates and commerce.[48]

The most dramatic impact Henry IV's 1602 reform of the Limoges town
government had on the municipality had to do with the reintegration of
formally ostracized ex-leaguers. Evidence shows that ex-leaguers, following their return in 1596, regained their economic viability quite rapidly. Yet
they were almost completely denied participation in the municipal government until 1602.[49] Of 92 individuals who served as municipal consuls from
1592 to 1602, only 3 managed to hold office in the 1602–10 period.[50] This
decrease in representation would not be especially significant if their sons
and/or nephews figured in the latter period. But in the case of Limoges,
there was a virtual changeover of personnel, so that of the 106 different
family names drawn from the overall 1592–1610 period, only 11 are common to both the pre- and the post-1602 categories.[51] Even more striking is
that while only a handful of ex-leaguers managed to hold municipal office
between 1592 and 1602, 28 out of 41 individuals, or 68 percent of those
who served as consuls between 1602 and 1610, were either ex-leaguers
themselves or related to the greatest league families.[52] Each year between
1602 and 1610 at least 3 of the 6 consuls were former leaguers, and in
1608 and 1610 all 6 consuls either had supported the league coup in 1589
or belonged to families that had done so. Finally, of the 7 persons who
held the consular office more than once between 1602 and 1610, all were
ex-leaguers.[53]

It should be clear that the *pancarte* riot of 1602 was far from a one-time
crisis that provoked Henry IV into action in Limoges, and his reorgani-
zation of the town's municipal government had an enormous impact. The
ex-leaguers in Limoges unquestionably owed their political reinstatement
into municipal power to Henry IV and the legislation promulgated after
the *pancarte* riot. Michel Cassan, the most recent historian of the town's
administrative and religious history, calls Henry IV's decision to favor
the ex-leaguers the "triumph of Catholicism."[54] Cassan notes that after
recovering political power the ex-leaguers went on to herald Catholic reform in the town.[55] This may have been the case, but it is important to
remember that Henry's decision to reintegrate ex-leaguers into the town's
consulate came only in 1602. The king had been observing and manipu-
lating elections in Limoges throughout the entire course of his reign, and

during the 1596–1600 period he clearly selected faithful royalists for municipal office. What was the reason behind this delay in the reintegration of former leaguers? One can only speculate, but perhaps a period of time was necessary for leaguers to prove their fidelity to Henry IV before they could be trusted in municipal office. In league towns in the 1590s Henry tended to promote men in municipal office who joined the royalist movement before a town's capitulation. But by the end of Henry's reign, in most of the largest former league towns, ex-leaguers, particularly those connected with families that had traditionally held municipal office, were reintegrated into city government.[56]

The great significance of 1602 in Limoges, therefore, is that of the six consuls Henry IV chose for municipal office, four were former leaguers.[57] Since these six consuls eventually selected the one hundred bourgeois, who in turn elected the succeeding six consuls, the enduring presence of ex-leaguers in municipal government was virtually guaranteed.[58] In one sense this restructuring of the municipal government was simply a return to the natural order of things, since many of the men who served as consuls between 1602 and 1610 came from families that had traditionally monopolized municipal offices since the fifteenth century.[59] More important, the 1602 restructuring of Limoges's municipal government was a conscious effort by Henry IV to end the electoral turmoil that plagued the town throughout his reign. Such effort proves the king to have been a serious and reform-minded ruler, who deliberately devised municipal policy (at least in Limoges) on the basis of his detailed understanding of town issues. Henry did not need the *pancarte* riot to rouse his interest in municipal matters in Limoges, but he used the event to his advantage and augmented his royal command of municipal affairs. While reestablishing order and stability in Limoges, Henry IV conditioned the town to greater intervention from the crown. In doing so he promoted his own power and established precedents for the emerging absolutist state.

NOTES

1. David Buisseret, *Henry IV* (London, 1984), 165; August Poirson, *Histoire du règne de Henri IV* (Paris, 1862), 3:29–30; François Bourçier, "Le régime municipal à Dijon sous Henri IV," *Revue d'histoire moderne*, n.s., 4 (1935): 118.

2. J. Russell Major, *Representative Government in Early Modern France* (New Haven, 1980), 380–81. The major Catholic League towns were Paris, Rouen, Marseilles, Lyons, Toulouse, Orléans, Dijon, Nantes, Reims, Amiens, and Troyes.

3. Jean-Pierre Babelon, *Henri IV* (Paris, 1982), 792–96; Orest Ranum, *Paris in the Age of Absolutism: An Essay* (New York: 1968), 53–56; A. Kleinclauz, *Histoire de Lyon,* vol. 2, *1595 à 1814* (Lyons, 1948), 3–8; Emmanuel Le Roy Ladurie et al., eds., *Histoire de la France urbaine,* vol. 3, *La ville classique de la Renaissance aux révolutions* (Paris, 1981), 169; Reverend Père Daire, *Histoire de la ville d'Amiens depuis son origine jusqu'à present* (Paris, 1757), 337; Pierre Deyon, *Amiens, capitale provinciale: Etude sur la société urbaine au 17e siècle* (Paris, 1967), 429.

4. See, for example, Buisseret, *Henry IV,* 165; and Major, *Representative Government,* 381.

5. Buisseret, *Henry IV,* 165.

6. Major, *Representative Government,* 381.

7. See particularly Robert Descimon, "L'Echevinage parisien sous Henry IV (1595–1610): Autonomie urbaine, conflicts politiques et exclusives sociales," in *La ville, la bourgeoisie et la gènese de l'état moderne, XIIe–XVIIIe siècles,* Actes du Colloque de Bielefeld (29 novembre–1 decembre 1985), ed. Neithard Bulst and J.-Ph. Genet (Paris, 1988), 113–50. After examining Henry IV's election intervention in Paris, Descimon concludes, "To sum up, the attitude of Henry IV referred to the most archaic possible political framework, far from all modernizing or absolutist will" (p. 150). In this author's opinion, the Paris example should not be used as a generalization for Henry IV's relationship with all French towns. For further discussion of Henry IV's municipal policy, see Annette Finley-Croswhite, "Henri IV et les villes," in *Henri IV, le roi et la reconstruction du royaume, colloque III, Pau-Nerac,* ed. J. Perot and P. Tucoo-Chala (Pau, 1990), 195–205; and idem, "Henry IV and the Towns: Royal Authority Versus Municipal Autonomy, 1589–1610" (Ph.D. diss., Emory University, forthcoming).

8. J. Russell Major, *Bellièvre, Sully, and the Assembly of Notables of 1596,* Transactions of the American Philosophical Society, n.s., vol. 64, pt. 2 (Philadelphia, 1974), 27–28. The Assembly of Notables was held in Rouen in 1596–97 to attack fiscal problems. It was similar in composition to an estates general but smaller. For more information, see ibid., 3–34.

9. Buisseret, *Henry IV,* 106–7.

10. Ibid., 107.

11. Noël Valois, ed., *Inventaire des arrêts du Conseil d'Etat, règne de Henri IV* (Paris, 1886–93), no. 7155.

12. Bonaventure de Saint-Amable, *Histoire de Saint Martial apôtre des Gaules, et notamment de L'Aquitaine et du Limosin, ecclésiastiques ou civils, des saints et hommes illustrés et autres choses depuis Saint Martial jusques à nous* (Limoges, 1685), 3:812; M. P. Laforest, *Etudes sur les anciennes provinces de France: Limoges au XVIIe siècle* (Limoges, 1862), 33–34.

13. Laforest, *Etudes,* 35.

14. Bonaventure de Saint-Amable, *Histoire de Saint Martial* 3:812.

15. Information on the revolt is slight. The deliberations of the municipality give

no detail whatsoever on the incident itself. See ibid.; Laforest, *Etudes,* 33–38; and Jean Levet, *Histoire de Limoges,* vol. 1, *Des origines à la fin de l'Ancien Régime* (Limoges, 1974), 251. A few letters found in the Bibliothèque Nationale and quoted below also shed some light on the aftermath of the riot.

16. Archives Municipales, Limoges, BB2, fol. 41r. Dates vary concerning when Jambeville actually arrived in Limoges.

17. Louis Guibert, ed., *Registres consulaires de la ville de Limoges, second registre (1592–1662)* (Limoges, 1884), 60; E. Ruben, "Changements introduits, en 1602, par Henri IV dans le mode d'élection et le nombre des consuls de Limoges," *Bulletin de la Société Archéologique et Historique du Limousin* 3 (1857): 147–48.

18. Act printed in Guibert, ed., *Registres consulaires,* 62–65; and in Ruben, "Changements," 149–51.

19. "Correspondance de Pomponne de Bellièvre," BN, MSS fr. 15899, fol. 849v.

20. Laforest, *Etudes,* 41–42; F. Marvaud, *Histoire des vicomtes et de la vicomté de Limoges* (Paris, 1873), 2:347.

21. Buisseret, *Henry IV,* 165.

22. The observation is discussed below. For a good town history of Limoges see Paul Ducourtieux, *Histoire de Limoges* (Limoges, 1925). For a short summary of civil disorder in Limoges during Henry's reign see Marvaud, *Histoire des vicomtes* 2:312–54.

23. Guibert, ed., *Registres consulaires,* 61.

24. Ibid.

25. Jules Berger de Xivrey, ed., *Recueil des lettres missives de Henri IV* (Paris, 1850), 5:597. For a similar observation about the kind of partisanship that existed in Limoges see Jambeville's letter to Bellièvre in BN, MSS fr. 15899, fols. 849r–50r.

26. Marvaud, *Histoire des vicomtes* 2:384–85.

27. Louis Guibert, *La Ligue à Limoges* (Limoges, 1884), 2–4.

28. Mauvaud, *Histoire des vicomtes* 2:202.

29. Ibid., 221–22. Charles IX asked for the names of twenty-four candidates, from which he chose the twelve consuls. He named only Catholics, who were inducted into office on 17 January 1564.

30. Henry de la Martonie became bishop of Limoges in 1585. In 1589 he adopted the cause of the league, but he became a loyal servant to Henry IV after the king's reconversion to Catholicism in 1594. Martonie's oath of loyalty to Henry IV is published in *Archives historique de la Gironde* (Bordeaux, 1879), 14:318.

31. See Guibert, *Ligue à Limoges,* 15–57. No documents exist in Limoges relative to the league. Guibert used a remarkable document drawn up by the *siège présidial* after the coup failed and now found at the Archives Nationales. See "Informations et procédures faites contre ceux de la Ligue, de la trahison et conspiration faite contre la ville de Limoges, pour la tirer hors de l'obéissance de Sa Majesté, le 15 Octobre 1589," AN, KK 1212. An excellent account of this 998-page manuscript is found in Guibert's *Ligue à Limoges.*

32. Quoted in Guibert, *Ligue à Limoges*, 21.

33. Ibid., 22–24.

34. Ibid., 22–28; Marvaud, *Histoire des vicomtes* 2:314–19; Emile Ruben, Felix Achard and Paul Ducourtieux, eds., *Annales manuscrites de Limoges dites manuscrit de 1638* (Limoges, 1867), 364–70.

35. Bonaventure de Saint-Amable, *Histoire de Saint Martial* 3:809; Mauvaud, *Histoire des vicomtes* 2:342; Michel Cassan, "Les lendemains des Guerres de Religion," in *Croyances, pouvoirs, et société des Limousins aux français*, ed. Michel Cassan (Le Louvanel, 1988), 267.

36. See examples of social tension provided by Michel Cassan in his article "Mobilité sociale et conflits religieux: L'exemple Limousin (1550–1630)," in *La dynamique sociale dans L'Europe du nord-ouest (XVIe–XVIIe siècles)*, Acts du colloque de L'Association des Historiens Modernistes des Universités, no. 12 (Paris, 1987), 80–83.

37. BN, MSS fr. 15899, fol. 849v.

38. Marvaud, *Histoire des vicomtes* 2:332; Ruben, Achard, and Ducourtieux, eds., *Annales*, 373.

39. A. Coissac, *Le consulat à Limoges au XVIe siècle* (Limoges, 1937), 34–36; Ducourtieux, *Histoire de Limoges*, 181.

40. AM, Limoges, BB2, fols. 46–47; Ducourtieux, *Histoire de Limoges*, 181.

41. Henry's letter is dated 7 December 1602 and printed in Guibert, ed., *Registres consulaires*, 66; and in Coissac, *Consulat à Limoges*, 37.

42. Regarding the December election of 1602 see letters in "Recueil de lettres originales et de pièces relatives aux affaires pendant le règne de Henri IV," BN, MSS fr. 23197, fols. 143, 187, 192, 195.

43. Printed in Ruben, "Changements," 149.

44. The *pancarte* issue in Limoges was finally resolved seven months after the riot when the tax was officially removed. See Valois, ed., *Inventaire*, no. 7155. Limoges paid a one-time subvention of 560 livres in place of the *sol pour livre*. Levet, *Histoire de Limoges* 1:251–52.

45. See act printed in Guibert, ed., *Registres consulaires*, 63. It reads, ". . . the said six consuls taken from the number of inhabitants contributing to our tailles . . ."

46. Laforest, *Etudes*, 44.

47. During the Middle Ages municipal governments were made up almost exclusively of merchants. By the sixteenth century regulations were devised to prohibit royal officeholders from municipal posts, but these were increasingly overridden and annulled as robe elite forced their way into the urban oligarchies and confiscated municipal offices. This transformation may not have been as dramatic as it sounds, however, since in many towns numerous powerful fifteenth-century families continued to control urban politics through their descendants in the sixteenth and seventeenth centuries. But while the oligarchic families of the fifteenth century

were solidly merchant-bourgeois, after the mid-sixteenth century they increasingly bought royal offices while maintaining interests in local municipal affairs. See Jacques Paton, *Le corps de ville de Troyes, 1470–1790* (Troyes, 1939), 76–92; Richard Gascon, *Grand commerce et vie urbaine au XVIe siècle: Lyon et ses marchands* (Paris, 1971), 1:409–13; Deyon, *Amiens, capitale provinciale,* 270–77; Philip Benedict, "French Cities from the 16th Century to the Revolution: An Overview," in *Cities and Social Change in Early Modern France,* ed. Philip Benedict (London, 1989), 35–36; and Le Roy Ladurie et al., eds., *Histoire de la France urbaine* 3:178–79.

48. This was the case in Amiens and Rouen. See Deyon, *Amiens, capitale provinciale,* 273–91; and Gayle Brunelle, "Rouen and the New World: Rouennais Investors in Commerce with North and South America, 1559–1629" (Ph.D. diss., Emory University, 1988). Archival documents dating from the sixteenth and seventeenth centuries in Limoges are quite scarce. Parish records are very incomplete, and no attempt was made here to utilize the thirteen *fonds* of notarial documents that exist for the 1550–1620 period. For a more detailed social analysis of certain key league families see Cassan, "Mobilité sociale," 71–92.

49. For the economic reintegration of the leaguers see Michel Cassan's articles "Lendemains," 266–82, and "Mobilité sociale," 71–92.

50. Guibert, ed., *Registres consulaires,* 21–22, 59, 115. The three consuls who held municipal offices in both the pre- and post-1602 periods were Durand-Brugière in 1594 and 1602–3, Joseph Croisier in 1597 and 1604, and Jehan Guerin in 1597 and 1607.

51. All statistical information is developed from the sources listed in the note to table 1. The eleven family names were Brugière, Benoist, Croisier, Descoutures, Douhet, Guerin, Martin, Petiot, Saleys, Vertamond, and Vidaud.

52. Information on league families is drawn from AN, KK 1212, and published in Guibert, *Ligue à Limoges,* 2–58. The list of exiled leaguers is printed in ibid., 47–48.

53. These observations were achieved by comparing Guibert, ed., *Registres consulaires,* 59, 73, 79, 113, 115, 117, 129, 133, with Guibert, *Ligue à Limoges,* 2–58.

54. Cassan, "Lendemains," 278.

55. Ibid., 278–82.

56. This point needs to be examined in detail and can only be fully explored by careful analysis of municipal history and elections in the major league towns. Most towns left the Catholic League once a royalist majority succeeded in taking over the town government, and Henry IV normally utilized the royalists in municipal office in the 1590s. See, for example, Deyon, *Amiens, capitale provinciale.* Henry manipulated elections almost immediately after the towns' capitulations to ensure royalist majorities. For a few examples see Archives Municipales, Amiens, BB54, fol. 3, and BB55, fol. 49; Archives Municipales, Dijon, B232, fol. 295; and Alexan-

dre Perthuis and Stephan de la Nicollière-Teijeiro, *Le livre d'oré de l'hôtel de ville de Nantes* (Nantes, 1873), 1:196.

57. Guibert, ed., *Registres consulaires,* 59. These were Jehan Bonin, Gaspard Benoist, Joseph de Petiot, and Pierre du Bois.

58. See the very interesting letter the consuls of 1602 wrote to the chancellor Bellièvre regarding the king's selection of one hundred bourgeois, in BN, MSS fr. 15899, fol. 644.

59. Cassan, "Lendemains," 277–78. The Petiot, Saxon, and Saleis families, for example, were three of those who traditionally sought consular office.

6. Popular Political Culture

and Mayoral Elections

in Sixteenth-Century Dijon

MACK P. HOLT

However one chooses to define the process by which the crown attempted to erode the powers and privileges of local municipalities during the course of the seventeenth century, it is nonetheless clear that the autonomy enjoyed by many towns during the Wars of Religion to tax their citizens and generally to police and administer their jurisdictions as they saw fit was not to survive indefinitely. That Henry IV (and later Louis XIII and Louis XIV) wished to control the independent and often powerful municipal magistrates who opposed the crown with much success during the latter stages of the civil wars is hardly in question; nor is the fact that the monarchy was generally successful in its attempts to curb the powers of these magistrates by the eighteenth century. Indeed, the process of an expanding central government pushing its way into the corridors of power at the local level is one of the keystones in J. Russell Major's analysis of the transition of the French crown from a weak, popular, and consultative Renaissance monarchy into a more centralized, absolute monarchy.[1] One of the most visible municipal privileges that Henry IV sought to undermine immediately after he made peace with the league in the 1590s was the right of a number of towns to elect their own magistrates, particularly their own mayors, and it is this process in the city of Dijon I wish to focus upon here.

A city's right to "create" or "name" its own mayor was the closely guarded privilege of a number of former medieval communes that survived the Middle Ages.[2] What historical attention has been focused on municipal elections has usually taken the form of an analysis of how long and under what circumstances the crown managed to wrest away these municipal privileges over the course of the sixteenth and seventeenth centuries. To be sure, the advancing arm of an ever-growing centralized state is one of the principal themes of early modern historiography, and contemporaries of the period reacted with hostility and sometimes violence when they perceived that the state was attempting to snatch away their traditional rights and privileges. In this essay I consider municipal elections from a different perspective, however: from that of the participants, the *échevins* or aldermen of the city council who supervised the annual mayoral elections, the candidates who stood for election and their supporters, and the bulk of the population (in Dijon largely artisans and *vignerons*), who turned out at six in the morning to cast their "voices" on the eve of Saint John the Baptist's Day every June. Although I cannot avoid mentioning the tension between town and crown, especially as it figured so prominently after the Wars of Religion, my main attention is on the participants in these elections, what it meant to participate, and the roles these elections played in Dijonnais society at all levels. I argue that these elections had a dynamic all their own, independent of the tensions between town and crown. Although they often served as a means for municipal elites to thwart the advances of an encroaching centralized state, they also provided an outlet for popular protest both in the form of selecting a mayor and in the opportunity to voice dissent during the events themselves. Furthermore, a study of these sixteenth- and early seventeenth-century elections demonstrates that the lower orders who made up the bulk of the voters had a political consciousness all their own. Though it rarely coincided with that of the elites they were electing each summer, and was entirely local rather than national, this consciousness clearly served as the foundation for the political values and sensibilities of the winegrowers and artisans who formed the majority of Dijon's population.

In order fully to appreciate the popular context of Dijon's elections in the early modern period, it is necessary to understand two essential premises. First, in a predemocratic age elections had none of the modern connotations of representative government. In fact, it is much nearer the truth to say that these elections were not a means to an end in the modern democratic sense, but an end in themselves. What mattered most was the event, or really series of events, that surrounded these annual rituals each June. To focus on the outcome or result, who was selected and by how much, is a limited way of looking at them. In this sense, the historical preoccupation with the crown's encroaching reach into municipal affairs is somewhat artificial, in that contemporaries were less concerned with royal attempts to place a loyal client in the *mairie* than they were with threats to alter the form of the election itself. It was the guarded privilege to select their own mayor in the traditional manner that they so zealously protected, not necessarily the ability to control the result. Moreover, the citizens of Dijon cast their "voices" rather than their "votes," with the early modern connotation stressing communal solidarity and harmony rather than the differences between or among factions within the community. Secondly, as Peter Burke and Keith Thomas among others have reminded us, we cannot fully appreciate early modern elections unless we realize that these events were *jours de fête* and periods of inversion and misrule.[3] Feasting and drinking were traditionally part of the electoral event all across western Europe, and this was all the more evident in Dijon, where the mayoral elections were held on the eve of the feast of Saint John the Baptist, the annual midsummer festival that culminated with fireworks and a large bonfire. Thus, to fully comprehend the reality of early modern elections for contemporaries, one not only must jettison modern democratic values but also must replace them with an understanding of carnival.

Dijon's right to elect its own mayor dated to the charter granted to the commune by Hugues IV, duke of Burgundy, in 1235.[4] And in the intervening centuries the procedure and format of these elections changed very little. Each year in mid-June the outgoing mayor handed over his symbols of office in a formal ritual that took place in the cemetery of the cathedral of Saint-Bénigne. These symbols included a manuscript copy of the Gospel of Saint John decorated with a gilded crucifix, which was turned over to one of the *échevins* on the city council, who then acted as the *garde des évangiles* and supervisor of the upcoming election. The election was held on 21 June, the traditional election day (unless it fell on a Sunday, in which case the election would take place one day early, on Saturday, 20 June), and the council members all assembled in the Jacobin convent near the cathedral at six o'clock in the morning in order to record the "voices" of the heads of household of the city. It was customary for local dignitaries and elites, such as the lieutenant general of the province or a representative deputed from the Chambre des Comptes, to name their choices first, in hopes of influencing the outcome. Then the outgoing members of the city council, twenty *échevins* plus four or more ecclesiastical members, named their candidates verbally to a recording secretary. Finally, the heads of household of the city of Dijon then filed into the convent one at a time to give their "voices" to the candidates of their choice in front of the assembled council. When all eligible participants had cast their voices, a process that could last all day and into the night in years of heavy turnout, the votes were tabulated and the candidate with the "plurality of voices" was declared the winner. The new mayor was then conducted back to his house, where he was expected to provide food and drink not just for his own supporters, but for all those who had participated in the election. Two days later, on 23 June, the eve of the feast of Saint John the Baptist, the newly elected mayor would select the twenty *échevins* to serve with him on the city council in the coming year: fourteen new members and six who had served the previous year. Six of the total had to be residents of the parish of Nôtre-Dame, three each from Saint-Jean and Saint-Michel, and two each from the remaining parishes of Saint-Nicolas, Saint-Philibert, Saint-Pierre, and Saint-Médard, proportional to parish population. And on the following day, the feast day itself, the new mayor would be presented with the Gospels by the *garde des évangiles,* and then in the parish church of Nôtre-Dame the mayor and *échevins* would all be required to swear their oaths of office before the altar.[5]

Although it is difficult to discern many clear-cut patterns over the course of these annual elections in the Burgundian capital, several conclusions seem warranted. First, the elections became more popular as more and more eligible voters turned out to cast their voices over the course of the sixteenth century. From 1545, when the recording secretary began listing individual voters by name, the lowest turnout was 52 in 1556, and the highest was 1,976 in both 1583 and 1607. This pattern becomes clearer when the figures are broken down further: the average turnout in the period 1545–60 was 194 voters; in the period 1561–80 it was 451 voters; in the period 1581–95 it was 1,050 voters; and in the period 1596–1610 it was 1,513 voters (see the figures for each election in table 1). Second, results of these elections varied widely, depending on several factors: the presence or absence of any volatile issues, such as religion in 1560 and after; the number of candidates seriously standing for office; and how successful the candidates were at mobilizing their supporters and getting them to the convent on election day. Many of the elections were very close, decided by only a handful of votes, while others were nearly unanimous. In all cases, however, a "plurality of voices" was all that was required to be elected mayor of the city. Though Chrétien Godran was elected easily in 1552, winning 80 of 82 votes (97.6 percent), he was defeated the following year by Guillaume Berbisey, who won only 116 out of 328 votes cast (35.4 per-

Table 1. Dijon mayoral elections, 1545–1615

Year	Elected mayor	Total votes	Votes for winning candidate	% of total
1545	Etienne Jaquotot	258	172	66.7
1546	Etienne Jaquotot	82	73	89.0
1547	Jean Jaquot	138	84	60.9
1548	Jean Jaquot	—	—	—
1549	Jean Jaquot	164	105	64.0
1550	Jean Jaquot	—	—	—
1551	Chrêtien Godran	299	166	55.5
1552	Chrêtien Godran	82	80	97.6
1553	Guillaume Berbisey	328	116	35.4
1554	Jehan Robin	357	158	49.9
1555	Chrêtien Godran	118	104	98.1
1556	Chrêtien Godran	52	50	96.2
1557	Bénigne Martin	252	181	71.8
1558	Bénigne Martin	121	118	97.5
1559	Bénigne Martin	224	130	58.0
1560	Jean Maillard	234	68	29.1
1561	Bénigne Martin	496	322	64.9
1562	Bénigne Martin	—	—	—
1563	Bénigne Martin	210	196	93.3
1564	Bénigne Martin	521	504	96.7
1565	Bénigne Martin	304	287	94.4
1566	Jacques Laverne	584	342	58.6
1567	Bénigne Martin	542	289	53.3
1568	Hugues Tisserand	511	274	53.6
1569	Hugues Tisserand	255	183	71.8
1570	Hugues Tisserand	567	370	65.3
1571	Guillaume Millière	363	156	43.0
1572	Guillaume Millière	521	443	85.0
1573	Bernard d'Esbarres	438	188	42.9
1574	Bernard d'Esbarres	491	454	92.5
1575	Hugues Tisserand	396	315	79.5
1576	Jean Petit	—	—	—
1577	Jean le Marlet	510	200	39.2
1578	Jean le Marlet	466	279	59.9
1579	Jean Petit	492	297	60.4
1580	Jean le Marlet	450	351	78.0
1581	Guillaume Royhier	422	201	47.6
1582	Pierre Bouhier	664	285	42.9
1583	Pierre Bouhier	1976	972	49.2
1584	Guillaume Royhier	1390	741	53.3

Year	Elected mayor	Total votes	Votes for winning candidate	% of total
1585	Guillaume Royhier	369	313	84.8
1586	Guillaume Royhier	969	452	46.6
1587	Jacques Laverne	463	449	97.0
1588	Jacques Laverne	475	470	98.9
1589	Pierre Michiel	1070	819	76.5
1590	Jacques Laverne	889	882	99.2
1591	Jacques Laverne	834	594	71.2
1592	Etienne Bernard	1984	558	28.1
1593	Jacques Laverne	1687	1084	64.3
1594	René Fleutelot	1922	1190	61.9
1595	René Fleutelot	634	632	99.7
1596	Bénigne Frémiot	1402	786	56.1
1597	Bénigne de Requeleyne	1277	823	64.4
1598	Bernard Coussin	1710	1240	72.5
1599	Jean Jacquinot	1396	899	64.4
1600	Jean Jacquinot	1792	1050	58.6
1601	Jean Jacquinot	1955	1450	74.2
1602	Michel Bichot	1806	1136	62.9
1603	Jean Frasans	1260	990	78.6
1604	Jean Frasans	1295	640	49.4
1605	Edme Joly	1449	1171	80.8
1606	Jean Perrot	1680	768	45.7
1607	Etienne de Loisie	1976	998	50.5
1608	Chrêtien de Masque	1591	674	42.4
1609	Etienne Humbert	823	470	57.1
1610	Nicolas Humbert	1290	383	29.7
1611	Nicolas Humbert	—	—	—
1612	Jacques Bossuet	772	476	61.7
1613	Jacques Bossuet	548	536	97.8
1614	Edme Joly	789	415	52.6
1615	Edme Joly	898	478	53.2

Source: Archives municipales de Dijon, B 183–253. This is a more accurate list of elected mayors than those published in Claude Courtépée and Edme Béguillet, *Description générale et particulière de duché de Bourgogne,* 3d ed., 3 vols. (Avallon, 1967), 2:28–32; or Pierre Gras, ed., *Histoire de Dijon,* 2d ed. (Toulouse, 1987), 409–12.

cent) in a very close four-man contest. While Jacques Laverne could win reelection convincingly in 1588 with 882 out of 889 votes cast (99.2 percent), Bernard d'Esbarres was elected by only 3 votes in 1573, garnering 188 out of 438 votes cast (42.9 percent) to edge out the incumbent, Guillaume Millière, who received 185 votes (42.2 percent), and several other candidates. Finally, it is clear that attempts by elites outside the *mairie* to influence the voting by making their choices known on election day when the convent opened were generally unsuccessful. Only during the first half of the sixteenth century did the governor of Burgundy, or his lieutenant general, nominate a candidate of his own. On the other hand, a representative of the Chambre des Comptes annually turned up at six in the morning to make known that body's nominee "in the name of the king." The chamber's track record was not an illustrious one, as from 1542 to 1610 its nominee was elected only 26 times in 68 elections: 38.2 percent. And it is very clear, moreover, that the chamber's nominee was not the king's choice, as the chamber invariably nominated one of its own deputies for mayor. In 1559 and in 1560, for example, the chamber's nominee was Antoine Brocard, a *conseiller du roi* but also a well-known Protestant, who could hardly have been the chosen candidate of either Henry II in 1559 or the Guise-dominated Francis II in 1560.[6] Thus, the result of the elections followed no discernible pattern of support by community notables. The outcome ultimately hinged on the candidates' own abilities to mobilize the city's voters, about which more will be said shortly.

But first, who participated in these elections? The sociology of those who sought the office of mayor is fairly straightforward, in that nearly all candidates were members of the municipal elites: wealthy merchants, professional men, or, increasingly by the late sixteenth century, men of the law. The office of mayor was a prized honor, not least because it carried automatic ennoblement after 1491. As it was extremely rare for any candidate to be elected who had not previously served for at least a year as an *échevin*, historians' insistence that the Dijon *mairie* was a self-perpetuating oligarchy is pretty close to the mark.[7] Several generations of some families, for example, served the *mairie* either as mayors or *échevins* or both: the Berbiseys, Tisserands, Humberts, Bossuets, Le Marlets, and Jolys, to name only the most obvious. Exactly how this oligarchy managed to maintain its political stranglehold on the commune is a more complex question, however, and raises the crucial issue of who turned out to cast their voices for them and why.

The sociology of the electorate is a much more difficult subject to assess.

Not only were individual votes not recorded before 1545, but occupations of the voters were indicated on the voter rolls for only a very few years after that date. Prior to 1545 the records of the *mairie* only described the election, indicated the winner, and listed the choices of the *échevins* themselves and other elites. Appended to this brief description was usually a note that "several other inhabitants of the said city [who] assembled in great number" also participated. How great that number was is unclear, however, until the council decided to record individual votes beginning in 1545. In that year 258 inhabitants (including the elites) out of a total of about 2,800 heads of household participated in the mayoral election: a turnout of less than 10 percent.[8] The voter turnout fluctuated but gradually increased to around 500–600 participants over the next three decades. In 1582, when 664 voters participated out of an eligible total of about 3,300 heads of household, the turnout had doubled to 20 percent.[9] The meager turnout was still so disappointing, however, that the *mairie* attempted to introduce a stiff fine the following year for any eligible voter who did not participate in the mayoral elections. From 1583 on, at least until the crown began to intervene seriously in the elections in 1630, participation numbered regularly over 1,000, and even approached 2,000 in peak years.[10] Thus, from 1583, turnouts of 50 percent and greater were not uncommon. But who made up these numbers?

The most striking aspect of Dijon's mayoral elections is that the electorate was composed overwhelmingly of winegrowers and artisans. The self-perpetuating oligarchy stayed in power not by mobilizing the elites of the city to turn out to support them, but by mobilizing the masses. Winegrowers and artisans headed more households in sixteenth-century Dijon than any other social groups. By the middle of the sixteenth century winegrowers constituted 18.7 percent and artisans 33.7 percent of Dijon's population of some 14,500 people.[11] These were by far the largest social groups on the tax rolls, and one would expect them to show up in large numbers at municipal elections. In reality they far surpassed their representation in the population at large, however, as winegrowers and artisans commonly made up from 75 to 90 percent of total participants in the annual elections. They so dominated the elections that merchants, professional men, and elites of all types deliberately stayed at home, not wishing to take part in an event dominated by the masses. It was the startling election of Pierre Bouhier in 1582, in fact, that provoked the attempt to fine any inhabitant who failed to turn up at the Jacobin convent to vote the following year. Bouhier, a lieutenant in the chancellery, was not sup-

ported by any of the elite officials. With the majority of the winegrowers
and artisans opting for Bouhier, however, he won a surprising victory. In
the hope of preventing a similar outcome in the future, the *mairie* requested
the Parlement of Dijon to change the qualifications of participation and
refuse admission to the convent to anyone who did not pay at least 40
sous per year in the personal taille. Moreover, the *mairie* decided to fine
anyone who was eligible who did not turn out. The primary concern of
the magistrates was that "worthy and notable inhabitants" were staying
away in droves, "seeing that the votes of the poor winegrowers and artisans counted for just as much as those of good and worthy inhabitants." [12]
The Parlement rejected the *mairie*'s request, as it happened, and the following year the largest recorded turnout in Dijon's history up to that time
occurred: nearly two thousand inhabitants of the city showed up to vote,
though artisans and winegrowers still made up the bulk of the numbers.

As an indication of the extent of popular participation in the elections,
the few voter rolls listing occupations show that the *mairie*'s concerns
about the low turnout of elites were justified. While winegrowers and artisans regularly made up the bulk of the electorate, the participation of the
former group commands particular attention. Numbering less than 19 percent of the population in the mid-sixteenth century, the *vignerons* regularly
made up the single largest occupational group participating in the elections. Moreover, they often made up more than half the entire electorate
(see table 2). In the election of 1561 there was a heavy turnout because
the Protestant candidate, Antoine Brocard, was running and garnered significant support. The heavily Catholic winegrowers turned out in record
numbers as a result, and they helped the ultra-Catholic Bénigne Martin
win the election. The winegrowers made up more than 40 percent of the
total electorate and nearly 60 percent of those who supported the Catholic Martin. Significantly, of all *vignerons* who participated that year, more
than 90 percent of them voted for Martin. Martin had been first elected
in 1557, largely because of a heavy turnout of winegrowers, and there is
little question that his ability to mobilize this social group was the foundation of his success. Whereas only a dozen or so winegrowers are listed as
having participated in the elections prior to 1557, 107 of them turned out in
that year, with half of them supporting Martin. The mayor was reelected
each successive year until 1560, when he decided not to mount a serious
campaign in order to let someone else hold office. Even then, Martin lost
to Jean Maillard by only 8 votes. When the Protestant Brocard offered a
serious challenge the following year, however, Martin and his supporters

Table 2. Winegrower votes in Dijon mayoral elections

Year	Winegrower votes	% of total	Winegrower votes for winning candidate	% of winner's total	% of winegrowers for winner
1555	16	13.6	16	15.4	100.0
1556	14	26.9	14	28.0	100.0
1557	107	42.5	89	49.2	83.2
1558	24	19.8	24	20.3	100.0
1559	48	21.4	33	25.4	68.8
1560	21	9.0	4	5.9	19.0
1561	203	40.9	188	58.8	92.6
1564	267	51.2	267	53.0	100.0
1565	161	53.0	161	56.1	100.0
1566	226	38.7	164	48.0	72.6
1567	234	43.2	115	39.8	49.1
1572	183	35.1	130	29.3	71.0
1580	247	54.9	226	64.4	91.5

Source: Archives municipales de Dijon, B 193–99, 201–4, 210, 218. The totals in this table are to be used in conjunction with those in table 1.

coaxed more than 200 winegrowers to turn out to vote to ensure Catholic control of the *mairie*. In the 1561 election they made up nearly 60 percent of his total support, as more than 90 percent of all winegrowers supported Martin in this election dominated by religion.[13] The Catholic mayor was reelected each year for the next five years, and the foundation of his support remained the *vigneron* community. In 1564 and 1565, for example, the winegrowers made up more than half the total number of voters as well as more than half those who supported Martin. Incredibly, their nearly solid support for the mayor became absolute in those years, as each of the 267 winegrowers who voted in 1564, and each of the 161 who participated in 1565, supported the mayor. Moreover, if the number of *vignerons* who participated in the municipal elections is compared to their total numbers on the tax rolls, it becomes clear that the winegrowers were the only occupational group in Dijon of which more than half regularly participated in the annual elections for mayor.

Why then did Dijon's winegrowers, and to a lesser extent its artisans, turn out in such unusually large numbers? And why did the winegrowers regularly cast their support so solidly behind one candidate as a block

vote? What motivated the masses to vote? All of these questions are prob-
lematical, not least because all of the surviving documentation has been
left by elites, who, as we have already seen, had a less than unprejudiced
view of their social inferiors. One thing is clear, and that is that Dijon's
winegrowers took participation in the municipal elections seriously. Not
only did they turn out to vote, but they often used the elections as a public forum in which they could express their discontent. Individual issues
such as religion in the 1560s naturally could arouse a large response from a
traditionally Catholic cohort such as winegrowers. For the most part, however, the elites on the town council did their best to mobilize the masses
for their own causes. In 1529, for example, a winegrower named Denis
Marquet led a noisy demonstration of *vigneron* support for the winning
candidate, Pierre Sayve, while the voting was going on.[14] The same thing
occurred in 1532, when in the midst of the voting "those of the *vignerons*
and other *gens de métier* . . . all began shouting together in great voice
[the name of their candidate]: 'Tabourot! Tabourot!' " The recording secretary made a point of fully describing all the "noise and tumult" created
by this disturbance, and he noted at the end of his entry that the victorious Pierre Tabourot departed after the votes had been counted "with many
of the said winegrowers and other men in great number, who followed
him home where they wined and dined in the accustomed manner."[15] In
1545 an even rowdier disturbance, with winegrowers who supported different candidates trying to outshout each other, caused the election to be
disbanded and continued two days later. The magistrates tried to prevent
such comportment of the masses in future. "Because some winegrowers
and mechanics come to the elections for mayor in order to go drinking
afterwards in the home of the one who is elected more than for any other
reason," noted the register of the city council, "it has been deliberated . . .
that the elected mayor and anyone else will be henceforth prohibited from
giving either drink or food to the said winegrowers and aforementioned
men on the day of the said election . . . under penalty of an arbitrary fine."[16]
The Parlement of Burgundy went one step further and made it an offense
to disturb the elections in any way, and this included attempts to solicit
votes; those who were caught were fined twenty livres *tournois*.[17] The
methods candidates were using to mobilize the winegrowers were spelled
out even more clearly in 1558 when the *mairie* declared "that it is prohibited and illegal for the one who gets elected mayor to give either bread,
wine, cherries, meat, or any other victuals to the voters under penalty of
arbitrary fine."[18] None of the threats of arbitrary fines seemed to be effec-

tive, however, because in June 1572, two days before that year's election, the Parlement published an even stronger measure: "The court, following several previous *arrêts,* has prohibited and declared it illegal . . . to interrupt the said election or to impede the voices and opinions of the voters. It is also illegal to create any disturbance or commotion on account of the said election, under penalty of death by hanging." This *arrêt* was required to be read aloud at the beginning of each successive election day to all assembled participants.[19]

Another insight into why *vignerons* and artisans participated in these elections emerges from the large number of them who were turned away at the polling place on election day. Though Parlement did not give in until 1612 to the *mairie*'s repeated requests to introduce a property requirement to prevent the poorest inhabitants from participating, there were always clear restrictions on who could vote. One had to be a head of household; and no outsiders were allowed in the convent on election day, nor were servants, beggars, those who lived in almshouses, women, children, students, or anyone who was armed, under penalty of imprisonment and arbitrary fine.[20] Nevertheless, a number of otherwise eligible voters were regularly turned away and their voices not counted in each election. In 1598 a winegrower named Nicolas Drouhin had his vote thrown out because he said that someone "gave him a present of some wine and one sou to vote for Monsieur Moisson."[21] This kind of campaigning was obviously commonplace, and the 1602 election witnessed the practice on a wide scale. Nine votes in Saint-Michel parish and 15 votes in Saint-Philibert parish alone—the two *vigneron quartiers* in the city[22]—were dismissed for various offenses. Léonard Forrot, for example, said that "he was given a pint of wine on behalf of [the candidate Michel] Bichot," who was elected mayor that year. Jacques Tridon told officials "that he had imbibed in return for giving his vote to Bichot." And Claude Petit "said that he had drunk on behalf of Monsieur Bichot, but that Etienne Coret made him do it." At the same time, a number of other votes were disqualified for similar offenses initiated by Bichot's principal challenger, Nicolas Gobin. And a few voters willingly volunteered that they had been offered gratuities, but they were less sure from which candidate they came. Guillaume Caillivet, for instance, "said that he had been given some money, but that he did not know from whom." Claude le Maigre "said that he had some drink with his neighbors, but he did not know where it came from." Claude le Follet "said that he had drunk two or three glasses of wine, but he was not sure where it came from." And one upstanding voter named Claude Laudriote told the magistrates "that he had been solicited to give his voice by those of [Monsieur] Gobin, nevertheless he was casting it for M[onsieur] Bichot." His vote was not counted all the same.[23]

What are we to make of this? Should we assume as the *mairie* and the elites of the city clearly did that the common people participated primarily because their votes were bought with drink or money? Should we accept at face value the implication that winegrowers and artisans dominated the electorate because their votes were the easiest to mobilize on election day with a little cheap wine? This all too easy assessment does appear to be the interpretation of the city fathers, and seems to be primarily what motivated their attempts to limit participation in the mayoral elections to what they deemed to be *gens de bien*: worthy men. Their efforts paid off in 1612, when they finally won approval from Parlement to limit participation to those inhabitants who had paid at least forty sous in personal taille each of the preceding three years and who had also paid a forty-sou poll tax. The new regulations seemed to have the desired effect, as campaigning among the winegrowers suddenly ceased. The result was not only a significant drop in the voter turnout (see table 1), but the dismissal of 192 inhabitants who did not qualify but who showed up at six o'clock in the morning to cast their voices anyway, even though much publicity had been given to the new requirements. Of those 192, 76 were understandably chagrined elites who were exempt from the taille, as in their zeal to enforce the new voter regulations the *mairie* enforced the letter of the law requiring participants to have paid the taille for the preceding three years.[24]

But why did the 116 others, largely winegrowers, turn out, knowing they would not be allowed to cast their voices? I would argue that they did so for the same reason that the tax-exempt elites did: to participate in the event of the election. The event itself was a political function of the commune to elect an honorable and worthy individual to serve as mayor. To take part in that process by definition bestowed honor on all who participated. For winegrowers and artisans, the elections were one of few opportunities where they could demonstrate their worthiness as citizens, where their voices really were the equals of those of their social superiors. In the Jacobin convent they could assemble and stand together with the lawyers, merchants, and noblemen of the city in common accord. Although the honor obtained by participating in the elections in no way garnered them any significant influence in the body politic, it gave the winegrowers considerable esteem in the body social. In their own *quartiers* and neighborhoods, participation translated into worthiness in the community. By way of illustration, the Sunday before the election of 1594 a Jesuit preacher named Père Christophe excoriated Dijon's *vignerons* in a sermon, claiming that "by their drunkenness and false promises they go to cast their votes corrupted by gluttony and money; and they should not be surprised if God destroyed their vines with hail, as it would be their own fault." The *vignerons* responded "that they were worthy men, not wicked [*gens de bien, non méchans*]." The priest repeated the charges the following Sunday, and a commotion broke out when "a wife of one of the *vignerons* shouted loudly that Père Christophe was lying, and that the *vignerons* were worthy men." [25] Though there were clearly issues of importance in particular elections—religion in the 1560s, for example—to participate as a member of the community mattered as much as campaign issues and even results. And that some voters took the trouble to go to the convent to cast their voices even though they were unable to name any of the candidates only underscores the premium placed on participation in the event at the expense of the result. [26] Thus, the elections served as an outlet of political expression for the masses, who were exclaiming and validating their own worth in the community.

To be sure, the magistrates were concerned about the widespread distribution of drink among the lower orders by the leading candidates, which dominated the campaigns before 1612. But surely this concern ought to be seen in the context of the *jour de fête* of Saint John the Baptist and accompanying festivities rather than as an intrusion into some nonexistent democratic process. The liberal distribution of wine, disturbances, tumults, and commotions always extended beyond the election for the next two days until the bonfire and fireworks on 23 June, the eve of the feast day. Things got so badly out of hand on bonfire night in 1600, for example, that the duke of Biron, the lieutenant general of the province, ordered the *mairie* to send an *échevin* to him in Beaune to report what had happened. And the following year the *mairie* declared that no one could assemble for eating and drinking in groups of more than three for the period of the election *and* the fête. [27]

In conclusion, this popular look at Dijon's mayoral elections from below has tried to establish that the winegrowers and artisans who made up the bulk of the city's electorate had a political consciousness of their own, although it did not necessarily conform to that of the elites who were trying to woo their support. The common people clearly took their participation in the political process seriously, as it validated their own worth in the body social. This realization ought also to force us to rethink the implications of the crown's attempts in the 1590s and early 1600s to re-strict Dijon's mayoral elections. As early as 1599 Henry IV requested that the city send him the names of the three highest vote getters so that he could personally choose the mayor from among them.[28] The magistrates balked at the suggestion and complained to Parlement for nearly a decade, when Henry finally issued an edict in June 1608 to that effect. His justifi-cation was that he wanted "to prevent the disturbances and seditions that take place during the elections in large towns throughout the kingdom and notably in Dijon." The king did promise, however, that having chosen the new mayor from among the three candidates with the most votes, "the said [candidate] will be received and installed [in office] in the accustomed manner." To the magistrates this was the whole point: the king's proposal was not "in the accustomed manner." When nearly a year later the *mairie* had still not agreed to this innovation, Henry issued letters patent dated 30 May 1609 and a *lettre de jussion* dated 31 May requiring the *mairie* to send him the names of the three candidates with the most votes in the forth-coming election so that he could name the next mayor.[29] Although the king did in fact select the candidate with the highest total that year, in the fol-lowing year, 1610, the regent for the young Louis XIII, Marie de Medici, did not; and the election in 1611 had to be postponed until an agreement could be reached between the city and the regent on the format of the election.[30] To be sure, the municipal officials in Dijon had shown little hesitation in attempting to alter the format of the elections themselves—introducing stiffer voting requirements, a poll tax, and so on—when their own control of the elections was first threatened in the election of Pierre Bouhier in 1582. But this is precisely the point. It was royal intervention that threatened the elites' domination of the *mairie* under Henry IV, and the *échevins* quickly came round to the same conclusion as the masses: that any alteration of the traditional format and ritual of the elections was anathema.

But is the best way to view these events necessarily from the perspective of a centralizing state's attempts to limit the independence of a local com-munity?[31] What bothered Dijon's citizens—particularly the winegrowers and artisans who made up the electorate—was not so much the crown's attempts to control the outcome of the elections as rather an innovation in the traditional right to hold elections in the traditional way. In July 1599, for example, when Henry IV first tried to change the format of the elec-tions, the *échevins* of the city council made their reservations known to the king immediately. They "resolved and deliberated that in this [matter] His

said Majesty will be rightly implored to continue the ancient form hereto-
fore observed for the election of the viscount-mayor of the said city, which
is that the plurality of the votes of the inhabitants will result in the choice
and election of one single person to carry out the said charge of mayor." [32]
Even in 1630, following the tax revolt led by winegrowers during carnival, when Louis XIII punished the *mairie* for not snuffing out the revolt
more swiftly by threatening to appoint the mayor directly, the issue was
not so much who had the right to select the mayor as it was a question of
interference in the format of Dijon's traditional elections. Thus, municipal
hostility toward the crown in 1630 was really the product of innovation in
the *event* of the elections much more than the king's ability to appoint his
choice as mayor. As the elections were not part of any proto-democratic
process, the result was clearly less important than the fact that the king
threatened to invalidate the civic participation of the inhabitants. And on
that occasion Louis removed the masses from the elections altogether. He
declared in April 1630 that although "the exercise of the vote remained
with the people . . . the king reserved for himself the nomination of the
mayor for the next six years." Moreover, "the winegrowers will be run out
of town [*chassés de la ville*] and will only be allowed to reside in the sub-
urbs or neighboring parishes . . . [and] the winegrowers and beggars will
be excluded from all elections." [33] Although the royal proscriptions lasted
only a year before the traditional format was restored, in the elections of
1630 the only inhabitants allowed to participate were those "who paid 30
sous in tax or more during the last three years they were on the rolls, except for the *vignerons* and manual workers," who could not participate at
all. Moreover, Louis demanded "the abolition of the Infanterie Dijonnaise
and Mère Folle," the group of young winegrowers who traditionally took
charge of the festivities for the feast of Saint John the Baptist. "Since the
king considers the assembly of the Mère Folle as a cause of debauchery
and scandal and wishes to uproot this evil, he is abolishing it and prohibits
those who have taken part in it from assembling." [34]

Thus, I would argue that the crown's attempts to control municipal elections in the seventeenth century have much to tell us about the relationship
between elite and popular culture and the extent of popular political consciousness, and do more than serve as illustrations of the rise of the modern state. After all, even though the crown was eventually successful in its
efforts to control Dijon's mayoral elections in the later seventeenth century,
the elections themselves survived more or less intact until the Revolution.
Although the municipal elites were naturally preoccupied by the growing

tensions between the crown and the provinces and the threat of the loss of municipal authority, these mayoral elections clearly had another dynamic all their own. For the masses who made up the bulk of the electorate, participation in the event was what ultimately mattered. By this light, it is still possible to argue persuasively that on the municipal level at least, the early modern state remained as popular and consultative as ever long after the rise of the so-called absolute monarchy.

NOTES

An earlier version of this essay was first presented at a session of the Western Society for French History in New Orleans, Louisiana, in October 1989, and I wish to thank all those who participated in that session for their useful comments, particularly Jim Farr, Sarah Hanley, and Samuel Kinser. I also wish to thank the National Endowment for the Humanities, the American Council of Learned Societies, and the American Philosophical Society for providing funds that made the research for this article possible.

1. See the discussion of Major's ideas in the Introduction. A useful example of this process at work is the analysis of Toulouse by Robert A. Schneider, *Public Life in Toulouse, 1463–1789: From Municipal Republic to Cosmopolitan City* (Ithaca, N.Y., 1989). Schneider's general thesis is summarized in his "Crown and Capitoulat: Municipal Government in Toulouse, 1500–1789," in *Cities and Social Change in Early Modern France,* ed. Philip Benedict (London, 1989), 195–220. Also, see chap. 5 above. I should point out that my general approach to and treatment of early modern French elections in the present essay owes much by way of inspiration to Mark A. Kishlansky, *Parliamentary Selection: Social and Political Choice in Early Modern England* (Cambridge, 1986), especially chap. 1.

2. For the medieval background to municipal elections, see the work of Susan Reynolds, *Kingdoms and Communities in Western Europe, 900–1300* (Oxford, 1984); Nicolai Rubenstein, *The Government of Florence Under the Medici* (London, 1966); and especially Jaime Vicens Vives, *Ferran II i la ciutat de Barcelona, 1479–1516,* 3 vols. (Barcelona, 1936–37), especially 1:40–74.

3. See Peter Burke, *Popular Culture in Early Modern Europe* (New York, 1978), 196–97; idem, *The Historical Anthropology of Early Modern Italy* (Cambridge, 1987), chaps. 6, 13; and Keith Thomas, "Social Differences in England, 1500–1750" (Paper presented at the Newberry Library, Chicago, 10 April 1989).

4. Archives Municipales de Dijon (hereafter AMD), B 12, cote 31 (carton), November 1235.

5. Examples of the format of the election procedure demonstrate how rigidly this pattern was followed from the mid-fifteenth to the mid-seventeenth centuries.

See AMD, B 11, cote 2 (carton), 24 June 1446; B 168, fol. 283r, 16 June 1514; B 210, fols. 1r–13v, 21–24 June 1572; B 12, cote 44, anonymous seventeenth-century copy; and Joseph Garnier and Ernest Champeux, *Chartes de communes et d'affranchissements en Bourgogne* (Dijon, 1918), 312–30. And for a more detailed discussion of the carnivalesque associations with the feast day of Saint John the Baptist, see the recent book of Jean Delumeau, *Rassurer et protéger: Le sentiment de sécurité dans l'Occident d'autrefois* (Paris, 1989), especially p. 46.

6. For the nominations of Brocard see AMD, B 197, fol. 2r, 21 June 1559; and B 198, fol. 1v, 21 June 1560.

7. See Henri Drouot, *Mayenne et la Bourgogne: Etude sur la Ligue, 1587–1596,* 2 vols. (Dijon, 1937), 1: 88–94; and Pierre Gras, ed., *Histoire de Dijon,* 2d ed. (Toulouse, 1987), 52–53, 89–90, 119–26. Patent letters of Charles VIII dated October 1491 according the elected mayor ennoblement are in AMD, B 11, cote 7 (carton).

8. The quotation is from AMD, B 167, fol. 35r–v, 24 June 1496. This is typical of election records until 1545, when individual votes were recorded by the clerk of the *mairie.* (See table 1 for figures on the 1545 election.) The nearest year to 1545 with a complete tax roll is 1553, which shows that Dijon had 2,888 total households: AMD, L 192, fols. 1r–237v, January 1552 (old style)/1553 (new style).

9. See table 1 for 1582 vote totals. The tax roll for 1579, the nearest complete year to 1582, shows 3,340 heads of household: AMD, L 205, fols. 97r–232r.

10. In 1607, for example, 1,976 voters participated out of 3,033 eligible voters on the tax rolls, for a turnout of 65.2 percent. The figure of 3,033 heads of household comes from the 1602 tax roll, the nearest complete year to 1607: AMD, L 213, fols. 57r–276r. Voting figures for 1607 are from table 1.

11. For winegrowers, see AMD, L 192, tax roll for 1553, which shows winegrowers heading 541 out of 2,888 households. For artisans, see James R. Farr, *Hands of Honor: Artisans and Their World in Dijon, 1550–1650* (Ithaca, N.Y., 1988), 75–83, which is based on AMD, L 170, the tax roll for 1556, and shows 950 artisan households out of a total of 2,822.

12. AMD, B 220, fol. 11r, 22 June 1582 (the day after the 1582 election).

13. AMD, B 195, fols. 2r–8v, 21 June 1557; B 198, fols. 1r–7v, 21 June 1560; B 199, fols. 1r–10r, 21 June 1561; and see tables 1 and 2. For details of the election of 1561 see James R. Farr, "Popular Religious Solidarity in Sixteenth-Century Dijon," *French Historical Studies* 14 (1985): 192–214; and Mack P. Holt, "Order and Community in Sixteenth-Century Burgundy," *Proceedings of the Western Society for French History* 16 (1989): 60–71.

14. AMD, B 173, fols. 43r–45v, 21 June 1529.

15. AMD, B 175, fols. 146r–47r, 21 June 1532: ". . . avec plusieurs desd[its] vignero[n]s et aultres gens en gros nombre que le suyverent en la maison dicelle ou ilz ont beu et mange en la mannie[re] accoustumee."

16. AMD, B 183, fols. 1r–7v, 20–22 June 1545, quotation from fols. 4v–5r.

17. AMD, B 183, fol. 10r, 26 June 1545; fol. 320v–21v, 20 June 1546.

18. AMD, B 196, fol. 2v, 21 June 1558.

19. AMD, B 210, fol. 9r–v, 21 June 1572.

20. For just two of many examples, see AMD, B 225, fol. 2r, 20 June 1587; and B 230, fols. 2r–3v, 20 June 1592.

21. AMD, B 236, fol. 22r, 20 June 1598.

22. In the first half of the sixteenth century Saint-Michel and Saint-Nicolas parishes were the most heavily populated with *vignerons*. Many moved out of the increasingly prosperous Saint-Nicolas parish during the Wars of Religion, however, and by 1600 Saint-Philibert had more winegrowers than any parish save Saint-Michel. See the tax rolls in AMD, L 163 (for 1500), L 192–93 (for 1553), and L 213 (for 1602).

23. AMD, B 240, fols. 11v–13v, 19v, 23v, 25r, 21 June 1602.

24. AMD, B 250, fols. 1r–22r, 20 June 1612.

25. *Journal de Gabriel Breunot, conseiller au Parlement de Bourgogne*, ed. Joseph Garnier, 3 vols. (Dijon, 1844), 2:128, 132.

26. There are numerous examples of otherwise eligible voters being escorted out of the convent because they were unable to name anyone to vote for. For just a couple of examples, see AMD, B 245, fol. 21r, 20 June 1607, when Jacob Caron's vote was not counted "pour navoir sceu nommer"; and B 250, fol. 4v, 20 June 1612, for "nayant seu personne nommer."

27. AMD, B 238, fol. 44r–v, 27 June 1600; fols. 229r–30r, 18 June 1601.

28. AMD, B 236, fols. 233v–93r, June–October 1599.

29. AMD, B 12, cote 41 (carton), June 1608, 31 May 1609; B 246, fols. 264v–66v, 18 June 1609.

30. AMD, B 248, fols. 1r–25v, 21 June 1610; fols. 42r–44v, 6–11 July 1610; fols. 257r–59r, 10 June 1611.

31. This is certainly the traditional approach. See Gras, ed., *Histoire de Dijon*, 88–94, 122–27; and especially Charles Bertucat, *La juridiction municipale de Dijon: Son étendue* (Dijon, 1911), particularly pp. 91–99.

32. AMD, B 236, fol. 252r–v, 29 July 1559.

33. "Suppression des privileges par Louis XIII à la suite de la sedition du Lanturelu," AMD, B 3, cote 60 (carton), 28 April 1630.

34. AMD, B 267, fols. 157r–60v, 28 February 1630; fol. 227r–v, 28 April 1630; fol. 265r, 10 June 1630; fols. 293r–94r, 2 August 1630; B 3, cote 60 (carton), 28 April 1630. On the Infanterie Dijonnaise, called La Mère Folle, and its domination by the winegrowers, see Gras, ed., *Histoire de Dijon*, 131–32; Natalie Zemon Davis, "The Reasons of Misrule," in her *Society and Culture in Early Modern France* (Stanford, 1975), 97–123; and Charles Rossignol, *La fête des fous et la Mère Folle de Dijon* (Paris, 1855).

7. Money, Dignity, and Self-Esteem in the

Relations Between Judges and Great Nobles

of the Parlement of Paris During the Fronde

OREST RANUM

To be able to render service to one's peers and superiors—that is, to be *dans l'état de pouvoir rendre service*—was a wellspring of dignity and self-esteem in seventeenth-century elite society. How one was perceived by those with whom one had social relations, and how one perceived one's own self-esteem, turned very powerfully on rendering service.

Among sword nobles, service remained an expression of willingness to fight at someone's side in battle or serve as second in a duel. When La Rochefoucauld's tenants gathered to offer their service to the duke, they needed a sword, armor, a horse, and a martial spirit sufficient to avoid shame in the company of men experienced at making war. When a judge or a household intendant offered to serve the duc de Guise by lending him money, he had to have the cash or a letter of credit to carry out the service, or lose some dignity.

Scarcely considered in the seventeenth century to mean mere household chores, though it involved that, service connoted such different activities as giving a prince or sovereign advice on matters of state or on private affairs, arranging a marriage for a relative or for a friend's child, repairing a breach of friendship (and there were many instances of this during the Fronde), and most important, speaking on behalf of someone to someone else. Pensions, posts in private households, ecclesiastical benefices, and state offices shifted from person to person and from family to family as a result of individuals speaking on behalf of others. The title of Charles Loyseau's *Traité du droit des offices* (1610) could be roughly translated as

"A Treatise on the Law of Service Rendering." Service could be both public and private, or one or the other, depending on the nature of the service and on the ranks of the persons exchanging services. Offered by a judge in the Parlement to a prince of the blood, service would have been considered routine and dignifying—until the prince was imprisoned by royal order or led troops against his king in rebellion.

At this point it is tempting to look at the instances of service that were central to the turning and changing of allied parties in the Fronde, some of which developed into lèse majesté; but instead I should like to explore some of the more prosaic activities of service by the *parlementaires* to their high aristocratic colleagues, who, by right, also sat in the Parlement. These services were more strictly social than professional and political, if the distinction is meaningful.

The dignity and moral rectitude of a judge were made fragile by the shifting alliances of the Fronde. A passing acquaintance, a small favor, a cosignature, an investment, a loan, attendance at the signing ceremony of a wedding contract, or being honored by a prince's presence at a *parlementaire* baptism might eventually force a judge to disqualify himself from voting or debating in the Grand' Chambre. But first let us take a glimpse at the long-term relations among the great nobles, the princes, and the high-ranking judges in the Parlement.

At the end of the Wars of Religion one of the more analytically minded participants concluded that one of the causes of the troubles had been the overly close ties between princes or other *grands* and some of the judges in the Parlement. Sully was emphatic on this point and favored the institution of the *droit annuel* partly for this reason. Grounding venality of office more deeply still in property rights, Sully argued, would give the judges a sphere of action more independent of the scions of the great aristocratic houses. Chancellor Bellièvre, as Roland Mousnier showed long ago, disagreed and argued that the *droit annuel* would degrade the judiciary by further confusing property and money with the virtue and merit needed to be a judge.[1] These conflicting views could not be reconciled at the time, as we all know, and as a result the same debate over the moral and professional foundations of the robe occurred every nine years when the renewal of the *paulette* prompted intense negotiations over all the issues dividing council and Parlement.[2]

During Marie de Médicis's regency—and beyond, as Jeffry Sawyer has shown in a recent paper[3]—charges that the judges on the royal benches were guilty of accepting gifts, of obfuscation, of peculation, of demanding excessive fees, and so forth turned up in the cahiers of the Estates General of 1614, and in the flow of aristocratically inspired pamphlets critical of Marie and her councillors over the next several years. There certainly was a tradition of criticizing the moral decay of the robe, but there may have been something more. To rally sympathizers in the country in 1617, Condé and other princely rebels harped on the theme of the corruption of royal justice to fan bitterness against the robe among the small nobles. Memories of these pamphlets were still vivid in midcentury. And the long-standing habit of service that linked judges to great nobles must be understood as a possible threat to confirming and reinforcing older charges about the corruption of justice.

How could a judge not express his willingness to carry out a service, and actually do so, when solicited by a prince de Condé or de Bouillon, or a duc de Nevers, de Guise, de Vendôme, or de Beaufort? The persistent quarrels within and without the ranks of the peerage, and the role of the Parlement in registering new titles, tended to cement ties of service and benefit into parties. How to vote on a law cleansing Beaufort of guilt after he had escaped from prison? What position to take concerning Bouillon's claims to Sedan? Or where to stand on Longueville's and Beaufort's prickly claims to higher rank and seats in the Parlement? Positions publicly taken on these and other issues were perceived by the princes and dukes as service, and a judge could not abandon these positions lightly without a loss of dignity, and perhaps other losses. And where to stand in 1650 on the various proposals favoring Condé's release from prison? Some issues were immediate and new, others lasted over generations. The flow of factums about the legitimacy and the rank of Vendôme and his competitive sons continued throughout the Fronde, throwing judges back to reviewing wardships and the like that had been set up in Parlement under Henry IV.[4]

During the Fronde every one of the prominent justices of Parlement, except President de Mesmes, was accused of being too favorable to one or another of the princes, or of having rendered one of them a service that compromised their professional integrity. The truth or falsehood of these accusations has never been researched, nor have the bonds of fidelity between the *grands* and the judges been carefully reconstructed. A cursory exploration at this point will suggest that the rivalry between the Bourbon Condé and the Bourbon Orléans branches of the royal family trickled down into a duel for controlling the greatest number of presidencies in Parlement. Jacques Le Coigneux's service to Gaston back in the early 1630s brought him a presidency.[5] Presidents Viole and Nesmond, in the

Parlement, and Perrault, in the Chambre des Comptes, had all served in the Condé household and continued to do so frequently, before moving along the usual tracks toward promotion in the royal government. Because the number of presidencies was limited, it took more than wealth to buy them. The princes' men often lacked the professional prestige of a long robe family heritage, a tradition of integrity.

As aristocratic household officials in service, while simultaneously holding offices in Parlement, these men were familiar with princely revenues from estates, pensions, debts, and dowries, and with the current litigation involving the princes and princesses they served. They were frequent moneylenders to their patrons as well. To my knowledge no historian has reconstructed the fabric of relations between household service and membership in the sovereign courts. Nor do we know the rules according to which a judge disqualified himself (*recuser*) when a case involving one of the princes to whom he gave counsel came before his court. And, for these *grands*, what distinguished a public matter from a private one? Since the changes in alliances during the Fronde prompted these links to be alluded to during debates in the Grand' Chambre, competition for new appointments in princely households may have intensified as a result of challenges to loyalty. But before turning to more precise illustrations of these relations, let us look at some background evidence about judges who served on household councils. Jacques Le Coigneux was, in every sense of the word, Gaston d'Orléans's creature. While in the Parlement, he served as the duke's chancellor and also as the head of his council.[6] During the minority of Gaston's daughter, the Grande Mademoiselle, Le Coigneux also served as superintendent of her household, receiving a pension of twenty-four hundred livres for his services. Upon reaching her majority in 1650, Mademoiselle decided not to appoint any of her father's household servants, according to one source, and proceeded to name a Monsieur d'Herbigny as her intendant.[7] Adolescent rebellion, political prudence, or extension of Orléans client networks? It is impossible to answer this question at the moment. The name d'Herbigny is quite obscure, but the important fact about his appointment is that he was the nephew of President Henri II de Mesmes. His other powerful relative was de Mesmes's brother, Claude, comte d'Avaux, the diplomatic statesman and superintendent of finance. In choosing d'Herbigny for her council, the Grande Mademoiselle gained not only a certain autonomy from her father's servants but also implicit support both in Parlement and in council. There would seem to have been no grounds for challenging d'Herbigny's appointment, but at the same time it marked a certain loss of dignity for the Le Coigneux family. Since

Le Coigneux had not done Gaston's bidding in Parlement during several critical attempts by the prince to shut off debate, it is possible that Gaston thought well of the way Mademoiselle clipped the Le Coigneux wings. The recent marriage alliance between Le Coigneux and the widow Galland, which involved a dowry of four hundred thousand livres and an alliance with a tax-farming family, also makes it possible to interpret Mademoiselle's choice of d'Herbigny as confirming robe, sword, and popular beliefs that judges are sullied by such marriages.

The services rendered in Condé's household council by presidents in the Parlement also illustrate how enhanced dignity could suddenly turn into shame and charges of treason. In 1650 Nesmond, Viole, and Perrault all held prominent posts on the household councils of the Condé family and were publicly known to be his men, yet they also presided over various chambers in sovereign courts and were charged by the king to help the first presidents "manage" these often stormy bodies.

Beginning his career in the Parlement of Bordeaux and subsequently becoming a master of requests in Paris in 1624, François Théodore de Nesmond had served as royal army intendant under Prince Henri II de Condé in Languedoc, in Dauphiné, and in Lyonnais in 1629.[8] There is little doubt that Nesmond was serving with the prince's entire approval, since Richelieu and Condé had long since become allies and the latter was helping carry out the cardinal's policies. Nesmond became a president in the Parlement in 1636 and, though I do not have his titles and the dates of his appointment in the prince's household, was certainly in the Condés' service by that date. Richelieu wrote Nesmond in 1640 to ask him to arrange a time for the prince and Nesmond to visit him at Rueil. The cardinal added that he wished to discuss some things that were advantageous to the public and to the person of the prince—"the one whom I desire to serve with sincerity."[9] Nesmond was clearly the prince's confidant.

Generations passed and services continued to be counted, indeed accounted, from one to the next. Nesmond's hotel on the Quai de la Tournelle would be the scene for many quasi-public and quasi-private turning points during the Fronde. In the spring of 1650, just after the Grand Condé's arrest, Nesmond nervously wrote Mazarin to express the hope that he would not be appointed the principal administrator of the prince's estate during the imprisonment. Was he sincere, or just trimming between the principal minister and the prince? A procuration from the prince giving Nesmond full power over all his financial and legal affairs arrived just a few days later.[10]

In April of the same year the dowager princesse de Condé fled house arrest in the château of Chantilly and made her way incognito to Paris and to the Grand' Chambre, where she presented a dramatic personal appeal for her sons' release. With Nesmond and Viole on the president's bench, she solemnly asked the court to designate either Nesmond's hotel, or Viole's,[11] as a place where her person would be secure from arrest or, failing one of these, the Palais de Justice itself.[12] It should be no surprise to find that Nesmond and Viole, and Perrault in the Chambre des Comptes, led the party that attempted to muster the votes needed for a resolution in favor of freeing Condé and Conti from prison. The order in which the princess listed the secure places may also be significant, not only because of the prestige of a president's residence and of the stoutness of doors and walls to resist rioters and small numbers of troops, but also because the Condés frequently stored papers, jewels, and ready cash at the Hôtel de Nesmond rather than in their own hotel.

When the dowager princesse de Condé died later that year, Nesmond announced to his colleagues in the Parlement that he had been named executor of her estate.[13] The social atmosphere in the city was certainly unstable at the time. The previous spring, Frondeur *parlementaires* had carried out *recherches* to find what they described as hordes of royal taxes illegally hidden in cellars, attics, and tombs. Gold, silver, and other precious objects were legally defined as *bonne prise* by the judges: twenty-five thousand livres were discovered under the flooring in the house of the widow Galand, the very lady who a few days earlier had put up four hundred thousand livres as a dowry for her marriage to Jacques II Le Coigneux, president-designate in Parlement and Orléanist householder. The twenty-five thousand livres were turned over to a public defense fund, while Le Coigneux and his allies in Parlement were accused by their Frondeur colleagues, Broussel, Benoise, and Pithou, of being polluted and *intéressé* in the odious administration of tax contracting—indeed, they were no more upright than President Thoré, the son of the hated superintendent Particelli d'Hemery and the son-in-law of President Le Coigneux.[14] In this atmosphere of partisanship and of accusations about corruption and pollution created by alliances with financiers, we should not be surprised to note that two judges solemnly visited the Hôtel de Nesmond after the dowager princess's death in order to affix special seals on the coffers containing money and documents from the Condé estate.[15] The possibility of an anti-Condé riot or a zealous anti-Condé *parlementaire* perquisition thus threatened the accumulated wealth of a deceased princess. Her fortune stood in jeopardy of immediate confiscation on moral and economic grounds, and this despite Nesmond's prestige, servants, and thick walls.

At no point were the presidents leading Condé's party in Parlement forced to leave their seats as a result of accusations about associating with tax farmers, a fate met by some of Gaston's *parlementaire* servants. This fact should not be interpreted as evidence that they were, indeed, free from associating with tax farmers, or speculating in royal tax farms. Quite to the contrary. It merely testifies to the greater strength of the Condé party in Parlement. Gaston's party had suffered reversals because of what was called, in the seventeenth century, an unfortunate "turn of events."

Some time after their release, Condé and Conti came to the Hôtel de Nesmond to divide their mother's estate according to the terms of her will, and all this under the eyes of President de Nesmond.[16] These were turbulent times for Condé. He was doing everything he could militarily and financially to mobilize forces to defeat the king's army. A dispute arose between the prince and the executor of his mother's estate over some one hundred thousand livres that Condé wanted immediately, in order to pay his troops.[17] Just how serious the dispute was is unclear, but it is evident that Nesmond's role had become virtually intolerable as he sought to sort out loyalties to his king, his deceased client, and her sons.

In the summer of 1650, still another incident occurred that sheds light on the roles a president could play. As the duchesse d'Orléans, that is, Gaston's wife, was about to give birth, the father dispatched a servant to summon Nesmond to witness the event.[18] On the surface this would seem to be a mere courtesy. Nesmond was, however, specifically singled out because of his reputation as a servant in the house of Condé, a rival collateral branch of the royal family. The president did not arrive in time. Did he wish to avoid the delicate duty of witnessing the birth of the sole male heir to the Orléans line? He may simply have been late. The incident suggests, however, that the prestige and probity of a presidential judgeship did not suffice to allay suspicions during kinship duels between princely houses. Testimony from a prominent judge who belonged to a rival party was stronger than testimony from a judge of the same rank, but belonging to one's own party, or to no party at all. A sieur de Cumont, also a well-known Condé servant, arrived in time to witness the birth. As it turned out, no one contested the legitimacy of the little duc d'Anjou, who died soon after, but the fact that Nesmond was summoned to witness his birth is a powerful indicator of how deep the ties of loyalty were perceived to go in Parlement.

With this evidence about Nesmond's attachment in mind, it is not surprising to learn that his colleagues named him to head the Parlement's delegation to negotiate a settlement of the princely Fronde with Condé.[19]

Nesmond probably was the focus of support by the prince's clients in the Grand' Chambre and the focus of the quite cynical hopes for an *accommodement* held by those judges who were for neither Condé nor the court. Nesmond reported several times to his colleagues about the course of the negotiations. When these talks proved fruitless, he may have suffered a loss of dignity as a result of the prince's decision to flout the authority of the sovereign court. When the judges were ordered to take up their duties in Pontoise, Nesmond declined to go and eventually presided over the rump Parlement in Paris. Living as he did until 1664, Nesmond saw the Grand Condé's return to favor. It would be interesting to research the relations between the two men after the prince's return from fighting at the head of a Spanish army combating French armies.

The careers of Presidents Viole and Perrault are somewhat better known than Nesmond's, thanks to Viole's tendency to make speeches and participate in rebellious military operations. Perrault's duels for Condé's favor with Pierre Lenet turn up in the latter's memoirs, and it is clear that a whole as yet unperceived layer of political and social history is still to be researched on the jockeying for power in the princely household itself. Here I wish to leave this cursory exploration of judicial princely relations in order to touch on other examples of these relationships and to reflect on the royal legislation at the end of the Fronde that aimed at prohibiting just the sort of relations I have been describing.

When First President Mathieu Molé carefully maneuvered to have the generalship of the Parlement's army fall to Conti, instead of to Elbeuf, during the crisis of 1649 that succeeded Louis XIV's flight from Paris and the blockade of the city by Condé and his troops, he may have been just a loyal servant of the royal family, in all its branches, rather than a servant of Elbeuf, of the house of Lorraine. This was not, however, the case when Molé attempted to find a middle ground in the negotiations over Condé's arrest in the spring of 1650. First President Molé's son, Champlâtreux, was a known Condé supporter, and in debates in the Parlement the judges loyal to the court (not necessarily Mazarinist) accused Molé of heeding his son's advice in Condé's favor and of eventually losing his independence and becoming a *Condéiste*.[20] Though known as a rock of loyalty to the queen regent, and though subject to abuse not only in the streets but also in the Grand' Chambre for his apparent refusal to join the ranks of the Mazarin-haters, Molé did, indeed, eventually support Nesmond and other Condé followers in their effort to use the court's prestige as a lever to force the regent to release the princes from prison. There is also evidence that Mazarin had warned Champlâtreux that promotion to his father's office by *survivance* might be in jeopardy should he continue to be so overtly *Condéiste*. The son continued to support the prince, and the triumphant cardinal Mazarin remembered: Champlâtreux never became first president of the Parlement, and the reason may lie at least partially in his support for Condé.

In the heady atmosphere of accusations about being *gagné,* or corrupted by favors dangled before their eyes to prompt a change in their positions, the *parlementaires* violated their usual comportment and descended to ad hominem accusations, slander, and rumor mongering. Accepting any office, pension, benefice, or gift for one's children could quickly weaken a judge's moral and political authority in the Grand' Chambre. The princes were giving out *grâces* in exactly the same manner as Anne and Mazarin; but either because the princes lacked the resources to compete with the crown in distributing favors or because princely favors were perceived as private while the crown's were considered public, the ad hominem accusation in Parlement centered entirely on the corrupting influence of favors coming from the court. The fact that princely patronage was not deemed odious or corrupting, while Anne and Mazarin's was, goes a long way toward clarifying why people on the side of the regent and her minister condemned the Parlement as partisan and Frondeur.

Molé suffered another loss of self-esteem and influence among his colleagues when Broussel accused him of accepting the treasurership of the Sainte-Chapelle for his son, Edouard, already bishop of Bayeux.[21] The first president's son did, indeed, become treasurer of the Sainte-Chapelle, an office in the royal gift, and there was probably no effective way to counter the accusations of bribe taking that the Frondeur president directed at his colleague.

Entering into the study of the perception of probity and corruption risks taking us far afield, but there are two quite powerful voices that deserve to be heard before this essay draws to a close.[22] The first is the voice of President Henri II de Mesmes, and the second, that of Advocate General Talon. The first statement appears as a homily presented at a *mercurial;* the second was proffered as private advice by a dying father to his son.

Manuscripts 523–24 of the Bibliothèque Nationale contain the *mercurial* homilies prepared by the de Mesmes over perhaps as many as three generations. Most of them date from the Fronde. Allusions to and citations of classical authors and church fathers abound in the speeches of these years, which address both current issues and the moral-philosophical questions affecting the judicial profession, its place in society, and the need to encourage judges to set a strict limit on their acquisitiveness.

De Mesmes argued forcefully that the avaricious judge was to be pitied as a *grand pauvre*, a totally impoverished person to whom wealth brought no sense of well-being or security. The mind of such a judge forced him to grasp desperately for every bit of wealth. The judge's hands, de Mesmes asserted, revealed the condition of his soul: in a dispute over money, a judge had no authority over the litigious parties if he himself had held his open hand out to one of those parties and had agreed to delay a case or turn a decision in one party's favor. De Mesmes's solemn evocation of hand positions in social relations was very powerful. We can imagine his colleagues staring discreetly at their hands as he spoke, or hiding them under a fold in their gowns. The literal and the metaphorical were pulled together in one meaning that pierced the boundary between private and public life. And, continued de Mesmes: "Are not the great and the powerful more daring about breaking the law with more insolence than other offenders? And do not those who are rich hope to win their cases by the power of their money? What fear have they of the uprightness and severity of the law? We must always keep our hands clean if we wish our offices to be revered and our judgments equitable."[23] Preaching, literally, in the *mercurial* the philosophy of equity, probity, and self-control over the passion for gain, de Mesmes appears not only as a survivor from the Humanistic learned company of Etienne Pasquier, Guillaume du Vair, and Charles Loyseau, but as a precursor of d'Aguesseau as well. His speeches on the importance of wearing gowns instead of court dress, on learning as a source of authority for judges, on the honor of holding a royal office, on pleading without fee for the poor, and so forth may not have moved the hearts of such colleagues as Le Coigneux and Thoré, men who came from social environments that had steeled them against accusations about loving money too much. But the shouts in the streets against the financiers, the *maltôtiers*, and the tax farmers certainly enhanced the power of what de Mesmes said in his *mercurials* during the Fronde.

Desperately ill in the summer of 1652, and humiliated by his failure to find a middle ground between the court and the Parlement, Omer Talon sat down to write a highly personal, intimate memoir for his son and successor, Denis. Echoing the themes about which de Mesmes had spoken so frequently, Talon went beyond ancient thought to evoke understandings of human nature formulated by Descartes, Pascal, Nicole, and La Rochefoucauld. The dying royal servant delved more deeply into the study of human nature than de Mesmes had, in order to interpret the comportment of the *parlementaires*. There was more to their behavior than acquisitiveness, though there certainly was that as well.

In dolorous tones, Talon observed the great difference between those who held dignities in a court of law and those who were attached to the royal court or involved in financial functions.[24] This link between the court and the *partisans* rested on a critique not only of Mazarin but also of the aristocracy surrounding the king. For the past five or six years, Talon told his son, he had witnessed a tendency among younger judges to cultivate relations with great nobles and princes and then to strengthen these ties, conduct that had had terrible consequences. He noted that he personally had never called upon the late king unless requested to do so, nor had he changed his conduct toward the present king or the queen regent, because "our masters desire service from us, not visits." He recalled: "I have seen the greatest among the robe officers scorned because they were too assiduous [in visiting the great]." Talon found that young judges from well-to-do families no longer worked or respected the gowns they wore; they sought out the court and wasted their time in entertainment, because their self-esteem had come to depend on the approval of great nobles and princes. The awareness that one's own amour propre might depend on recognition by a *grand,* or on his affection, marked Talon's anguished attempt to comprehend the turmoil that the Fronde brought to robe families. And he added: "The great nobles and princes who receive [the young judges] do so agreably . . . considering them like their dogs and their slaves, and when they want something that their votes on public matters can produce, they require a kind of blind deference that they believe is due because of their rank." [25] In other words, judges could lose their probity and independence by seeking to found their self-esteem and dignity upon the approval of princely houses.

Talon concluded in an almost formally stoic vein as he exhorted his son to live modestly and uprightly—neither sordidly nor cheaply nor too luxuriously, but according to his rank. His final exhortation was a repetition of his father's advice to him: "Never make an alliance with the family of a financier or a *partisan*." [26]

Below these surface meanings, much is left to be interpreted by the specialist not only of clientage, but of kinship and professionalism. One of Talon's first cousins worked as secretary to the duc de Beaufort during the Fronde, and another worked for Condé. None of the guests who signed his wedding contract on 8 January 1626 were high-ranking nobles; but his wife's dowry included *rentes constituées* on the duchies of Vendôme and Nevers. Back in the 1620s the Doujat family had agreed to render service, yet it is highly doubtful that this service came back to haunt Talon as he strove to enhance the authority of the robe and to maintain civil order.[27] Still, the Fronde coincided with that age when French moralists explored the meaning of *intérêt*, and it is just possible that the advocate general occasionally speculated about whether payments on his rentes would be forthcoming if he took too strong a stand against Vendôme-Beaufort.[28] But that is another story, and for another essay at another time.

Let us conclude. When the young king entered Paris on 21 October 1652, preparations were well along for the *Lit de Justice* to be held the following day. Eleven members of the Parlement did not attend that august ceremony, so they did not hear the royal proclamation that became the law of the realm on that day. In it we read:

> The greatest amount of these disorders came from the liberty that our officers took in interesting themselves in the affairs of the princes and the great nobles of our realm, whether in taking up their direction, whether in receiving pensions or gifts, whether in paying regular court to them to the prejudice to the duty and honor of their *charges*, whether in attending their councils, which then engaged them in a blind compliance toward them and their plans, including revealing secrets from debates in violation of their own oaths and the service they owe us. . . . [29]

In *Lit de Justice,* the king had spoken in his parlement concerning the *commerce* between the great nobles and his judges.[30] For him, and for a great number of his contemporaries in the *classes politiques*, this *commerce* had been the principal cause of the late troubles.

NOTES

1. Roland Mousnier, "Sully et le Conseil d'état et des finances . . . ," *Revue historique* 192 (1941): 68–86; J. Russell Major, *Bellièvre, Sully, and the Assembly of Notables of 1596*, Transactions of the American Philosophical Society, n.s., vol. 64 (Philadelphia, 1974), 29. With great satisfaction and enhanced social dignity, Arnauld d'Andilly records how his father, a prominent *parlementaire*, received great nobles and princes at his home to confer with them. See my "Father and Sons: Social Values in Seventeenth-Century Robe Society," in *Proceedings of*

the Tenth Annual Meeting of the Western Society for French History, ed. J. F. Sweets (Lawrence, Kans., 1984), 219.

2. A. Lloyd Moote, The Revolt of the Judges: The Parlement of Paris and the Fronde, 1643–1652 (Princeton, 1971), passim.

3. Jeffry Sawyer, "Judicial Corruption and Legal Reform in Early Seventeenth-Century France," Law and History Review 6 (1988): 95–117. See also Robert Harding, "Corruption and the Moral Boundaries of Patronage," in Patronage in the Renaissance, ed. G. F. Lytle and S. Orgel (Princeton, 1981), 47–64.

4. See the factums in BN, F^m 32226, a powerful attack mounted in the Parlement by the Vendôme-Beaufort family and its allies against First President Mathieu Molé, his son, and their "relatives and allies," through arguments that all of them had to disqualify themselves from judging the Vendôme inheritance case, on the grounds that they were interested parties.

5. Jacques I Le Coigneux was one of Gaston's favorites and was implicated in the Chalais Conspiracy and subsequent plots. Avenel perceived him as a real threat to Richelieu's political survival in 1630. Richelieu, Lettres, instructions diplomatiques et papiers d'état (Paris, 1853–77), 3:126, 128, 662–63. Omer Talon notes that Le Coigneux had been chancellor in Marie de Médicis's household. He also remarks that it was Richelieu who made him a president in the Parlement. Was Talon unaware of the tremendous pressure that Gaston exerted on Richelieu in favor of Le Coigneux? He says that "Le Coigneux avoit l'esprit fin, mais timide et suspicieux ne voulant jamais prendre confiance avec M. le Cardinal de Richelieu." Mémoires, Collection Michaud et Poujoulat (Paris, 1839), 2.

6. E. Griselle, ed., Maisons de la Grande Mademoiselle et de Gaston d'Orléans, son père (Paris, 1912), for the year 1627, 11, 24.

7. BN, MSS fr. 25025, fol. 332v, and 25026, fol. 168.

8. Richelieu, Lettres 3:216.

9. Ibid. 7:256.

10. Mazarin wrote: "M. le Président de Nesmond m'a prié formellement d'empêcher que l'administration des biens de M. le Prince lui fût commise, au cas qu'il le nommoit pour cela, avec cette reserve neanmoins qu'il ne parut point qu'il m'en eût parle." Mémoires de Mathieu Molé, ed. A. Champollion-Figeac (Paris, 1857), 4:370.

11. Her requête is printed in the Journal du Parlement (Paris, 1650), 67–68; and in Jean Vallier, BN, MSS fr. 10274, fols. 429–31.

12. She arrived at the Palais de Justice in President de Viole's coach. BN, MSS fr. 25025, fol. 207.

13. Ibid., fol. 329, and MSS fr. 6704, fol. 159; Dubuisson-Aubenai, Journal des Guerres Civiles (Paris, 1883), 1:345.

14. See my "L'Argent du roi: Pillage populaire et recherche parlementaire pendant la Fronde parisienne," in the papers of the Centre Méridional des Recherches

du XVIIe Siecle, forthcoming; and Françoise Bayard, *Le monde des financiers au XVIIe siècle* (Paris, 1988), 341 ff.

15. AN, U185, fol. 148. See Albert N. Hamscher, *The Parlement of Paris After the Fronde, 1653–1673* (Pittsburgh, 1976), 67ff., for a pioneering exploration of royal patronage in the Parlement.

16. Dubuisson-Aubenai, *Journal* 2:36. He notes that Condé also took all the funds in the royal treasury, including those allocated for the *maison royale*.

17. BN, MSS fr. 25025, fol. 401. A rumor also circulated to the effect that Turenne received three hundred thousand livres for his rebellious troops, and that the money came either from the princesse de Condé or from President Perrault, that is, from the superintendent of Condé's household, also a president in the Cour des Aides. Molé, *Mémoires* 4:365.

18. Dubuisson-Aubenai, *Journal* 1:306.

19. Ibid. 2:202–72. He quite frequently reported to the Grand' Chambre on his efforts.

20. Molé, *Mémoires* 4:359. The various summaries of the debates held in the Grand' Chambre provide evidence of these accusations, e.g., Councillor Dorat's speech of 13 April 1652: ". . . qu'il estoit honteux d'entendre ses [*sic*] discours d'un homme qui a voulu parestre et esclatter en vertu jusqu'à present, mais que l'on vovoit bien que scavoit [i.e., cela avoit] esté de fausse couleur, et que l'ambition et l'aveuglement pour ses enfans l'avoient honteusement precipité à suivre le party du Cardinal. . . ." Journal du Parlement, COD Geulph 3.1.72.2, Wolfenbuttel Library, n.p.

21. As a result of his son's appointment as treasurer of the Sainte-Chapelle (15 May 1649), Molé was attacked by Broussel in the debate over who should be disqualified on grounds of financial interest and connections with partisans. *Procès de la Boulaye* (Paris, 1862), 307. There was really little anyone could say in reply to such charges. Only systematic refusal of pensions, offices, and gifts could legitimate one's stature in the court when a wave of debate about corruption washed over the judges.

22. The question of gifts and gratitude has often been noted by historians but has never been systematically researched in the context of the loss of power and of self-esteem that might result from the acceptance of a gift. Hubert Mailfait, *Omer Talon* . . . (Paris, 1902), 198, captures Talon's ambiguity on this subject when he raises the issue of his attitude about wealth.

23. BN, MSS fr. 523, fol. 2. His French is an example of the "plainstyle" philosophy: "Les mains signifient autant que la voix, car elles demandent, elles promettent, elles appellent . . . , elles adorent. Les oeuvres de la main sont des preuves certaines de la disposition de l'âme. Et si les magistrats ont les mains toujours ouvertes. . . ."

24. Mailfait, *Omer Talon*, 359–60.

25. Ibid., 349.

26. Ibid.

27. Ibid. I owe this reference to Patricia M. Ranum. His Doujat relative in the Parlement nonetheless either accepted service when appointed or sought to serve when the move came to *perquisitionner* Mazarin's silver, rings, and jewels. *Journal contenant ce qui s'est fait et passé en la cour du Parlement*, 156, copy in the Stanford University rare-book library.

28. Holding an order of payment for a gage, a pension, or a rente was, of course, one thing; actually receiving payment was another. This was true of payments made by others than the royalty or the aristocracy. Mazarinist supporters in Paris were systematically denied interest due them by the Hôtel de ville, which was just another way of pressuring them to rally to the Fronde. The Frondeurs claimed that Mazarinists administering the rentes had emptied the bureau's coffers and had left the city. See O. Ranum, *The Fronde* (New York: W. W. Norton, forthcoming).

29. Quoted in Victor Cousin, *Madame de Longueville* (Paris, 1859), 227.

30. See Sarah Hanley, *The Lit de Justice of the Kings of France: Constitutional Ideology in Legend, Ritual, and Discourse* (Princeton, 1983), for a brief account of this ceremony.

8. The Parlement of Toulouse

and the Fronde

WILLIAM BEIK

Sovereign companies restrict themselves within the rules of their procedures except when the hope of increasing their authority or the fear of having it completely crushed causes them to transcend the limits set by these rules. But if for either of these reasons they begin to leave their usual path, they easily take up extreme positions because those who are most prudent do not ordinarily prevail in number, and they are considered suspect when they try to oppose excessively bold deliberations.

—Pierre Lenet, procureur general in the Parlement of Dijon and mastermind of the prince of Condé's rebellion, *Mémoires*

We still know relatively little about the Fronde, especially out in the provinces. This was a major struggle over political power, but it was far from a conflict over modern "constitutional" issues, and the very concept of power as it was then conceived is elusive to the modern observer. How could experienced leaders change sides so many times, express such contradictory sentiments, undermine the very authority they were trying to develop? Why did some provincial parlements rebel and others remain loyal? How, indeed, could learned judges steeped in the law find themselves encouraging illegal activities and issuing incendiary rulings? [1]

I would like to take up this question of motivation with respect to the Parlement of Toulouse and its conduct during the Fronde. Most authors rank the Toulouse Parlement as a loyal court in a city where the necessary conditions for revolt did not prevail. Standard authorities regularly ignore the Fronde in Toulouse altogether, presumably because a loyal parlement is considered an unimportant parlement. [2] And yet, the Toulouse court was "loyal" only in a relative sense. This imposing body of judges, located strategically in a proudly independent city halfway between the rebellious Parlement of Aix and the insurgent Parlement of Bordeaux, was actually seething with subversive activity between 1648 and 1653 and teetered on the brink of revolt many times, a fact left out of even the best local histories.[3] Its story needs to be resurrected, not only to correct the larger picture of the Fronde, but, more important, to grasp the dynamics of *parlementaire* politics in a setting where the judges were able to act out their own inclinations relatively unhindered by outside encroachments.

The Toulouse Parlement was an austere company of almost a hundred royal officers distributed among five chambers. Its first president, Jean de Bertier de Montrave, was a loyal supporter of Cardinal Richelieu with an important set of provincial connections and a long history of supporting the royal position while trying to protect his company's interests.[4] The court was by far the most prominent authority in the region, but its resounding influence stemmed partly from the fact that it was geographically removed from significant rivals. It had an immense district with something of a split personality, spanning both Languedoc and parts of Guyenne and the territories of two, sometimes three, different intendants. Even the annual Estates of Languedoc usually met far away on the Mediterranean coast. Governors, intendants, and military commanders who impinged on the interests of Toulouse were always coming from somewhere else, and none of them had jurisdiction over the court's whole territory.

On the eve of the Fronde the Parlement had already been through thirteen years of turbulence involving rejection of unpopular taxes, battles with intendants, and a major conflict with the *capitouls* of Toulouse over taxation and decision making within the city.[5] During this period the *parlementaires* had acted aggressively, but they had always been forced onto the defensive: members had been suspended from office, summoned to court, and punished with fines and creations of offices. Every tax they had avoided had been adopted later in some other form, but they had nevertheless maintained the company intact, and they remained angry and resentful.

When the news of the Parisian Fronde began to arrive in Toulouse in the summer of 1648, the *parlementaires* reacted by attempting to translate the actions of the Chambre Saint-Louis into terms that fit local circumstances. "This prodigious example of the Parlement of Paris, combined with the poverty of our company, is pushing us into disorder," wrote Bertier.[6] The more belligerent members were calling for declarations of "union" in imitation of the Paris Parlement—at one point for union with the Estates of Languedoc, and at another for union with the Parlement of Bordeaux.[7] By 6 July broadsheets from Paris and letters "full of fire" were inspiring the radical members to devise plans of action. On 18 July the court went ahead and suspended intendants, *commissions extraordinaires*, and the collection of tailles by force, pending the completion of remonstrances. On 22 and 26 August it took the next step and named two commissioners, Hughes de Vedelly in Languedoc and Pierre de Caumels in Guyenne, to tour around investigating abuses in the lodging of troops. Soon it sent Philippe-André de Forest de Carlincas to punish judges in Privas who had disobeyed the Parlement.[8]

On 10 September the *parlementaires* drew up a list of thirty-two remonstrances to the king. This comprehensive statement of concerns makes an interesting contrast to the declarations of the Chambre Saint-Louis in Paris.[9] For the province of Languedoc the court demanded cessation of all extraordinary taxes and all extraordinary commissions. In the future only those registered by the Parlement would be valid. Commissioners from the Parlement would prosecute any violations. All tax farmers were to be eliminated from the collection process and their profits returned to the people. The taille was to be reduced by one-fifth and arrears from past years canceled, in view of the considerable military burdens the province had recently supported.[10] Many articles were devoted to the various forms of illicit charges levied in the form of *étapes*, lodging of troops, fees in the *assiettes* (diocesan tax assemblies), and exactions of *traitants*. *Parlementaire* commissioners should monitor assessments in the *assiettes*. The Estates of Languedoc should be restored to their traditional form by the abolition of the "unverified" Edict of Béziers and allowed "freedom of voting." Toulouse should regain its special tax *abonnement*, granted in 1596 by "Henry the Great."[11] For the province of Guyenne the *parlementaires* wanted tax abuses similarly curtailed and the intendants—viewed as interlopers who collected large sums illicitly to support grand retinues of servants and soldiers in order to "enhance their authority"—forever abolished.

Another section treated the interests of officers. Newly created *présidial* courts should be abolished; officers' gages and fees should be restored, especially the gages, *franc-salé,* and *paulette* of the *parlementaires* themselves; and the Chambre de l'Edit of Castres should be reincorporated into the Parlement. Future reductions of gages were invalid until they were registered by the court. A particular concern was *évocations-générales,* the decrees removing whole classes of citizens (notably the bourgeois of Toulouse) from *parlementaire* jurisdiction. The Parlement also disliked *évocations* granted by the royal council to individuals whose legal adversaries had relatives in the court, and it denounced the facility with which *arrêts de conseil* suspending the court's proceedings were readily granted upon the request of litigants. No more lettres de cachet should be issued concerning annual elections in the towns of Languedoc, because the Parlement should have jurisdiction over all election appeals. There were also specific requests: that the officers of the *présidial* of Toulouse be protected from the *traitant* Boudon; that the professors of the University of Toulouse, "one of the most celebrated in Europe" have their full privileges restored; and that customs duties at Argentan in Berry be eliminated because they obstructed communications between Paris and Toulouse.

These demands are extremely interesting. The Parlement was following Paris in suspending intendants, reducing taxes, and seizing control over legislation by accepting only verified edicts. Its rejections of every manner of tax farm, of reductions of gages, and of creations of offices without registration were a dramatic assertion of regional control against all the monarchy's innovations. But the differences from the declarations of the Chambre Saint-Louis are also striking. The Parlement was a single company, not a "union" of corps, and it was not at the center of power, so no issues of "national" scope were raised: no general civil liberties, no joint chamber of justice to reform finances, no concern about "liberty of commerce" or foreign competition. Many of the *parlementaires'* demands were selfish in the extreme. They focused on their own customs duty, their own *présidial,* their own university (no mention of the professors of Montpellier, also in their district), and their own *franc-salé.* It was as if their ambitions to dominate the region were boundless, but their political sights were myopic, focused on their immediate area and the concerns of Toulousains like themselves.

At the heart of the matter was a struggle against every measure that diminished the *parlementaires'* role as the principal arbiters of public authority. They wanted to eliminate all alternative judicial and regulatory channels; handle all major disputes without appeal or evocation; monitor the towns via municipal elections; monitor the taxes via the *assiettes.* Unlike Paris, where the declarations focused on power at the center and made no mention of the territory outside the capital, the Toulouse Parlement focused on its domination of the region and prescribed the sending out of commissioners—a tactic never mentioned in the Paris declarations.

In September 1648 these were just aspirations. The question was going to be whether the Parlement, left to its own devices, could assert its hegemony over provincial affairs, given that it was not the only royal authority. The naming of commissioners was one practice that could be developed, since *parlementaires* on mission could mobilize support for the court. In October Vedelly spent ten days in Montpellier investigating the affairs of prior intendants and announcing loudly that he had discovered great abuses, "in order to make the name of intendant odious to the people and at the same time raise the authority and power of the Parlement."[12] It was later reported that in his mission to regulate troops he had traversed six dioceses accompanied by a syndic general from the Estates, a substitute procureur general, a clerk, and a *huissier;* held 63 trials in 150 days; heard 1,000 witnesses; and issued 50 final sentences: an impressive show of provincial influence exerted in collaboration with the Estates.[13]

In 1649 the Parlement of Bordeaux began to agitate. Pushed mightily by popular demonstrations, it began organizing resistance to its governor, Epernon, in March; led an expedition against his fortress at Libourne in May; declared war in July; and withstood a siege until December. In Aix an uprising against the governor, Alais, and the newly created semester Parlement (20 January) was followed by an armed rebellion of provincial nobles in June and July.[14] The Toulouse Parlement was thus surrounded by "bad examples," but it gave no formal support to the Paris Parlement, or to Bordeaux or Aix. It had no equally aggravating governor, since Gaston d'Orléans, governor of Languedoc, was far away in Paris. Instead, the Toulouse *parlementaires* continued to assert their influence over the region and attempt to realize their programs.

On 20 May 1649 the Parlement forbade royal agents to collect any taxes in Toulouse except the city's traditional *abonnement* and unilaterally suspended the Edict of Béziers, which had restricted the functioning of the Estates since the rebellion of 1632, declaring that "subject to the king's pleasure the province of Languedoc will enjoy its ancient liberties and privileges."[15] This move prodded the Estates of Languedoc, recently called into session, to start negotiating the same thing. On 13 June a distinguished delegation from the Estates arrived in Toulouse to salute the Parlement. Such a visit was unprecedented. The Estates presented two requests: first, that the roving commissioners continue to investigate "unworthy exactions" being collected in the province, including the violence being committed by the sieur de Vallon's regiment of Languedoc; second, that the 20 May *arrêt* be modified because it was making collection of the taille impossible and causing "trouble and disorder."[16] Rivalry of authority was already emerging, even as a distinctive "union" was contemplated.

In August agitation mounted. Broadsides attacking the Bertier family and Procureur general Fieubet, viewed as Mazarinists, appeared in the streets of Toulouse and on the doors of the men themselves, while people refused to pay the taille in various parts of the province. No doubt news had arrived of the riot in Bordeaux on 26 July that had expelled Epernon and the king's agents from the city.[17] On 14 August the Toulouse Parlement decreed against Epernon's raising of troops in its district. On 18 August an agreement with the Estates was announced whereby each body would consult the other before taking major steps. Victor de Fresalz was named, along with Jean-Antoine Du May and President François-Antoine de Garaud de Donneville, to continue visiting "the towns of the province to strengthen the people's dedication to their duty" and "return the courtesies of the Estates."[18] This group visited Montpellier in October and was viewed as having encouraged the Estates to resist high taxes, saying that "one should take advantage of the favorable conjuncture of general conditions in the kingdom to give relief to the province."[19]

The year 1650 was dominated by the arrest of the princes in Paris on 14 January, an act that placed Orléans even closer to the center of power. In June the princesse de Condé set up a government-in-exile in Bordeaux that was enthusiastically embraced by the population of the city, launching a second war against the duc d'Epernon and the king. At the end of July the king, queen, and Mazarin moved toward the region with an army; a siege of Bordeaux was undertaken; and another peace was signed on 28 September. These events caused excitement upriver in Toulouse, but with Orléans still on the side of the crown and the Estates not in session until late October, the Parlement was once again free during most of 1650 to pursue its particular interests.

The nature of its ambitions is made evident by the Morant affair. In 1650 Thomas Morant was sent to Montauban by the government as a *maître des requêtes en chevauchée* for Guyenne. The radical *parlementaires* viewed his arrival as a challenge to their authority, and he was linked to Bordeaux since he was acting on behalf of Epernon. They anticipated his appearance by issuing an *arrêt* on 30 April prohibiting all *maîtres des requêtes* from executing *commissions extraordinaires*. On 5 May Morant came to Toulouse to demonstrate that his commission was in full conformity with the rules banning intendants. He was admitted to the Grand' Chambre, but when he started to give a speech about his mission the councillors all got up and walked out. Shortly after, thirty to thirty-five of them filed back into the room without warning, issued a new *arrêt* commanding Morant to leave Toulouse within twenty-four hours, and commissioned Guillaume de Masnau and Jacques de Foucaud to look into any abuses he might commit.[20] Two days later the Parlement similarly attacked Breteuil, "so-called intendant of Languedoc." [21]

On 16 June Morant went to Lectoure to try a man accused of spying for the Spanish. The Parlement, obviously monitoring his every move, sent a councillor from the Requêtes to organize resistance in Lectoure by spreading the word that Morant had come to impose the cost of two companies of troops on the town. On 21 June a new *arrêt* called for his arrest and imprisonment because "the people have frequently experienced the *foules,* oppressions, vexations, violence, and fraud formerly perpetrated by intendants" and "they are starting to stir." [22] Morant was exasperated. "What connection," he asked, "can there be between an intendant and a *maître des requêtes* who comes to tour a province and investigate disorders?" [23] But it was precisely the exercise of preemptory royal authority by someone else that made the *parlementaires* jealous, and they did not really care what the mission was about.[24]

The siege of Bordeaux in August 1650 brought both Mazarin and the supporters of Condé close to Toulouse and intensified the convictions of their followers within the Parlement, "poisoning many people," as Bertier put it.[25] Diehard royalists now urged the cardinal to bring the king to Toulouse so that the position of *gens de bien,* as they saw themselves, would be reinforced. But most of the judges had reason to dislike Mazarin and at least to sympathize with the Parlement of Bordeaux, which was denouncing pseudo-intendants in a manner parallel to their own. In mid-August the court declared a union with the Parlement of Paris, which was then advocating a moderate solution along the lines suggested by Orléans. This union was controversial and was rejected by the Paris Parlement in September. In Toulouse, however, it was a compromise that placated the radicals by taking a stand that implied rejection of Mazarin (who was furious), while staying in the good graces of the governor and avoiding the perils of supporting the princes.[26]

The departure of the royal party from the region without visiting Toulouse was the signal for new agitation that lasted from the fall of 1650 through 1651. Earlier, in January 1650, the Parlement had reiterated its insistence that the cost of troop excesses suffered by communities be subtracted from the tailles they owed, after verification by commissioners from the Parlement.[27] Here was a perfect opportunity to intervene in local affairs by sending out more roving investigators. The marquis des Ouches, one of Mazarin's informants, was shocked: "This invention without precedent or foundation is a loss for the state, and it is impossible to answer for the conduct of a parlement with this sort of 'officers' created by itself."[28] The flight of Mazarin and the freeing of the princes in February 1651 added the final touch to the independence of the *parlementaires,* who issued a decree calling for the trial of Mazarin and the confiscation of all his properties.[29] But meanwhile the Estates, back in session since October, had struck a major blow at the Parlement. On 15 November 1650 they declared that the Parlement had no authority to monitor taxes, instructing all local officials to disregard its rulings and appealing to the crown against the Parlement's violation of the "rights and liberties of the province." The merchandise of private citizens from Toulouse was to be seized on the roads to pay three hundred thousand livres in back taxes owed by the city.[30]

This was a call to battle. The Parlement counterattacked on 16 February 1651 with a major list of abuses perpetrated by the Estates.[31] Four more commissioners were named to tour the towns, commandeer financial records, and cancel illicit impositions. One of them, Carlincas again, distributed a printed manifesto announcing that "the oppressors of the people" were trying to persuade the taxpayers that the Parlement was abrogating legitimate tax rolls in order to charge high fees for doing so. On the contrary, he asserted, such vilifiers were "trying to obscure by the blackness of their falsehoods the luminous globe of the justice of the Parlement," the purpose of which was to act on behalf of "the weak and [as he put it] the scum of the people" and to expose the "public thieves" who were selling votes in the Estates and concealing payoffs in the *étape* funds.[32]

Wherever Carlincas and his colleagues went they spread rhetoric of this sort, polarizing communities and encouraging rejection of the tax mandate from the Estates.[33] In Castelnaudary Carlincas called a council of inhabitants, which removed the deliberations of the last Estates from their registers. In Béziers he forced the bishop to retire into his fortified palace, corrected the registers, and held a public bidding for the *étape* contract. He proceeded on to Carcassonne and later started a riot in Narbonne in which cries of "Vive le Roy, le Parlement, et la Liberté" were heard in the streets. Jacques Caulet entered the diocesan tax assembly at Fanjeaux and told the deputies not to obey the Estates' tax roll; in Castres he commandeered the papers of the diocese and arrested several who resisted. Christophe Maynier de Lestang did the same thing in Bagnols. At the same time the

Parlement's warrants for the arrest of most of the bishops of the Estates occasioned a spirited protest from the general assembly of the clergy.[34]

The Parlement was meanwhile stirring up further corporate resistance to the Estates. It encouraged a meeting of the cathedral chapter of Toulouse at which the canons denounced the bishops in the Estates and demanded representation for themselves, suggesting in a circular letter that other chapters do the same. A meeting of the local nobility modeled after the one in Paris in March and April also demanded representation.[35] The Parlement commanded the bishops (who were prominent in the Estates) to devote a sixth of the fruits of their bishoprics to the feeding of the poor, and communities were instructed to seize that sixth out of benefices in their area if the bishops did not comply.[36] Attacks on the form of the Estates (from which *parlementaires* were constitutionally excluded), the nature of the tax accounts, and the role of the bishops were measures that went beyond the remonstrances of 1648. The radicals were asserting their administrative control over the province and trying to counter the alliance of bishops, great nobles, and royal agents by supporting the urban chapters (no doubt containing many of their relatives) and the lesser nobles, while shifting control of the town consulates from the bishops to themselves. On 31 July they responded to a negative *arrêt de conseil* with a major defense of their authority. The king, they stated, transmitted his power to them in undivided form, and it was their duty to use it to maintain the people in respect. "To this end the magistrates believe it necessary to carry their authority *anywhere in the district* where public affairs require it, without benefit of *any commission* other than that creating their offices." Defying the council, they proceeded to name a president, procureur general, and eight councillors to continue touring the province.[37]

These activities clearly had to be stopped. On two occasions, in July and then in August 1651, the comte d'Aubijoux, *lieutenant-particulier* of Languedoc and favorite of Orléans, arrived in Toulouse with Alexandre de Sève and Louis de Boucherat, royal commissioners to the Estates, to try to work out a compromise. The first mission, on 1 July, failed. The second, from 8 to 24 August, was more intensive. Negotiations went back and forth for several weeks. The royal commissioners heard from the deputies named by the assembled chambers of the Parlement, who were in fact the roving commissioners themselves, that three matters required urgent attention. First, the taille *abonnement* of Toulouse had to be restored. Second, a representative of the second order of clergy and the lesser nobility from each diocese should be admitted to the Estates. Third, the *trésoriers de France* should be admitted to the diocesan tax meetings with power to monitor the interest charged by the receiver generals. The deputies pleaded that they had *proof* from their investigations of overtaxing and profiteering, and argued passionately that the only solution was to give them jurisdiction over the Estates' rules of admission and tax policies. They were obviously deeply committed to their position. The commissioners reminded them that the *parlementaires* had no authority over the Estates and that their opposition to *arrêts de conseil* was obstructing reform. They were urged to transfer their disputes to the crown so that the king could do them justice. The next day the assembled chambers debated this option in a heated session accompanied by "angry words and blows" to the point where two members were suspended for six months. After this the deputies' position hardened. Transferring disputes to the crown, they said, "would diminish their credibility and authority with the people," who were awaiting justice from them. Negotiations were broken off.[38]

The fall of 1651 saw no moderation of the *parlementaires'* binge of assertions of authority. In the diocese of Castres Commissioner Caulet arrested two officials in an attempt to requisition papers; in Albi the bishop raced back from the Estates to counteract agitation by *parlementaires;* in Saint Papoul Carlincas had the clerk of the diocese seized while his office was searched for the registers of the *assiette.* On 12 October three commissioners were dispatched to Albi to rally resistance. On 9 November and 4 December Hughes Rudelle went twice to Montpellier and sent his servants circulating through the streets trying to incite the citizens to hold a general assembly and suspend the taille.[39]

Between December 1651 and August 1652 the situation changed. In September 1651 Condé had left the court and retired to Guyenne to raise a new, serious rebellion, in alliance with Spain. His follower the comte de Marsin deserted the royal war in Catalonia and led eight hundred cavalry and eight hundred infantry through Languedoc to Guyenne to join the mutiny. This military threat helped draw the province together.[40] Then royal troops from the army of Italy also started crossing the province. As news arrived of rebels raising forces and royal soldiers committing atrocities that only the intendants could stop, a compromise of necessity was arranged between the Parlement and the Estates.[41]

Paradoxically, the second moderating force was the slipping of Languedoc *into* rebellion. On 24 January 1652 Orléans and Condé formed an alliance to oppose the return of Mazarin. On 15 and 27 February the Parlement of Toulouse followed suit and, indirectly at least, declared for Condé, while calling for the seizure of Mazarin dead or alive.[42] Its *arrêt* stated that the court had a history of loyalty to the crown and had fought to uphold the royal declaration of October 1648 even when the Estates, egged on by Mazarin, had blocked it. Now, however, the return of Mazarin had made the province completely impossible to govern, forcing the loyal judges to take the necessary step of opposing the source of the trouble, the cardinal himself.

This "rebellion" created temporary chaos in the province, but the factionalization of provincial authorities did more to immobilize the situation than to generate resistance. As long as Orléans and his subordinates had been on the side of compromise, it had been possible to agitate effectively under the pretext of loyal service. Now everyone worked at cross purposes. In Montpellier "most of the principal people" were for the princes, "but all agree that they do not want to declare themselves unless they are extremely pressed because they don't want a war in their province."[43] In Toulouse the atmosphere is well captured by a letter to Mazarin dated 13 March:

> Plans are openly discussed and conferences are held in the very houses of the officers of the Parlement. People are scheming down to the lowest artisans. The streets are covered with broadsides saying to kill the mazarins. People assemble at night in companies and go around town carrying torches, threatening to burn and beat up our followers. Numbers of nobles and soldiers have been introduced into the city. Aubijoux has taken up residence in the *sénéchaussée* right near the wall, and in the Palais all these things are making the *gens de bien* apprehensive, since they are without a leader and barely dare to confer with one another for fear of arousing jealousy in their enemies.[44]

In May 1652 the agitation in the Parlement reached its peak.[45] Maugiron, Mazarin's latest envoy, reported that the company was split into six camps: totally loyal to the king and Mazarin; loyal to the king except for the interests of Mazarin; loyal to the king and the state; avid partisans of the princes; frondeurs for the interests of Orléans; frondeurs for their own sake. The party of the princes had the upper hand for the moment. President La Terrasse openly admitted writing and distributing a "book of maxims" that Maugiron called "criminal"; Maugiron added that if this was not stopped the Parlement would be "full of republicans." Meanwhile Baltasar de Cambon proposed to the assembled chambers on 8 May that they hold a general meeting of the corps, métiers, and clergy of Toulouse to deliberate Mazarin's departure from France—almost a meeting of "union" like the ones that had organized the rebellion in Bordeaux.[46] In fact, on 23 May Maugiron said that only twenty-five or thirty of the officers were loyal and the rest were so "bedeviled" that they might "make a Fronde worse than Bordeaux and Paris combined."[47]

But all this seditious activity petered out during the summer, as the plague gripped Toulouse. On 9 August the Parlement abandoned its position by registering an *arrêt de conseil* of 23 July that nullified the naming of Gaston as lieutenant general of the kingdom.[48] Switching positions, *parlementaires* now favored payments to the comte d'Harcourt's royal troops by towns downstream on the Garonne for fear that soldiers might threaten the environs of Toulouse, in which case there would be "no safety in any *maison de campagne*."[49] During 1653 the court continued to move toward a more loyal stance, largely because of the scramble of the judges to join Mazarin's "team," which was clearly the winning option at this point, and the presence of a large number of royal troops in winter quarters in Languedoc.[50] But the return to obedience was only partial. Throughout 1653 there was new talk of joining with the Estates to resist the troops, and the same phenomenon recurred in 1657. While some *parlementaires,* like Hughes de Vedelly, were initiating correspondence with Mazarin, the Parlement was denouncing the intendant Machault in October the same way it had denounced Morant in 1650, and in November Fieubet and five leading officers were summoned before the royal council to explain this action.[51] Like Bertier before him, Fieubet wrote to Mazarin defending the justice of his company's position: "The officers in our district, the nobility, and the people are all of virtually the same mind, and no one hesitates to proclaim that the reestablishment of the intendants is an evil that is hardly less serious than civil war."[52]

But what had really been happening inside the court between 1648 and 1653? The Parlement should be thought of as a collection of individuals motivated by a common point of view but increasingly split over how far to go in asserting that viewpoint. A "dissident" parlement was simply one in which the majority of votes in the assembled chambers had been won over to a "dissident" *arrêt* at a particular moment. The company was always divided. Conservatives believed in the merits of humble re-monstrance alone. Radicals became excited, wanting to act more, to go farther, to force obedience to the court. At first Bertier struggled to guide the plenary sessions into issuing more innocuous resolutions than the agi-tators wanted, as he had done in earlier days, but they insisted on holding meeting after meeting to draw up strident remonstrances.[53] By 1649 they had extended their consultations into a sort of "chambre Saint-Louis," as Bertier called it, consisting of one deputy from each of the five chambers, who met every day,

> looking for reasons to hold assemblies of chambers, drawing up *arrêts*, and seeking us out at all hours to demand assemblies of chambers to approve them, remaining so united in their false generosity that not a single one can be detached from the rest except by sending him away. I would break up this monopoly if I thought the royal authority were strong enough to support me. It must be done another time. All justice is being lost. Respect is already lost. And I consider it a major achievement if I just hold the line and avoid our falling even lower.[54]

By 1650 Toulouse, like the rest of France, was filling with intrigue. The marquis de Fontrailles, a longtime follower of Orléans, was there "getting drunk and debauching the young men of the Enquêtes, inspiring them with seditious sentiments and getting them to do all the evil he can," according to Mazarin, while the cardinal's agents the marquis des Ouches, the chevalier Terlon, and a certain Brachet were all trying to do the opposite. Meanwhile a man named Alliez connected to the tax farms was distributing money on behalf of the princes, and letters were being smuggled in from the princesse de Condé.[55] The same sort of effervescence intensified each time troops or factional conflicts approached Toulouse.

How powerful was this agitation? In the period of the Fronde the Parlement consisted of eleven presidents and slightly more than eighty councillors. In 1639 two controversial votes had been tallied in which those supporting the king won by 36 to 32 and 38 to 23, for a total of 68 and 61 votes respectively. In 1652 a frondeur vote on giving cannons to the royal army went *against* the royalist position, 39 to 34, for a total of 73 voting. Thus in 1652 the balance had tipped toward the dissidents, but only by 5 votes, and the fact that the total number voting was roughly the same indicates that the court was not suffering from significant numbers of abstentions or expulsions. In May 1650, 30 insurgents voted for the decree against Morant. In March 1651, 25 councillors allegedly voted to annul *arrêts de conseil*. Other reports indicate that the votes in 1652 fluctuated around majorities of only 1 to 5. On 17 April the royal position won by 2 votes. On 23 May it was reported that only 25 to 30 members were "loyal."[56] Thus the court was probably split into thirds, with one-third agitating, one-third loyal, and one-third passive or fluctuating. Under these conditions casual influences like a shift of mood, the arrival of news, or the lobbying of individuals could be decisive.

There are no lists of factional membership, but I have drawn up a list of the fifteen surest agitators and the fifteen clearest loyalists—hardly a scientific sample, but one permitting a few rough generalizations.[57] Both "parties" were a combination of respected elders and younger activists with similar *parlementaire* pedigrees. The one difference was generational. Most of the frondeurs had become councillors around 1632, and a few of them had entered much earlier. By contrast the loyalists were newer arrivals, with admission dates polarized around the 1620s (a few "Richelieu loyalists") and the 1640s (the Mazarin clients). Only four of the loyalists entered in the period 1625–38, compared to nine of the frondeurs. This frondeur group had entered the chambers at a time when the plague of 1630–32 had decimated the company. They had then been directly hit by the consequences of the Montmorency rebellion and the Thirty Years' War. Perhaps their expectations had been dashed. Already in 1635 Bertier had complained that the plague had taken most of the "ancients" from the Parlement and that the company was filled with "young people full of license who have retained nothing of the morals of those who formerly won a little honor for this Parlement."[58] Led by several considerably more senior men, including Carlincas, who had entered in 1614, these dissidents seem to have felt a tremendous loss of influence and the need to fight to regain it. At the hub of this group were President François-Etienne de Donneville and his son-in-law President Pierre Potier de la Terrasse, who died in 1649 and left his office to *his* son Etienne, author of the "Maxims" of 1652. Other frondeurs, such as Jean-Antoine Du May and Christophe Maynard de l'Estang, were related by marriage. The Potiers had considerable contacts in the province and belonged to the camp of the princes. Other frondeurs had closer ties with Aubijoux and Orléans.

On the other side of the fence, the loyalists fell into two groups. Some belonged to the waning sphere of First President Bertier. But the younger ones, those with longer careers ahead, were already scrambling to tie themselves to Mazarin. In this respect 1652 was a turning point—the year when the future servants of Mazarin and Louis XIV got into position. The post of advocate general was vacant, and people were talking about who would succeed Bertier as first president, while Mazarin's agents watched to see who would prove the most reliable. On 31 May Orléans wrote to the Parlement opposing the appointment of Guy de Maniban for the former post, on grounds that he was a "creature of Mazarin," but he was appointed anyway.[59] In May 1653 Bertier died and was replaced by neither his own choice, his nephew, nor any of the three Frondeur presidents nominated by the court. Instead, Gaspard de Fieubet, the creature of Mazarin, ran the company for the next thirty years in conjunction with other relatives by marriage like the Cirons, Torreils, and Manibans.

The Fronde in Toulouse had indeed been serious, even in the absence of the armed rebellions and popular demonstrations that put some cities on the map. Its distinctiveness lay in the *parlementaires'* intense quest for influence, an almost pathological desire to command and control that was shared by most of the company and probably by other provincial parlements as well. Like its Parisian counterpart, the court started by trying to undo most of the ministerial innovations of the past fifty years. But in order to make such reforms effective it had to expand its interventionism into new, questionable areas like tax accounting, municipal deliberations, and ecclesiastical responsibilities, and these moves set it on a collision course with other authorities like the Estates and the bishops. Soon the *parlementaires* were pestering the province with regulatory decrees, roving commissioners, and warrants for the arrest of recalcitrant rivals. Records were seized, budgets changed, extraordinary assemblies convoked.

These efforts flourished in the absence of some of the conditions that focused conflict elsewhere, as Sharon Kettering has indicated.[60] There was no antagonistic governor to draw fire. Intendants and royal agents did not live in the same city. Conflicts with the *capitouls* of Toulouse existed, but they remained low-key because a destructive battle had already taken place before the Fronde and because both sides were engaged in a common battle against the Estates in defense of municipal privileges.[61] The company *was* split into factions, but allegiance to national "parties" was muted by the ambivalent position of Gaston and the fact that none of the principals ever came to Toulouse. Client ties helped to stir up belligerence without unifying it around action; and without military targets like Epernon for the Bordelais, there was no strong advantage in drawing troops into a relatively peaceful region.

Were the judges irresponsible demagogues? From the perspective of a centralizing "absolutism," much of the court's agitation was certainly questionable, even illegal. But close study suggests that the judges of Toulouse, themselves fervent "absolutists," meant what they said. *Parlementaires* truly believed that they spoke with the authority of king, God, and judicial tradition behind them, and they must have felt deeply the psychological force of decisions taken by so many powerful individuals assembled collectively. They understood something about the dictates of government, but they were very far from Paris and extremely sure of themselves. It was easy for them to be suspicious of the dealings of manipulative commissioners and to assume that the king was not aware of the magnitude of the mismanagement taking place or the problems being caused. Their exasperation was heightened by the fact that they were excluded geographically and institutionally from the agencies with the power to do anything about these evident abuses.

When Pierre de Fermat, the famous mathematician, wrote to Séguier in 1648 that the Parlement had suspended tax practices "that violated both the ordinances and humanity itself," and that these measures had been necessary to keep Guyenne calm, since "plots and assemblies were taking place on all sides against the [taille] brigades," he was probably being perfectly sincere.[62] Similarly, when Carlincas was criticized by the royal council for his activities in Privas, he did not hesitate to reply that he had done nothing wrong: "I only avenged an insult done to the authority of the [Parlement] by subordinate officers, since it seems to me that [the Parlement's] authority should serve as a shield placed between them and the highest offices of the state."[63] Obviously, he felt secure in the belief that it was perfectly proper to maintain authority by chastising inferiors. Nor was Bertier any less serious when he told Mazarin in 1651, at the height of the Parlement's agitation, that the crown should protect the Parlement from the Estates and the Cour des Comptes: "Our provinces, even those far removed from the enemy, feel a great need for domestic [change] because of the uprising of inferior companies against the Parlement, the extraordinary impositions that do not return any profit to the king, and the oppressions of military men. These things are no less ruinous or painful than the entrance of foreign armies into Picardy or Champagne."[64]

Reading such pronouncements, it is hard to escape the conviction that these men were sincere, however defensive their arguments, and that they saw themselves as spokesmen for the community. They really thought they knew where the tax money was going and what was best for the crown. Yet at the same time their perspective was severely limited by their selfish vantage point. Again and again the theme of maintaining authority crops up in their pronouncements, along with illicit taxation and control over troops, but these were precisely the issues where their selfish instincts had been aroused by the recent loss of Toulouse's special tax and military status.

The Toulousain Fronde thus fits into recent attempts to view the national Fronde as a serious debate over modes of domination within the framework of absolutism. To the extent that the *parlementaires* were rejecting recent ministerial innovations, they were joining their compatriots elsewhere in calling for a more accommodating, traditional form of absolutism.[65] But unlike the Paris Parlement, which could attempt a union with other Parisian sovereign courts and negotiate a modus vivendi with the royal council and the financiers, the Toulouse Parlement had no way of influencing events except by arrogating leadership to itself, the organs of decision making all being elsewhere. The *parlementaires'* critique was negative and lacking in sophistication. This was not a call for constitutional reform, nor was it a "traditionalist" return to a past golden age, because it meant inventing new tactics and violating the equally traditional rights of the Estates of Languedoc. How could there be a provincial "union" when a select circle of prelates, barons, and town councillors—provincial neighbors, so to speak—was deeply implicated in the abuses being attacked, in alliance with financiers who were also "regional?"

The judges of Toulouse were confirmed absolutists, jealous of rivals and hungry for influence. What they really wanted was a more assured position within the king's system of delegated, hierarchical authority. In order to establish this position, some of them were willing to stir up corporate opposition to the Estates and resistance to royal agents, but only with the counterproductive goal of stalemating rivals. The logic of their position suggested that they should trade renewed loyalty *to* the crown for better support *from* the crown, now that they were in a position to bargain. Perhaps the importance of the Fronde was precisely that it forced the king to pay more attention to the aristocratic forces that had been neglected by his cardinal predecessors and to invent new ways of accommodating them, even while continuing to develop the tools of centralized government. This was to be the agenda of Louis XIV.

NOTES

1. These "political" questions have recently been revived in Robert Descimon and Christian Jouhaud, "La Fronde en mouvement: Le développement de la crise politique entre 1648 et 1652," *XVIIe siècle*, no. 145 (1984): 305–22; and in Christian Jouhaud, *Mazarinades: La Fronde des mots* (Paris, 1985). See also Sharon Kettering, "The Causes of the Judicial Frondes," *Canadian Journal of History* 17 (1982): 275–306.

2. None of the major histories discuss Languedoc. Ernst H. Kossmann, *La Fronde* (Leiden, 1954), barely mentions events in Toulouse and dismisses the events of 1651 and 1652 in a footnote: 125–26, 171, 179, 242 n. 1. There is nothing in Pierre-Georges Lorris, *La Fronde* (Paris, 1961); or in Georges Dethan, *Gaston d'Orléans, conspirateur et prince charmant* (Paris, 1959), even though Gaston was governor of Languedoc; or in the excellent brief summary by Hubert Méthivier,

La Fronde (Paris, 1984). By contrast, A. Lloyd Moote, *The Revolt of the Judges: The Parlement of Paris and the Fronde, 1643–1652* (Princeton, 1971), stands up extraordinarily well and brings Languedoc into the story at a number of points: 144, 240, 263–64, 284–85, 312–13, 322, 335, 346.

3. The standard *Histoire de Toulouse*, edited by Philippe Wolff (Toulouse, 1974), reports that "the troubles of the Fronde did not extend to the Toulouse region," and says nothing further about the matter (p. 293). The history of the Parlement, Jean-Baptiste Dubédat, *Histoire du Parlement de Toulouse*, 2 vols. (Paris, 1885), does include a sketchy section on some of these events but without any clear analysis. On the other hand, good information has been available for a century in the comprehensive survey by Ernest Roschach, *Histoire générale de Languedoc*, vols. 13 and 14 (Toulouse, 1876) (vol. 14, documents, is hereafter cited as Roschach 14). The situation is analyzed from the provincial vantage point in William Beik, *Absolutism and Society in Seventeenth-Century France: State Power and Provincial Aristocracy in Languedoc* (Cambridge, 1985), 206–15. See also the excellent analyses by Robert A. Schneider, "Crown and Capitoulat: Municipal Government in Toulouse, 1500–1789," in *Cities and Social Change in Early Modern France*, ed. Philip Benedict (London, 1989), 195–220.

4. Bertier was thus a classic "broker" of clientage: see Sharon Kettering, *Patrons, Brokers, and Clients in Seventeenth-Century France* (New York, 1986), 40–60.

5. This history is discussed in William Beik, "Magistrates and Popular Uprisings Before the Fronde: The Case of Toulouse," *Journal of Modern History* 46 (1974): 585–608.

6. Bertier to Séguier, 27 May and n. d. 1648, BN, MSS fr. 17388, fols. 31, 55.

7. Garibal to Séguier, 4 June 1648, ibid., fol. 66.

8. Trésoriers de France of Montauban to agents in Paris, 6 September 1648, ibid., 7686, fol. 22; Bertier to Séguier, 16 September, ibid., 17390, fol. 211.

9. Toulouse remonstrances: ibid., 18830, fols. 113r–21v; Paris declarations: François-André Isambert et al., eds., *Recueil général des anciennes lois françaises depuis l'an 400 jusqu'à la révolution de 1789*, 29 vols. (Paris, 1822–33), 17:72–84.

10. On the taille-reduction process, see Jean-Paul Charmeil, *Les trésoriers de France à l'époque de la Fronde: Contribution à l'histoire de l'administration financière sous l'ancien régime* (Paris, 1964), 285–86.

11. The Edict of Béziers was a law restricting the independence of the Estates and imposing a heavier tax burden on the province after the unsuccessful Montmorency revolt in 1632. The Toulouse *abonnement* was an arrangement whereby the city paid a miniscule fixed sum in place of the taille.

12. Breteuil to Séguier, 27 October 1648, BN, MSS fr. 17390, fol. 260.

13. Procès-verbaux of the Estates of Languedoc (hereafter P-V), 7 January 1651, cited in Roschach 14:354–55.

14. Sharon Kettering, *Judicial Politics and Urban Revolt in Seventeenth-Century France: The Parlement of Aix, 1629–1659* (Princeton, 1978), 261–85.

15. AD, Haute-Garonne (hereafter ADH-G), B 1879, fol. 543 (19 May 1649).

This move also represented cooperation with the *capitouls* of Toulouse: Barnabé Farmian de Rozoi, *Annales de la ville de Toulouse*, 4 vols. (Paris, 1771–76), 4:445.

16. P-V 31 July 1649, cited in Roschach 14:268–75.

17. "Extrait des registres de la maison de ville de Toulouse," BN, MSS fr. 18830, fols. 129–30.

18. Deburta to Séguier and Donneville to Séguier, 25 August 1649, ibid., 17394, fols. 202, 205.

19. Breteuil to Séguier, 6 October 1649, A.D. Lublinskaya, ed., *Lettres et mémoires adressés au Chancelier Séguier (1633–1649)* (Moscow-Leningrad, 1966), 218.

20. The Morant episode is described in Edmond Esmonin, "Un épisode du rétablissement des intendants: La mission de Morant en Guyenne," in his *Etudes sur la France des XVIIe et XVIIIe siècles* (Paris, 1964), 53–70. Morant's correspondence is in BN, MSS nouv. acq. fr. 1081. See also ADH-G, B 1879, fol. 494; Roschach 14:303–5; and Trésoriers de France of Montauban, 12 May 1650, BN, MSS fr. 7686, fol. 180.

21. Roschach 14:306–7.

22. Ibid., 311–13.

23. BN, MSS nouv. acq. fr. 1081, fol. 12.

24. Roschach 14:311–13 (*arrêt* of 25 June).

25. Bertier to Mazarin, 6 July 1650, Archives des Affaires Etrangères, Mémoires et Documents, France (hereafter AAE), 1634, fol. 444.

26. Mazarin to Le Tellier, 25 August 1650, *Lettres du Cardinal Mazarin pendant son ministère*, 9 vols. (Paris, 1872–1906), 3:744; Mazarin to someone in Toulouse, 26 August 1650, AAE, 1632, fol. 497. On Paris see also Moote, *Revolt of the Judges*, 273–74; and Richard Bonney, *Political Change in France Under Richelieu and Mazarin, 1624–1661* (Oxford, 1978), 64.

27. ADH-G, B 1879, fol. 487 (22 January 1650). This *arrêt* alluded to earlier ones on 27 February and 13 September 1649 and to contrary *arrêts* of the vacation chamber on 20 and 22 October.

28. Des Ouches to Mazarin, 13 September 1650, AAE, 1634, fol. 467.

29. *Arrêt* of 18 April 1651, Dubédat, *Parlement de Toulouse* 2:249.

30. ADH-G, C 2306, P-V 15 November 1650. This whole exchange is well analyzed in a memo drawn up for Séguier, BN, MSS fr. 18830, fol. 123. The Estates' attack was partially in response to the refusal of the *capitouls,* supported by the Parlement, to pay back taxes on grounds that the traditional *abonnement* made them illegal.

31. *Arrêt* of 16 February 1651, Roschach 14:357–61.

32. "Manifeste de Monsieur de Carlincas," bound in BN, MSS fr. 18830, fol. 86.

33. Procès-verbaux of Breteuil, 14 May and 2 June 1651, ibid., fols. 141, 148; ADH-G, C 2306, P-V 29 August and 3 October 1651; Germain Mouynes, ed., *Inventaire des Archives Communales, ville de Narbonne*, ser. BB, vol. 1 (Narbonne, 1872), 12 September 1651 (p. 638); AN, E 1696, 406, 432, 442.

34. Dubédat, *Parlement de Toulouse* 2:250–51.

35. On the politics of the nobility, see Jean-Marie Constant, "La Troisième Fronde: Les gentilshommes et les libertés nobiliaires," *XVIIe siècle*, no. 145 (1984): 341–62.

36. Roschach 14:364, 380–81, 384, 386; ADH-G, B 1880, fols. 81, 87.

37. *Arrêt* of 31 July 1651, Roschach 14:391–96 (my italics).

38. "Relation," BN, MSS fr. 18830, fols. 87–95.

39. The Parlement took this matter seriously enough to send Councillor Puymisson to the king with a memorandum charging the Comptes with inciting a riot. Ranchin case, AD, Hérault, B 9831; *arrêt* of 18 November 1651, Roschach 14:431–33; *arrêt de conseil,* 9 February 1652, AN, E 1700, fol. 45.

40. ADH-G, C 2306, P-V 4 October; *arrêt de parlement,* 5 October, Roschach 14:423–24.

41. ADH-G, C 2306, P-V 28 November, 5 and 24 December, and 6 January; Bertier to Estates, 30 December, Roschach 14:445–46; *arrêt* of 17 February 1652, ibid., 453–54.

42. Dubédat, *Parlement de Toulouse* 2:255.

43. Boissac to Mazarin, 29 March, AAE, 1634, fol. 585.

44. Fresalz to Mazarin, 13 March 1652, AAE, 1636, 51.

45. Major factional conflicts continued in a number of towns, especially Béziers, Albi, and Nîmes, exacerbated by the agitation of *parlementaire* commissioners, the bishops from the Estates, and various military commanders. In March the court created a scandal in Narbonne by lifting the suppression placed by the royal council on payment of *charges* by the gabelles agents so that the gages of the court (some 106,076 livres) could be seized. Roschach 14:459–61; AAE, 1636, fol. 51.

46. Maugiron to Mazarin, 8 May and n.d., ibid., fols. 48, 66.

47. Maugiron to Mazarin, 23 May, ibid., fol. 59.

48. Roschach 14:466–67.

49. *Arrêt de parlement,* 9 September 1652, ibid., 468.

50. Trelon to Mazarin, 24 September, AAE, 1636, fol. 91.

51. Vedelly to Mazarin, 15 November 1653, ibid., fol. 219; Trelon to Mazarin, 5 and 11 October, ibid., fols. 207, 212; interdictions, 16 November, BN, MSS fr. 18830, fol. 173.

52. Fieubet to Mazarin, 15 November 1653, AAE, 1636, fol. 200.

53. Bertier to Séguier, 9 June 1648, BN, MSS fr. 17388, fol. 197.

54. Bertier to Séguier, 18 August 1649, ibid., 17394, fol. 182.

55. Mazarin to Le Tellier, 8 August 1650, Mazarin, *Lettres* 3:670; Bertier to Mazarin, 3 September 1650, AAE, 1634, fol. 451; Trelon to Mazarin, 5 September 1650, ibid., fol. 452.

56. "Mémoires" of Malenfant, ADH-G, MS 148, fols. 189, 202; BN, MSS nouv. acq. fr. 1081, fol. 8; Fresalz to Mazarin, 7 April 1652, AAE, 1636, fol. 25; Maugiron to Mazarin, 23 May 1652, ibid., fol. 59.

57. The lists of faction members are drawn up from a wide variety of casual

mentions, mostly in correspondence. The best list of entrance dates is ADH-G, MS 193.

58. Bertier to Séguier, 8 August 1635, BN, MSS fr. 17369, fol. 111.

59. AAE, 1636, fol. 63.

60. For a discussion of these conditions, see Kettering, "Causes"; and Kossmann, *Fronde*, 125–26.

61. In July 1650 Mazarin granted Toulouse a new taille exemption for twenty years, but there still remained conflicts with the Estates over payment of back taxes and *étapes*. The Parlement collaborated with the *capitouls* in these matters, but they conflicted over control of municipal elections, payment of taxes by *parlementaires*, and the city's *évocation* to the Parlement of Grenoble. Rozoi, *Annales* 4:448–49, 458–59.

62. Fermat to Séguier, 18 August 1648, BN, MSS fr. 17390, fol. 115.

63. De Forest to Séguier, 29 November 1648, ibid., fol. 327.

64. Bertier to Mazarin, 26 April 1651, AAE, 1632, fol. 523.

65. Descimon and Jouhaud, "Fronde en mouvement," 309.

9. The Shadow of the Sixteenth Century in

Seventeenth-Century Absolutist France:

The Example of Molière

ELLERY SCHALK

Absolutism and the emergence of the absolutist state in France have drawn a good deal of scholarly attention recently.[1] Much of the impetus for this attention, and the resultant rethinking and reworking of the problems involved, stem from a series of related works that have led to major reevaluations of older assumptions and approaches. Recent work on elites and nobilities in the sixteenth and seventeenth centuries, for instance, has led most historians to abandon the concept of a declining nobility over the period,[2] and they also tend no longer to accept that there were fundamental differences between noble and "bourgeois" or noble and nonnoble or sword and robe in the sixteenth and seventeenth centuries.[3] Thus, older concepts used for helping to understand the emergence of absolutism, such as the "rise of the bourgeoisie," have had to be essentially abandoned. Also important in this reevaluation of absolutism has been work that has emphasized major differences in political structures between those of the sixteenth and those of the early and middle seventeenth centuries,[4] as well as work that has focused on the significance of the effects of the Wars of Religion in leading to major changes in French society.[5] In this case, accordingly, the chronological shift for the early crucial years has gone from the age of Francis I in the early and mid-sixteenth century to either the end of the sixteenth and the beginning of the seventeenth centuries (the age of Henry IV) or the early and middle seventeenth century.

Many older assumptions about absolutism, then, have had to be abandoned. In the meantime, several new frameworks are beginning to take shape. One, built around the impressive work of William Beik, argues for crucial differences between the first half of the seventeenth century and the period of the majority of Louis XIV and emphasizes the more fruitful co-operation between the aristocracy and the monarchy in the later period.[6] Another, which does not reject the main insights of Beik but simply tries to absorb them into a somewhat larger chronological period, is built around the work of the late Denis Richet and others working with him at the Ecole des Hautes Etudes en Sciences Sociales in Paris. This framework, which forms the groundwork for the present article, is social, political, and reli-gious. It assumes that fundamental structural change took place in French society with the development of the absolutist state, and sees the period of the religious wars and just after as the watershed between the "pre-absolutist" and the "absolutist" periods. It emphasizes the importance of the transformation of elites for understanding the phenomenon of absolut-ism, arguing that different kinds of elites ran the absolutist system and the absolutist state from those that dominated before, and that this transfor-mation reflected a combination of old elites changing and new ones taking over.[7] It also emphasizes the importance of the Catholic League as offering a serious alternative in the 1580s and early 1590s for the future of French society.[8] The year 1594 is especially important here, for even though at one level the process of change is seen as long-term and evolutionary from the sixteenth into the seventeenth centuries, at another level it is considered to be more abrupt. In a sense, two conflicting worlds, which had differ-ing social and political programs, faced each other in the 1580s and early 1590s; and one of these (the *politique*, Henry IV, royalist one, of course) won out. The new group of elites that represented this world then put into place a social and political regime that was to last basically unbroken (with, of course, developments and modifications) for two hundred years, or until 1789.[9]

This particular framework in its entirety (and especially the idea of an absolutist "regime" lasting from 1594 to 1789) has not yet been widely accepted in the United States and Britain, and one of the purposes of this article is to encourage scholars there to consider it more carefully. It seemed that one way to help understand it better and test it would be to analyze its relationship to what could be called the "fear of the pre-absolutist period" or the "fear of the sixteenth century"; and this is what is attempted in a preliminary way here. If a different set of elites, either trans-formed old ones or new ones, was responsible for putting this new regime into place, one of the reasons it did so, it would seem, was the great fear among these elites of what they perceived to be the chaos and disorders of the period of the religious wars. This, in fact, is known in general terms, but the extent to which these attitudes and myths dominated the minds, not only of the political and social elites, but also of the intellectual ones of the period, is only coming to be understood now. Among the main intellectual elites of the period, for instance, from 1594 on, and especially from the 1620s on, it could be argued that no really viable alternative to absolutism was ever *seriously* proposed, even perhaps until as late as the 1680s.[10] In the great literature of the time, alternative views were, of course, often presented, but they seem to have been used just for literary purposes, to create a confrontation or struggle (as in some of Corneille's plays), and they always lost out in the end to the "absolutist" answer.

These views, then, of the fear of the pre-absolutist period—of the need to remain within the structures of the new so as not to risk a return to the chaos of the period before—seem to be either emphasized or at least assumed by all the great intellectual figures of the early seventeenth century. Descartes, for instance, in the 1630s and 1640s, despite the revolutionary nature of so many aspects of his thought, emphasized strongly—and with quite clear reference to the period of the religious wars—that one should not risk touching or meddling with the social hierarchy or the political system and should, instead, "conform" in these areas.[11] Corneille, also in the 1630s and 1640s, despite the often titanic struggle in some of his plays between the forces of noble independence on the one hand and of "absolutist" authority on the other, always ends up with the latter winning. Corneille (in these plays) and Descartes were writing before the Fronde, of course, with the memory of the religious wars still fresh, and certainly few scholars would question the existence of the "shadow" of the sixteenth century here. But in light of the Richet framework for understanding absolutism outlined above, it seems useful to try to determine if these ideas continued later in the century. In other words, if the shadow of the sixteenth century did continue into the 1670s and 1680s, then this would seem to offer further evidence that there was indeed an "absolutist regime" that grew out of the period of the Wars of Religion, and that making such an assumption is thus a useful way to help us understand absolutism. Molière seemed an ideal person with whom to begin the examination. And a rereading of his major plays has suggested that a fear of the sixteenth century, similar to that found in Corneille and other writers of the first half of the century, can indeed be found in him.[12]

These ideas are not so visible in Molière, of course, as they are in Corneille. The struggle in Corneille between the absolutist and pre-absolutist periods is, as suggested, "titanic" and heroic. The struggle of the Cid, for instance, to avoid submitting to absolutism and being under the law and the monarch like everyone else thunders across the stage; and the confrontation in *Cinna* between absolutism and noble independence, although framed differently, is similarly heroic. It will be argued in this article, however, that even though not so immediately visible, and presented in a different context, the struggle in Molière between these two periods—between what will be called the sixteenth and the seventeenth centuries—is equally titanic, even if it is more subtle and presented in the framework of comedy instead of tragedy. This implies a certain reinterpretation of Molière's relation to absolutism and to the sixteenth century; and considering the massiveness of that question and the short space available here, the main purpose of this essay—even if the conclusions are stated rather categorically—is simply to open the discussion and suggest a rethinking of the question.

There is, in almost all of Molière's plays (and seven of his greatest plays—*Le misanthrope, Dom Juan, L'école des femmes, Tartuffe, L'avare, Le malade imaginaire,* and *Le bourgeois gentilhomme*—will be examined here), an emphasis upon what can be called, for want of a better term, "conformity." As Alban John Krailsheimer has shown,[13] all seven "heroes" in the plays just mentioned (Alceste in *Le misanthrope,* Dom Juan in *Dom Juan,* Arnolphe in *L'école des femmes,* Orgon in *Tartuffe,* Harpagon in *L'avare,* Argan in *Le malade imaginaire,* and Monsieur Jourdain in *Le bourgeois gentilhomme*) overstep the normal bounds—but, it should be emphasized, not the legal bounds—of prescribed action in their familial and societal situations; and all are brought back (in different ways each time) to conformity or "normality," to moderation and to common sense, by the end of the play. In each case, thus, they are acting with what is portrayed as an unbridled egoism, which harms those around them.

When these plays are examined in relationship to the views of absolutism outlined above, it becomes quite clear that Molière, in portraying this unbridled egoism and its downfall, was making a conscious comparison and parallel with what could be called the "unbridled egoism" of the sixteenth century and *its* downfall, that is, its being mastered and put under control by the seventeenth-century absolutist state. In other words, an overdose of unbridled egoism is how Molière apparently understood what had gone wrong in the sixteenth century and what was responsible for its disasters (whether this is an accurate historical portrayal of what actually happened, as we understand it today, is, of course, immaterial). And then this unbridled egoism was replaced by the reasonableness and conformity and moderation of his own "absolutist" century. This century of his, he felt, had not conquered egoism (to try to conquer it was in fact one of the illusions of the sixteenth century and indeed in some ways the ultimate form of egoism), but rather had *given up* trying to conquer it. In other words, his own century did—and should—accept egoism, and vice, as long as they stayed within the bounds of prescribed behavior and moderation. The sin of his seven heroes—and of the sixteenth century—is thus not egoism but *unbridled* egoism. If left unmastered, it would, in the case of the plays, have led to familial and societal disasters and, in the case of the sixteenth century, did lead to chaos and disorders—results that were unnecessary, unfair to innocent people, and unreasonable.

This contrast and parallel between centuries is portrayed the most clearly, probably, in the contrast between the characters of Alceste and Philante in *Le misanthrope*. Alceste, at first reading, seems very modern or right out of Rousseau. He is against hypocrisy and demands honesty and sincerity ("Je veux qu'on soit sincère, et qu'en homme d'honneur / On ne lâche aucun mot qui ne parte du coeur").[14] He wants to be judged upon merit alone ("Je refuse d'un coeur la vaste complaisance / Qui ne fait de mérite aucune différence").[15] But when one looks further, it becomes clear that Alceste is in fact portrayed as a symbol of the *past,* of past ages, and in particular the previous century (aspects of which could, of course, have continued into the seventeenth century), which is regularly contrasted with "ce siècle ou nous sommes."[16] Alceste, in fact, represents the "vertu de vieux ages,"[17] a close parallel with the sort of vertu that dominated the thinking of nobles about themselves in the sixteenth century.[18] Alceste wants merit, freedom, and independence, or a sixteenth-century form of vertu, which "est une vertu rare au siècle d'aujourd'hui,"[19] but his present century will not allow it to exist.

It has been argued that this vertu and freedom of the sixteenth-century nobles had to be mastered or modified (partially with a greater emphasis upon birth) before the civil and religious wars could be brought to an end and absolutism put into place.[20] It seems that Molière also saw a similar change away from this vertu and emphasis upon liberty and being a "law unto oneself."[21] He adds to this an emphasis that would define this vertu, in its extreme, as unbridled egoism, an unbridled egoism that had to be mastered for the good of society (or, in the case of Alceste, not allowed to flourish as he gives up and goes off to his "desert island"). Molière, thus, offers further evidence for the view of nobility as virtue in the sixteenth century, and its change to something else; but he also shows—because of his negative attitude toward this vertu and the century that it represents— a definite fear of that century, a fear that leads directly to his acceptance of the new view of nobility and of the absolutist state that went so well with that new view.

For this vestige of the sixteenth century who is Alceste, then, "Trop de perversité règne au siècle ou nous sommes." [22] But for Philinte (or Molière), who represents the new century:

La parfaite raison fuit toute extrémité
Et veut que l'on soit sage avec sobriété
Cette grande raideur des vertus des vieux âges
Heutre trop notre siècle et les communs usages:
Elle veut aux mortels trop de perfection:
Il faut fléchir au temps sans obstination.
Et c'est une folie à nulle autre seconde
De vouloir se mêler de corriger le monde
J'observe, comme vous, cent choses tous les jours,
Qui pourraient mieux aller, prenant un autre cours;
Mais quoi qu'à chaque pas je puisse voir paraître,
En courroux, comme vous, on ne me voit point être;
Je prends tout doucement les hommes comme ils sont,
J'accoutume mon âme à souffrir ce qu'ils font,
Et je crois qu'à la cour, de même qu'à la ville,
Mon flegme est philosophe autant que votre bile. [23]

The shadow of the sixteenth century in seventeenth-century absolutist France, with the resultant demand for "conformity" and for accepting people as they are instead of as they should be, as well as the accepting of the political system that seemed to reflect those ideals best, could hardly be shown better.

This contrast in Molière between the sixteenth and seventeenth centuries is also shown in *Dom Juan* in the discussion between Dom Juan and his father about the nature of nobility,[24] a passage that offers as well another interesting insight on the question of changing conceptions of nobility between the two centuries. Although in the story as a whole Dom Juan represents the sixteenth century just as the other six heroes do, he is, in this particular argument, on the side of acceptance of the realities of the seventeenth century, while his father defends the vertu of the sixteenth-century nobility. The long speech of Dom Louis (the father) trying to call Dom Juan back to vertu from his evil ways has, indeed, interesting parallels with—along with some illuminating differences from—the many calls for a return to virtue of the nobles of the 1570s and 1580s, nobles who in this latter case, however, were watching their raison d'être of virtue and action crumbling around them in the crisis years of the Wars of Religion:[25]

> Ah! quelle bassesse est la vôtre! Ne rougissez-vous point de mériter si peu votre naissance? Etes-vous en droit, dites-moi, d'en tirer quelque vanité? Et qu'avez-vous fait dans le monde pour être gentilhomme [the equivalent of "noble" for the time, of course]? Croyez-vous qu'il suffise d'en porter le nom et les armes, et que ce nous soit une gloire d'être sortis d'un sang noble lorsque nous vivons en infâmes? Non, non, la naissance n'est rien où la vertu n'est pas. Aussi nous n'avons part à la gloire de nos ancêtres qu'autant que nous nous efforçons de leur ressembler; et cet éclat de leurs actions qu'ils répandent sur nous, nous impose un engagement de leur faire le même honneur, de suivre les pas qu'ils nous tracent, et de ne point dégénérer de leurs vertus, si nous voulons être estimés leurs véritables descendants. Ainsi vous descendez en vain des aïeux dont vous êtes né: ils vous désavouent pour leur sang, et tout ce qu'ils ont fait d'illustre ne vous donne aucun avantage: au contraire, l'éclat n'en rejaillit sur vous qu'à votre déshonneur et leur gloire est un flambeau qui éclaire aux yeux d'un chacun la honte de vos actions. Apprenez enfin qu'un gentilhomme qui vit mal est un monstre dans la nature, que la vertu est le premier titre de noblesse, que je regarde bien moins au nom qu'on signe qu'aux actions qu'on fait, et que je ferais plus d'état du fils d'un crocheteur qui serait honnête homme, que du fils d'un monarque qui vivait comme vous.[26]

Here, on the one hand, virtue seems to be the basis of nobility; and Dom Juan should, it would appear, cease being noble if he is not virtuous. And that indeed is what the writers of the 1570s and 1580s mentioned above, using their inherited view of nobility as virtue and action, seem to have been arguing. But what is different here is the contrast with birth, something that is *not* found in the writers of the 1570s and 1580s; and it is not found, it seems, because the new emphasis and reliance upon birth did not really take shape until the 1590s and after.[27]

Molière, then, is indeed contrasting the sixteenth and seventeenth centuries here (put in this case in generational terms because of the needs of the story). Dom Louis stands for what Molière understands to be the view of nobility of the earlier period, but Molière adds to this view of virtue an emphasis upon birth as being the opposite view, something that had, in fact, not taken shape in its modern form yet in the sixteenth century. In other words, the sixteenth-century writers emphasized the virtue without contrasting it particularly with birth, but it is understandable that Molière would add birth, since the latter had become much more the basis of nobility by his time.

Molière, therefore, does in fact accept seventeenth-century views of nobility of birth. Taking away Dom Juan's nobility for not being virtuous is not an actual option in his time, and he knows it (even though it still seemed at least an assumed possibility in the 1570s and 1580s). Dom Juan answers his father rudely and then pays no attention to him, and remains just as noble. In the same way, other corrupt as well as not so corrupt nobles can be found sprinkled throughout Molière's plays, and they remain just as noble no matter how corrupt they may or may not be. What Molière is doing, then, is contrasting the sixteenth and seventeenth centuries and using an example (nobility as virtue) that he *thinks* does reflect—and in fact it does with modification—the sixteenth century. But he also knows that that vertu (and its comcomitant liberty and independence) would not fit in his own century; he knows, instead, that nobility of birth, corrupt or not corrupt, but always under the monarchy, is much less of a problem (and not that much of a threat to nonnobles in the form in which it existed in seventeenth-century France).[28] The old noble virtue, thus, seems also for Molière to be a part of the "threat" of the sixteenth century that needs to be suppressed.

The contrast of the sixteenth to the seventeenth century, of pre-absolutist to absolutist, is also found in the five other plays under consideration, as well as in the main story of *Dom Juan*. It is not so obvious in them, at least at first reading; but it becomes more so when the plays are looked at as a whole. All seven stories (including that of *Le misanthrope*) follow a similar pattern. In each case, there is a relatively powerful individual, who holds ascendancy and influence over others and who in most aspects seems normal and reasonable, but who seems to follow in one particular area a course of action that outsteps the bounds of normalcy. If permitted to carry out his desires, he will harm those around him. In a sense, his unbridled egoism will not allow the normal or controlled egoism—often of young people who are in love and who wish to marry and who should, logically, be allowed to marry—to run its course.

There appears to be a parallel here, in Molière's mind, with the sixteenth century. It does not seem surprising that someone like him, whose society had lost touch with the fundamentally religious concerns of many of the main religious actors of the sixteenth century, whether Protestant or Catholic, might see these whole movements as being led by unleashed egoism. In other words, individual leaders—whether they were Protestant reformers, leaders of the Catholic League, powerful and independent nobles, unscrupulous leaders like Casaulx of independence-seeking cities such as Marseilles,[29] or others—viewed from outside as selfish and thinking only of themselves, would be understood from this point of view as trying to impose their wills upon society, or sections of it, while only making things worse for people and often producing chaos and destruction. The tendency that can be found in almost any period for people who are opposed to widespread popular movements to turn them in their own minds into the products of a few self-promoting leaders is well known. In this case, it would be the historical distance, the results of the rewriting of the past done by the early royalists after 1594 that has been so brilliantly brought to light by Robert Descimon,[30] and simple fear of the unquestionable violence and destruction of the period that would have led Molière to parallel the unbridled egoism of his seventeenth-century characters with the perceived unbridled egoism of the leaders of the sixteenth-century "troubles."

The similarity of the seven plots joined with the clear contrast in one, *Le misanthrope*, seems to be strong evidence that Molière was in fact paralleling the sixteenth and seventeenth centuries with his plots and thus making the same historical point in each case. And there are other indications in the plays that seem to offer further evidence for the existence of this parallel. In *L'école des femmes*, for instance, Chrysalde, the sensible friend of the "unsensible" hero, Arnolphe, makes the parallel between the craziness and extremes of Arnolphe—in this case his excessive fear of being cuckolded—and other more "sixteenth-century" forms of excess: "être avare, brutal, fourbe, méchant et lâche."[31] Chrysalde counsels moderation, the advice that is found regularly throughout Molière's plays and that fits well, of course, with the needs and desires of the absolutist state:

Car pour se bien conduire en ces difficultés
Il y faut, *comme en tout*, fuir les extrémités.[32]

Arnolphe has kept the young Agnès prisoner for years in order to save her for himself, and although he loses her in the end, he does get off relatively unpunished. This could seem unfair if one expects Molière not to allow for vice at all, but if one sees him accepting vice as long as it stays within normal bounds—and when that staying within normal bounds assumes submission to good sense *and* to absolutist authority—then it does appear logical. After all, absolutism in its early years after 1594, and perhaps even until the 1680s, almost always offered forgiveness for submission.[33]

Orgon, the hero of *Tartuffe,* has, of course, a different problem from Arnolphe's: he does not recognize religious hypocrisy in others (and again it is not difficult to imagine that seventeenth-century observers could see those who would use religion for their own purposes as representing a sixteenth-century stereotype). But his problem is also similar to Arnolphe's in that his blindness could lead to great hardship for his family and those around him (and himself too, in fact, since he even signs over his goods to Tartuffe). Orgon is "saved" first, by returning to reasonableness, when he learns of Tartuffe's real nature (by being hidden under a table). But in this particular case he is also saved, in that he gets his goods and house back, by a *direct* intervention of the king (the ostensible reason is that he had supported the royal cause during the Fronde).

Absolutism, thus, enters directly here, and with full and positive acceptance. In the context of the rest of Molière's work, it seems clear that this should not be taken as hypocrisy—not, for instance, just as an attempt to flatter a king and the regime he stands for (which Molière theoretically then would not like or accept) in order to get his own plays performed and *Tartuffe* accepted. It rather reflects one more deus ex machina, like those at the end of the other six plays, that helps bring a hero back to reasonableness and sanity; and like the other six it uses the framework of the absolutist state—even if here a bit more directly—to do so, that framework being the only one, it is argued here, known and accepted by essentially all the dominant elites of the time, including Molière.

The hero in *Dom Juan* may represent the new century against the old, as demonstrated earlier, in the confrontation with his father about concepts of nobility, but he represents the old century, as Molière's other heroes do, in his excesses. For his "sins," like those of Arnolphe and Orgon, are also sins of extremes. These are first of all his constant seductions and then abandonments of women, whose lives he often ruins, and then, in his attempts to explain or justify his actions, his open statements of religious hypocrisy. Also, he may be right at home with his time in arguing that "un sage esprit" should "s'accommode aux vices de son siècle,"[34] but he parts company with Molière (and rejoins the sixteenth century) by prefacing that statement with the claim that one should use this accommodation to "profit from the weaknesses of men."[35]

Dom Juan, then, has to be brought down, and in this case it is a heavenly intervention that performs this task at the end. Orgon's problem (in *Tartuffe*) is that he does not *recognize* religious hypocrisy; it would seem that Molière can allow religious hypocrisy to exist as long as it does not act upon or influence other people, but when it does act upon others—as Dom Juan suggests—the situation is potentially that of a sixteenth-century religious war. Molière feels that he must remind his society of this potential, and thus Dom Juan is sent off to hell.

Harpagon in *L'avare* also outsteps the bounds of normalcy, this time the passion being for money instead of for women, as it is for Dom Juan. He seems a ridiculous figure in the play (as do all the seven heroes, in fact, in their excesses), until one remembers that if he has his way—and he theoretically has the means and the authority—he will wreak havoc on the rest of his family. At this point he becomes more serious and more dangerous. Building, maintaining, and integrating the paternally dominated family into the absolutist state—and in so doing taking away some of the freedom of the sixteenth century—has been seen as a basic part of the constructing of that state;[36] but if that family, and that state, were to function well and fairly (and liberally and compassionately even if with authoritarianism, as Molière certainly believed they should), then the excesses of people like Harpagon could not (or should not) be allowed. And similar ideas of the need to submit to the demands of the "authoritarian" family on the one hand, while on the other hand encouraging respect, within this inequality, for the rights of women, and also children, can be found throughout Molière's plays (especially strongly, for instance, in *Les femmes savantes*). Harpagon is also brought back to normalcy or "egoism within bounds," and the others in the family are left free to marry whomever they wish (again egoism within bounds). The resolution is accomplished in this case with another outside intervention (the temporary stealing of his money box), an intervention that could be taken just as silly but that also could perhaps be understood as being all that is needed for a return to reason, because of the extreme silliness of Harpagon.

Unbridled egoism is also the fault of Argan in *Le malade imaginaire*, and again what is needed is a return to a certain conformity or normalcy, an escape from excess. His mania (to have even better than the absolutely best medical care possible) leads him—we find again the common theme—to wish to marry his daughter against her wishes and her happiness. And again, by a ruse he is brought back to a certain sanity and reasonableness, and his daughter is allowed to marry the one whom she loves. With this she should obtain relative happiness, relative because she will still have to conform, like others in the society, to the basic structures of that society. In her case this will mean, among other things, that she will have to live in a husband-dominated family, but one in which (Molière hopes) the husband will act, not like Argan and the other six "heroes," but rather with reason and common sense. The husband, in other words, in spite of his greater power, must also conform, just as must the other dominant members of absolutist society (as opposed to those [elites] of pre-absolutist sixteenth-century society, who lived lives theoretically freer and more independent—but also more destructive to those around them).

Monsieur Jourdain in *Le bourgeois gentilhomme,* in his attempt to take on the noble accoutrements of his time, is as silly as the other heroes in his excesses, although this play is certainly lighter in tone than the others. But the same harm can fall on those around him if he pushes his folly beyond sensible or reasonable bounds. In this case his excess would be forcing his daughter to marry the wrong or "illogical" person just because he is noble, but he is blocked and reason prevails at the end through the elaborate ruse with the supposed son of the Grand Turk. Monsieur Jourdain continues to keep his same ideas, but these are harmless enough as long as they do not threaten others too seriously. Once again, thus, the "sixteenth century" is suppressed. And it is done this time in a context that reflects the replacement of more "dangerous" sixteenth-century concepts of nobility with the less dangerous seventeenth-century ones of "culture" and "civilization," a replacement that also suggests the existence in the latter period of a society of elites without any major or fundamental distinction between noble and nonnoble.[37]

The shadow of the sixteenth century, then (including that century's more feeble remnants in the first half of the seventeenth century, such as the noble revolts and the Fronde),[38] hung heavily over Molière and led to his making significant parallels in his plays between the unbridled egoism of his heroes and the perceived unbridled egoism of the sixteenth century; and in the end this helped lead to his strong support and acceptance of the absolutist regime. And in this conscious and positive support of absolutism he seems, from all indications, to have been typical of the main elites of his time, social and political as well as intellectual, and both noble and nonnoble—although these groups must be distinguished here from "local" elites that could and often did oppose absolutism.[39] In the 1680s, however, this shadow of the sixteenth century, which had hung so heavily over so many for so long, at last began to lift. Serious opposition to absolutism became possible and started to surface.[40] People began to forget the seeming horrors of the sixteenth century and notice more of the apparent excesses of the king (which perhaps in fact resembled the excesses of the seven heroes described here), such as the revocation of the Edict of Nantes. But it was now too late. All the years of almost unqualified support for absolutism had enabled it to become too deeply entrenched. The French for the next century could imagine alternatives; they could struggle—often heroically but without substantial success, as we know—to make fundamental reforms in the system; but in the end, of course, they seemed to have no choice but to turn to revolution. And the great upheavals of the late sixteenth century, and the shadow they laid over the seventeenth century, must take some of the blame (or credit) for that later course of events.

NOTES

1. See, for instance, the extensive review article by Richard Bonney, "Absolutism: What's in a Name?" *French History* 1 (1987): 93–117. Significant works that have appeared since the publication of Bonney's fine article include Lawrence M. Bryant, *The King and the City in the Parisian Royal Entry Ceremony: Politics, Ritual, and Art in the Renaissance* (Geneva, 1986); Albert N. Hamscher, *The Conseil Privé and the Parlements in the Age of Louis XIV: A Study in French Absolutism,* Transactions of the American Philosophical Society, vol. 77, pt. 2 (Philadelphia, 1987); William H. Beik, "Urban Factions and the Social Order During the Minority of Louis XIV," *French Historical Studies* 15 (1987): 36–67; Paul Sonnino, *Louis XIV and the Origins of the Dutch War* (Cambridge, 1988); James B. Collins, *Fiscal Limits of Absolutism: Direct Taxation in Early Seventeenth-Century France* (Berkeley, 1988); Mack P. Holt, "The King in Parlement: The Problem of the *Lit de Justice* in Sixteenth-Century France," *Historical Journal* 31 (1988): 507–23; Sarah Hanley, "Engendering the State: Family Formation and State Building in Early Modern France," *French Historical Studies* 16 (1989): 4–27; and Mark Greengrass, "The Public Context of the Abjuration of Henri IV," in *From Valois to Bourbon: Dynasty, State and Society in Early Modern France,* ed. Keith Cameron (Exeter, 1989), 107–26.

2. For instance, William A. Weary, "The House of La Trémoille, Fifteenth Through Eighteenth Centuries: Change and Adaptation in a French Noble Family," *Journal of Modern History* 49 (1977): on-demand supp.; J. Russell Major, "Noble Income, Inflation and the Wars of Religion in France," *American Historical Review* 86 (1981): 21–48; James B. Wood, *The Nobility of the Election of Bayeux,*

1463–1666: Continuity Through Change (Princeton, 1980); Jean-Marie Constant, *Nobles et paysans en Beauce aux XVIe et XVIIe siècles* (Université de Lille III, Service de reproduction des thèses, 1981); and this is strongly implied in Kristen B. Neuschel's impressive new study, *Word of Honor: Interpreting Noble Culture in Sixteenth-Century France* (Ithaca, N.Y., 1989).

3. For a few examples see Denis Richet, "Autour des origines idéologiques lointaines de la Révolution française: Elites et despotisme," *Annales E.S.C.* 24 (1969): 1–23; Robert R. Harding, *Anatomy of a Power Elite: The Provincial Governors of Early Modern France* (New Haven, 1978); Jonathan Dewald, *The Formation of a Provincial Nobility: The Magistrates of the Parlement of Rouen, 1499–1610* (Princeton, 1980); Wood, *Nobility of Bayeux;* and Denis Crouzet, "Recherches sur la crise de l'aristocratie en France au XVIe siècle: Les dettes de la maison de Nevers," *Histoire, économie et société* 1 (1982): 7–50.

4. J. Russell Major has been among the most important in leading the way here, from his early statement of the concept of the "Renaissance monarchy" (which was set against the later absolute monarchy) in *Representative Institutions in Renaissance France, 1421–1559* (Madison, 1960), 3–20, to his great work of summation *Representative Government in Early Modern France* (New Haven, 1980).

5. The list is long here, but certainly especially important has been the work of J. H. M. Salmon; see his *Society in Crisis: France in the Sixteenth Century* (New York, 1975), and the recently published collection of his articles, *Renaissance and Revolt: Essays in the Intellectual and Social History of Early Modern France* (Cambridge, 1987). See also James B. Wood, "The Impact of the Wars of Religion: A View of France in 1581," *Sixteenth Century Journal* 15 (1984): 131–68.

6. See William Beik, *Absolutism and Society in Seventeenth-Century France: State Power and Provincial Aristocracy in Languedoc* (Cambridge, 1985).

7. See, for example, Denis Richet, "Aspects socio-culturels des conflits religieux à Paris dans la seconde moitié du xvie siècle," *Annales E.S.C.* 32 (1977): 764–89; Robert Descimon, *Qui étaient les Seize? Etude sociale de deux cent vingt-cinq cadres laics de la Ligue radicale parisienne (1585–1594)* (Paris, 1983); and idem, "La haute noblesse parlementaire parisienne: La production d'une aristocratie d'Etat aux xvie et xviie siècles," in *L'Etat et les aristocraties (France, Angleterre, Ecosse), XIIe–XVIIe siècle,* ed. Philippe Contamine (Paris, 1989), pp. 357–84.

8. The list of recent work here is long and growing steadily each year. Much of the impetus for this new work on the League has come from Denis Richet and those working with him: see the works by Richet and Descimon cited in notes 7 and 9; also especially important is the recently published *thèse d'état* of Denis Crouzet, *Les guerriers de Dieu: La violence au temps des troubles de religion (vers 1525–vers 1610),* 2 vols. (Seyssel, France, 1990).

9. For example, Denis Richet, "Elite et noblesse: La formation des grands serviteurs de l'état (fin xvie–début xviie siècle)," *Acta Poloniae Historica* 36 (1977): 47–63; Denis Richet and Norman Hampson, "Révolution anglaise et révolution

française, 1640 et 1789," in *Dix siècles d'histoire franco-britannique: De Guillaume le Conqérant au Marché commun*, ed. François Bédarida, François Crouzet, and Douglas Johnson (Paris, 1979), 94–113; Richet, "Autour des origines idéologiques"; Denis Richet, *La France moderne: L'esprit des institutions* (Paris, 1973); Descimon, *Qui étaient les Seize?*; Denis Crouzet, "Henry IV, King of Reason?" in *From Valois to Bourbon*, ed. Cameron, 73–106; Christian Jouhaud, *Mazarinades: La Fronde des mots* (Paris, 1985).

10. More work is clearly needed here, but some recent work seems to point in this direction. For an example of opposition to Louis XIV before the 1680s, for instance, which turns out to be more disagreement on policy than serious opposition to the regime, see the fine study by Paul Sonnino, *Louis XIV*. For a contrast between the overall support of Louis XIV in his early years by historians and serious opposition by them later (from the later 1680s on) see, for the first, Orest Ranum, *Artisans of Glory: Writers and Historical Thought in Seventeenth-Century France* (Chapel Hill, N.C., 1980); and for the second, Phyllis K. Leffler, "French Historians and the Challenge to Louis XIV's Absolutism," *French Historical Studies* 14 (1985): 1–22. Similar conclusions on the developing of serious opposition only later can also be drawn from the older study of Lionel Rothkrug, *Opposition to Louis XIV: The Political and Social Origins of the French Enlightenment* (Princeton, 1965); and from Klaus Malettke, *Opposition und Konspiration unter Ludwig XIV: Studien zu Kritik und Widerstand gegen System und Politik des französischen Königs während der ersten Hälfte seiner persönlichen Regierung* (Göttingen, 1976).

11. See, for instance, René Descartes, *Discours de la méthode: Pour bien conduire sa raison, et chercher la vérité dans les sciences* (Paris, 1987), 18–19, 24–25.

12. The following works have proposed approaches for understanding Molière and the other great intellectual and cultural figures of the time in relationship to their society; and they—and especially, but not only, the works of Krailsheimer and Bénichou—have been quite helpful: Paul Bénichou, *Morales du Grand Siècle* (Paris, 1948); Mikhail Bulgakov, *The Life of Monsieur de Molière: A Portrait*, trans. Mirra Ginsburg (New York, 1986); Erica Harth, *Ideology and Culture in Seventeenth-Century France* (Ithaca, N.Y., 1983); Nannerl O. Keohane, *Philosophy and the State in France: The Renaissance to the Enlightenment* (Princeton, 1980); Alban John Krailsheimer, *Studies in Self-Interest from Descartes to La Bruyère* (Oxford, 1972); and Carolyn C. Lougee, *Le Paradis des Femmes: Women, Salons, and Social Stratification in Seventeenth-Century France* (Princeton, 1976).

13. Krailsheimer, *Studies in Self-Interest*, especially pp. 152–72.

14. Molière, *Le misanthrope*, act 1, sc. 1, vol. 2, p. 40: "I want people to be sincere, and, as men of honor / never to utter a word that does not come from the heart." The citations and volume and page references to Molière's works are taken from the Pléiade edition, *Oeuvres complètes*, 2 vols., ed. Maurice Rat (Paris, 1951). The English translations are mine unless otherwise indicated.

15. Ibid., p. 41: "I reject completely the enormous complacency / which pays no attention to differences of merit."

16. Ibid., p. 43: "this century of ours." See also, for instance, ibid., act 1, sc. 2, p. 53, and act 3, sc. 5, pp. 79–80.

17. Ibid., act 1, sc. 1, p. 44: "the virtue of past ages."

18. Ellery Schalk, *From Valor to Pedigree: Ideas of Nobility in France in the Sixteenth and Seventeenth Centuries* (Princeton, 1986), especially chaps. 2–5.

19. Molière, *Misanthrope,* act 4, sc. 1, p. 83: "is a virtue which is rare in today's century."

20. Schalk, *From Valor to Pedigree,* especially pp. 115–44.

21. On nobles being seen as laws unto themselves in the sixteenth century see Ellery Schalk, "Under the Law or Laws unto Themselves: Noble Attitudes and Absolutism in Sixteenth and Seventeenth-Century France," *Historical Reflections/ Réflexions Historiques* 15 (1988): 279–92.

22. Molière, *Misanthrope,* act 5, sc. 1, p. 95: "Too much perversity reigns in our century."

23. Ibid., act 1, sc. 1, p. 44. The emphasis is mine. The following English translation of this passage is by Charles Heron Wall in *The Dramatic Works of Molière* (London, 1908), 2:155: "A sound judgment avoids all extremes, and bids us be wise with moderation. The unbending severity of the virtues of olden times clashes too much with the customs and manners of our century [here I have translated the word "siècle" as "century" instead of "age"]. It requires too much perfection in mortals: we should yield to the times without obstinacy, and it is the greatest of follies to wish to reform all mankind. I, like you, notice every day a hundred things which would be better if ordered otherwise. But whatever I may discover at each step, men do not see me breaking forth into anger as you do; I take them quietly as they are, I accustom myself to bear with what they do, and I believe that, whether at Court or in the city, my placidity is as philosophical as your wrath."

24. Molière, *Dom Juan ou le festin de Pierre,* act 4, sc. 4, vol. 1, pp. 809–10.

25. See Schalk, *From Valor to Pedigree,* 65–93.

26. Molière, *Dom Juan,* act 4, sc. 4, pp. 809–10. The following English translation of this passage is by Christopher Hampton (with my changes in brackets) in Molière, *Don Juan* (London, 1974), 70–71: "How can you be so contemptible? Aren't you ashamed of not living up to your position [your birth]? Or perhaps you're proud of it, is that it? When have you ever behaved like a gentleman [nobleman]? Do you think it's enough to come from a noble family and to have a name and a coat of arms, when you live like a criminal? It isn't, there's no such thing as aristocracy without virtue [No, birth is nothing without virtue]. We can only inherit the glory of our ancestors if we force ourselves to resemble them [to follow their virtues], and your ancestors wouldn't recognize you as their offspring. Don't think all their achievements give you any privileges [your birth has no meaning]: on the contrary their distinction simply accentuates your disgrace, it's a torch lighting up the shamefulness of your behaviour. Let me tell you something, an aristocrat

[noble] who lives badly is an unnatural monster, the only title worth the name is virtue [virtue is the first title of nobility], the way you behave [act] is much more important than the name you sign, and I'd have more respect for a burglar's son if he were a man of honour, than I'd have for a king's son who lived like you."

27. Schalk, *From Valor to Pedigree,* chaps. 5–8.

28. See, for instance, the works cited above in note 3 on the lack of any fundamental difference between noble and nonnoble in the seventeenth century.

29. Attempting to determine the significance of Casaulx has been part of a larger project I have been working on concerning Marseilles in the sixteenth and seventeenth centuries.

30. See Descimon, *Qui étaient les Seize?* especially pp. 18–45.

31. Molière, *L'école des femmes,* act 4, sc. 8, vol. 1, p. 496: "to be miserly, brutal, deceitful, wicked and cowardly."

32. Ibid., pp. 496–97. The emphasis is mine. "Because, in order to guide yourself well through these difficulties / one must, as with everything, avoid the extremes."

33. The examples of Henry IV forgiving those who had submitted are well known. And the examples, analyzed by Beik in *Absolutism and Society,* of aristocrats and king working together during the period of the majority of Louis XIV also suggest to me a similar, if more complex, relationship of submission and forgiveness.

34. Molière, *Dom Juan,* act 5, sc. 2, p. 818: "a clever person [should] adapt himself to the vices of his century."

35. Ibid.; the entire passage reads: "C'est ainsi qu'il faut profiter des faiblesses des hommes, et qu'un sage esprit s'accommode aux vices de son siècle."

36. See, for instance, Hanley, "Engendering the State."

37. Schalk, *From Valor to Pedigree,* 174–201.

38. On the noble revolts see Arlette Jouanna, *La noblesse française et la gestation de l'Etat moderne, 1559–1661* (Paris, 1989). On the Fronde see, as an example, Jouhaud, *Mazarinades,* which suggests a Fronde that did not offer a serious program of opposition. To call the Fronde a "remnant" of the sixteenth century, however, which is my term, is obviously a gross oversimplification; the purpose is not to negate the complexity and importance of the Fronde, but only to try to put it into the context of this article and to see it in relation to sixteenth-century events.

39. The contrast between "national" elites (the use of this term is not at all meant to imply the existence of modern nationalism in the sixteenth and seventeenth centuries) and local ones is a complex question that needs to be explored further, I think. We see these local elites in action attempting to resist absolutism, for instance, in Daniel Hickey's *Coming of French Absolutism: The Struggle for Tax Reform in the Province of Dauphiné, 1540–1640* (Toronto, 1986); and we also see them resisting in Marseilles in ways that I have been exploring in the project mentioned above in note 29.

40. See the works cited above in note 10 and also Richet, *France moderne,* especially pp. 141–50.

10. The Family and Early Career

of Michel de Marillac (1560–1632)

DONALD A. BAILEY

After Cardinal Richelieu, Marie de Médicis, and the king himself, the most important political personage in the reign of Louis XIII was the *garde des sceaux*, Michel de Marillac. This widely experienced royal servant oversaw the writing of the last great law code of the ancien régime, participated in several aspects of the Catholic revival, and set himself against France's active participation in the Thirty Years' War—for which opposition he lost his post at court and his brother Louis his life. More significantly, he had an absolutist vision for French government that went beyond the more pragmatic approach to political policy shared by his king and the great cardinal and that involved a program of systematic undermining of the quasi-independent *pays d'états*. J. Russell Major has extensively sketched this program in his *Representative Government in Early Modern France* and thereby done more than any other scholar to bring Marillac into his rightful place in French studies.[1] At this stage of my current biographical study, I would add only that I think Marillac's absolutist approach was significantly driven by his personal sense of religion and morality, a sense of rectitude and integrity that he thought was widely lacking among royal servants and provincial officials and that only a well-coordinated monarchy could ensure for the kingdom of France. An investigation of his family and early career can serve no more than as an introduction to this interpretation.

Who, then, was Michel de Marillac? Until very recently, very few could answer that question, at least beyond recalling his connection to the Code Michaud and perhaps to the saints of the Catholic Renaissance. The small nineteenth-century studies of his attempts to reform the laws and judiciary of Louis XIII's France did not hold scholarly attention for long, and most

devotees of Mme Acarie's pious circle were outside the scholarly community. Thus, Georges Pagès's 1937 article, "Autour du 'Grand Orage,' " was
a major event in French historical studies, for it forcefully demonstrated
that Marillac's almost total obscurity was inversely proportional to his real
significance.[2]

The article pointed out that the "Grand Orage," which in 1630 culminated in the famous Day of Dupes, was about far more than a mother's
jealousy over who held influence with her royal son. The Great Storm was
created by the clash of two conflicting policies for the future of France.
On the one side were *les bons Français,* led by Cardinal Richelieu, whose
primary concern was the Hapsburg threat to both the peace of Europe
and the security of France. These good Frenchmen were prepared to put
the triumph of the Counter-Reformation at risk and to postpone necessary reforms within France in order to end Spanish hegemony in western
Europe. On the other side were *les dévots,* led by Garde des Sceaux Marillac since the recent death of Cardinal Bérulle, whose emphases were the
triumph of a reinvigorated Catholicism and the thorough reform of French
laws and finances. These devout men cheered the victories of Spanish
arms, for their Catholic Renaissance uncritically embraced the Counter-
Reformation Europe-wide. They were convinced that a reformed France
could never be endangered by even an enlarged Hapsburg power, as indeed
France had demonstrated by surviving several sixteenth-century invasions
of frontier provinces.

Georges Pagès described these two positions with novel clarity and balance. Furthermore, he suggested that Louis XIII's choice on that fateful
11 November decided more than the outcome of the Thirty Years' War; it
confirmed French political institutions on a course that led inexorably to
the Revolution. Even Colbert's fiscal and legal reforms were only a partial implementation of Marillac's intentions. The French monarchy's hegemony both at home and abroad was achieved through unreformed institutions and unremitting peasant exploitation. Clearly, Marillac's defeat at
the end of 1630 was, in the words of the French series, one of the "Trente
Journées qui ont fait la France."[3]

Yet Marillac's reputation survived World War II in continued relative
obscurity. The wide-ranging institutional studies of Roland Mousnier and
his students have brought to light several aspects of Marillac's career, en
route to all the other contributions they have made to our current understanding of early modern France. But no member of that *équipe* has directly
concentrated on Michel de Marillac, and the sweeping titles covering some

of their works have obscured how scant has been the attention given to the actual reign of Louis XIII.[4]

In 1966, however, J. Russell Major's "Henri IV and Guyenne" made the first important contribution to Marillac studies since Pagès's "Autour du 'Grand Orage.'"[5] The article examined royal policy in Guyenne and demonstrated how Henry IV gradually undermined the provincial estates, even in the *pays d'états*. But it also illuminated the role of a then younger Michel de Marillac, *maître des requêtes,* as royal agent on mission in Guyenne, struggling to overcome local resistance to the king's objectives.

In spite of Richelieu's well-established reputation as the turning point for French absolutism, Major argued that Marillac was in fact more of an "absolutist" than Richelieu. The latter's belligerent policy and his 1630 triumph in the royal council not only brought domestic reform qua reform to an end; it also removed from office a man whose approach to reform was more rigidly and uncompromisingly centralist than was Richelieu's. To deny Richelieu's title to primary architect of Louis XIV's later absolutism would be going too far. But the implications of Major's work, especially after its extensive development in *Representative Government,* force us to see that the nature and quality of that absolutism might have been very different had Marie de Médicis, Marillac, and the *dévots* emerged victorious on the Day of Dupes. Imagine an absolutism less dependent upon Versailles as a dissipator of noble energies, less dependent upon venality of office, and based on extensive redesigning of the tax structure. Imagine an absolutism implemented by a Louis the Just through Chancellor Marillac rather than through Cardinal Richelieu.

It cannot be imagined, can it? Marillac in 1630, at age sixty-seven or perhaps seventy, probably did not have Cardinal Richelieu's (or, for that matter, the eighteenth-century Cardinal Fleury's) remaining dozen years of life. Nor did he have Richelieu's dexterity and resourcefulness. But he did articulate a viable alternate policy for the future of France. He also had the experience and dedication to have continued to serve his king well. It is time that posterity knew more about him.

Studies are not yet sufficiently advanced to improve much upon the recent work of Mousnier, Major, and Richard Bonney concerning Marillac's political career, but some of my and others' investigations into his family and early career might be usefully fed into the mainstream at this time. The foundations of his later prominence are obviously owed to his family and early professional experience. Furthermore, what the student of politics would call Marillac's support of absolutism might better be credited to his personal rectitude and religious scruples than ascribed to convictions derived directly from reflections about governmental policy.

Marillac's family was originally from the Haute Auvergne, but his own birth in Paris (on 9 October 1563 or more probably on 28 August 1560)[6] made him one of the few royal councillors who were natives of the capital city. In Auvergne, the family followed the pursuits of the old sword nobility, often as dependents of the ducs de Bourbon. This was the path of Pierre de Marillac, *capitaine châtelain* de Lastic, and of his eldest son, Guillaume, seigneur de Saint Genest, de la Motte-Hermart, and de Riom, who was a secretary to the duc de Bourbon and who was buried at the ancestral home at Aigueperse.[7] This governor of the town of Montpensier in Auvergne had six sons, the last of whom was to be the father of our Michel. The eldest of Guillaume's sons was Gilbert de Marillac, baron de Poisac and a *secrétaire* of the constable de Bourbon. Another son, Bertrand, doctor in theology and abbé de Saint Symphorien de Thiers, became a bishop. The other four sons, however, sprinkled themselves broadly among the royal offices to be sought in the capital, thereby offering one more illustration of the dubiousness of sharp distinctions between sword and robe families.[8]

The most important among them, Charles de Marillac, had been one of the four abbés (of Saint-Père, near Melun) in Roland Mousnier's list of *maîtres des requêtes* in the period 1515–47, an office he held in the years 1541–57.[9] Previously, as was true of 29.6 percent of Mousnier's sample, he had been a member of a sovereign court, in his case as a councillor in the Parlement de Paris. More exceptionally, he had served as ambassador to the court of Charles V. He later became bishop of Vannes, in Brittany, and eventually archbishop of Vienne, and was a member of Henry II's *conseil secret*. Another brother was Gabriel de Marillac, an *avocat général* in the Parlement de Paris, while Julien de Marillac served as *commissaire ordinaire des guerres*, in 1551 being treasurer and paymaster of two companies of men.[10]

Michel de Marillac's father, Guillaume, *seigneur en partie* de Ferrière, was a *valet de chambre ordinaire du roi*, who became a *maître des comptes* in Paris (10 March 1555) and then rose to the position of *contrôlleur général des finances* only four years before his death in 1573. At the time of Guillaume's intention to marry, in mid-1549, Ambassador Charles gave him all his furniture and chattels located in Auvergne and the duchy of Montpensier.[11] By the marriage contract between Guillaume de Marillac and Renée (or Marie?) Alligret, the couple were to receive from the bride's tutor, Louis Hennequin, an *avocat au parlement*, thirty-five hundred livres *tournois*, and from the groom's brothers Charles and Gabriel, the land and lordship of Bicon, lands at Denone and Effiat, and the *maison pater-nelle* at Aigueperse, all situated in the duchy of Montpensier, *sénéchaussée* of Auvergne.[12] By the end of the year, the couple had sold "une maison" (the *maison paternelle?*) at Aigueperse to Julien, Guillaume's brother in the military.[13]

This marriage produced five sons (Michel was the third) and then a daughter. The three eldest sons all became *conseillers au parlement*, Michel perhaps doing so reluctantly, in order to maintain there the family's posi-tion after his elder brother Charles's death in 1580. The two younger sons also appear to have died young, without children. Their mother died on 8 June 1568, and Guillaume remarried, this time to Geneviève de Bois-Levesque, to whom were born the later marshal Louis (1573–1632) and another sister, Valence (15??–1617).

Michel studied at the Collège de Navarre, where he knew Jean-Pierre Acarie, the future husband of the extremely pious woman with whom Michel was to share so many religious activities after 1602. At age eigh-teen, Michel wanted to join the Carthusians and spend his entire life in religious works.[14] He trained in the law, however, like Saint Thomas More, with whose life his was to share numerous parallels, and eventually entered the Parlement de Paris. His religious proclivities were also revealed in the modest way of his being a churchwarden (*marguillier*) in 1594. Descimon states that in 1595, at least, he was a *capitaine*, though he does not tell us of what.[15]

Guillaume's widowed second wife and his surviving sons continued to reside in Paris through the turn of the century. Is the family representa-tive of others of similar station in the number of times it moved house? As a widow, Geneviève was living in the rue de Thorigny, parish of Saint-Gervais, in 1588, and in the rue de Paradis in 1594.[16] In 1587, at the age of twenty-seven and recently married, Michel was living in the same parish as his stepmother, but in the rue des Rosiers, where he still resided seven years later.[17] The next year, however, he moved to the Vieille rue du Temple, still in the parish of Saint-Gervais, where he appears also to have been in 1605.[18] By 1619, he had moved to the rue Quincampoix, in the parish of Saint-Nicolas des Champs, where he could still be found as late as 1622.[19] By 1629 he had moved to an *hôtel* in the faubourg Saint-Jacques, and only in 1631, when he was under house arrest in the château at Châteaudun, could he be found "living" outside Paris.[20] Four residences, in three different parishes, suggest only a modest restlessness for someone who in these same forty-plus years moved from being a simple *conseiller au Parlement de Paris* to exercising the highest judicial functions in the royal council.

On 12 July 1587, Michel married Nicole, *dite* Marguerite Barbes de la Forterie, daughter of Jehan Barbes, an *échevin* of Le Mans and, Descimon thinks, a merchant there.[21] Everat writes that the Barbes were one of the "familles les mieux apparentées du Maine."[22] Having become a widower on 6 February 1600 (Marguerite's inventory of estate after death being registered on 13 September 1601), Marillac remarried on 6 September 1601, to Marie de Saint-Germain, the daughter of Denis de Saint-Germain, a *maître des comptes*. Marie was the widow of Jean Amelot, seigneur de Carnetin, a royal councillor, who was also a president of the Chambre des Enquêtes in the Parlement de Paris.[23] Lasting until Michel's death in 1632, this marriage seems to have enjoyed mutual devotion, although one of his posthumous pamphleteer enemies accused Marillac of having too intimate a friendship with Madame du Fargis, whose husband was ambassador to Spain in the 1620s.[24]

Michel's remaining elder brother, Louis, was not so faithful, for we find him in 1595 settling a rente of eighty-three écus upon his natural daughter Louise,[25] no doubt an action evoked by his imminent or recent marriage to Antoinette Le Camus, with whom he was to settle into a new home in the rue Saint-Antoine, in the parish of Saint-Paul.[26] Born in 1591 and living until 1660, Louise was to become the renowned nun Mme Legras. Michel's half-brother, another Louis de Marillac, had lived in his teens at Ferrières-en-Brie, a *seigneurie* he shared with Michel, and later lived with his widowed mother in the rue de Paradis, in Paris.[27] In 1607 the younger Louis married Catherine Cosme de Médicis, Queen Marie's cousin and maid of honor, a marriage no doubt signaling his rise in influence and a help to its furtherance.

In 1588 this Louis's sister (and Michel's half-sister), Valence de Marillac, contracted a marriage to Octavien de Douy, seigneur d'Attichy, a councillor to Queen Mother Catherine de Médicis, who then lived in the Vieille rue du Temple, perhaps at the corner of the rue des Francs Bourgeois.[28] Thirty years later, Michel is found monitoring the financial relations between the tutor of the remaining minor children of this marriage (Antoine Le Gras, *secrétaire* of the queen mother's) and their grandmother, Geneviève de Marillac.[29]

The homes and marriages of Michel de Marillac appear to have emphasized the piety that his public life exemplified. Indeed, imagining their domestic and spiritual harmony calls to mind the better-known family scenes of Thomas More in the same decades of the preceding century. Father Pierre Bérulle (1575–1629) counted both Marillacs among his closest friends and advisers, and Marie celebrated mass along with Mmes de Maiguelay, Séguier, and Acarie on the occasion of the founding of the Oratory in Paris in November 1611.[30] Of the three surviving children whom Michel reared with Marguerite until her death, and then with Marie, two entered the religious life, as did the wife of the third and *their* three daughters.[31] Octavien (born 26 December 1597) became a Capuchin and was later nominated to the see of Saint-Malô, while the five women (Michel's daughter Valence, born 5 February 1599, his daughter-in-law, and his three granddaughters) all became Carmelites.

Michel's eldest son, René, was born on 15 December 1588 and reached the age of nine years before another child was born who survived infancy. He followed his father into a legal career, becoming a *maître des requêtes* in 1617, when his father was a *conseiller d'état*. Before contracting a mortal illness in the royal siege of Montauban in 1621, René had married Marie de Creuil, with whom he had two sons and three daughters. As already noted, the three daughters preceded their widowed mother into the Carmelite order, while the second son, Louis, died without issue as a *chevalier de Malte* in 1635. It was Michel II, the eldest child, who became a councillor in the Parlement and obtained the title seigneur d'Ollainville before dying in 1684. After two more generations, through René II and Michel III, the family died out in the male line, all but the last generation continuing to divide its issue between the law and the church.

If a survey of the family reveals several religious connections, Michel de Marillac's avocational scholarly interests show a similar proclivity. At the College of Navarre, Marillac had mastered the classical languages, as well as Italian and Spanish. He already displayed the spiritual intensity that remained a central thread of his life. Despite the numerous tasks that his judicial and governmental career forced him to shoulder later, Marillac found time to translate the *Imitation of Christ* (the first of four editions appearing in his lifetime was published in 1621) and soon thereafter, into French verse, the Psalms. Later, under house arrest at Châteaudun, he was to produce two more pious works, *Histoire de Job*, in verse, and *Traité de la vie éternelle*.[32]

In 1604 Marillac helped Pierre de Bérulle and Mme Acarie (Barbe Jeanne Avrillot, wife of Jean-Pierre Acarie, 1566–1618) bring the Carmelite order from Spain to France, an order that the later widow was to join in 1615 as *la bienheureuse* Marie de l'Incarnation. By 1602 Marillac had become a prominent member of Mme Acarie's circle. As he became more devout and even mystical, he gave more hours to contemplation and prayer, and fewer to his responsibilities as *maître des requêtes*. Major states that Mme Acarie persuaded Marillac not to resign from his life in the world in 1608, but to remain where he was, because of all the good he could do in that office.[33] However, an analysis of his work as *rapporteur* in the Conseil Privé suggests that he may have slackened off in mid-decade. From reporting between at least 32 and 71 *arrêts* a year from 1600 to 1603, he reported only 8 (that I can identify) in 1604, signed none in 1605–7 (perhaps 1), 5 in 1608, and only 24 and 27 in 1609 and 1610, respectively.[34] Of course, the possibility exists that he was reassigned to other responsibilities in these years.

After Marillac and Bérulle worked to establish the Oratorians on the Italian model in France in 1611, the two men again cooperated, this time along with Vincent de Paul and François de Sales (the later saints), to found the Company of the Holy Sacrament in 1620.[35] This company was to concentrate the energies of the *dévots* in pious and charitable works after Richelieu had removed its political leaders from the royal council, but initially its members had indeed been interested in the broad reform objectives associated with its founders.[36]

Marillac appears also to have been one of the early discoverers of Philippe de Champaigne (1602–74). When Marie de Médicis commissioned Marillac to establish the Carmelites in the faubourg Saint-Jacques, he proposed to her that Champaigne paint the vaults, as well as do other paintings and sculpture, in the church.[37] For the Carmelites in Paris, Champaigne executed the *Nativité* in 1628 and the *Présentation au Temple* the following year. He also painted many personages at court, as well as most of the participants in his generation of the Catholic Renaissance in France, not only the Cardinals Bérulle and Richelieu and our current subject, Michel de Marillac, but the large Arnauld family and most of the other inhabitants of Jansenist Port-Royal.

With this understanding of Michel de Marillac's religious and family commitments, we are better able to appreciate one of the age's leading political figures. Marillac took communion several times a week, in an age still absorbing the Tridentine exhortation to celebrate mass more than once a year, and devoted many hours each week to prayer, reading, and acts of religious service. And yet, despite his early yearnings for a religious life, all these interests were avocational, pursued alongside a career in the law and judiciary, then in royal government, and eventually at the very heart of the formation of public policy.

The death of one of the last Marillacs holding office in the Parlement de Paris brought the family to dissuade the twenty-six-year-old Michel from his religious intentions and to obtain for him the office of councillor in that Parlement in 1586. We know very little so far about his activities there, except, peripherally, that his *ligueur* sympathies kept him opposed to the Bourbon accession until Henry IV acted upon his announced intention to convert.[38] His intervention on Henry's behalf thereafter had a certain significance for Parlement's declaration heading off the Guise attempt to declare the throne vacant, and Henry's appreciation for that support undoubtedly lay behind Marillac's becoming a *maître des requêtes* in 1595.

The statesman known to us as rigid in his views, and restrained in his deliberations, was less moderate in his youth. He was devoted enough to the Catholic League that he accompanied the armed Bussy-Le-Clerc into the Grand' Chambre on 16 January 1589 in the latter's attempt to transport the faithful magistrates to the Bastille—a high-handedness for which the Parlement never forgave him and which was to trouble his dealings with that body as late as the registration of the Code Michaud in 1629.[39] And in his short memoirs for these years, Marillac tells us that he later helped deliver Paris's Porte Neuve over to Henry IV in June 1595.[40]

Once it seemed clear that Henry IV was sincere in his promise to return to Rome, Marillac helped initiate the resolution in the second Chambre d'Enquêtes (June 1593) that reaffirmed the Salic Law and headed off the duc de Mayenne's intention to use a dubiously called Estates General to declare the throne vacant; from the Enquêtes, he was a leader of the delegation that introduced the resolution to each of the other chambers of the Parlement de Paris.[41] Léon Desjonquères argues that Marillac did not support Henry per se earlier than the beginning of 1594, but he was concerned about Spanish ambitions within France and in general preferred order and tradition to a continuation of the previous years' tumults.[42] It may help us better understand Marillac's later opposition to Richelieu's arguably aggressive war against Spain to remember this earlier reaction to a *Spanish* aggression in France. Throughout these years, he was struggling to balance his religious zeal against his instincts for order and authority.

We should therefore view Henry IV's suggestion that he leave the Parlement in favor of a mastership as more than an opportunity for an ambitious career. Marillac had come to be resented by many *parlementaires*, including Achille de Harlay, for initiatives that were deemed unbecoming a magistrate or at least threatening to the corporative body, and for being among those originally factious *ligueurs* to whom Henry had merely rendered a severe reprimand, in March 1594, followed by forgiveness.[43]

The records of the decisions in the Conseil Privé remain only exiguously extant for the sixteenth century, so Marillac's total absence from them before 1600 tells us nothing about his activities there. But in these first five years of his mastership, Marillac traveled many times to the various provinces as a *commissaire*. By 1601, he had visited Normandy, Agénais, Brittany, Bourbonais, Auvergne, and Guyenne, and contributed to the royal supervision of the Assembly of Notables at Rouen in 1596–97. With the help of his friend M. Denitz, a councillor in the Parisian Cour des Aides, he developed during these and subsequent years an aptitude for financial affairs.[44] On missions such as these, he became familiar with the inefficiencies of much local government and with local resistance to royal policies, experiences that cannot but have sharpened the personality traits that would contribute to his absolutist attitudes.

Marillac reflected the minority of *maîtres des requêtes* whose fathers had been royal councillors or members of the sovereign courts—15 out of the approximately 50 masters in the 1590s.[45] He was more typical of his generation in having served close to the average of 9.9 years in the Parlement before his appointment to a mastership.[46] To estimate what Marillac paid for his mastership, we have only the benchmarks suggested by Colin Kaiser: the 27,000 to 30,000 livres that L'Estoile gave for 1584, and the 50,000 to 55,000 livres that were paid by 1607.[47] Under Henry IV, a master was paid 300 livres per quarter, another 100 for his *robe de pacques,* expenses and augmented salary when sent into the provinces, and perhaps various *épices* and other augmentations of income depending on the circumstances.[48]

Colin Kaiser tells us that in 1583, at least, about a third of the company served each quarter at the *requêtes de l'hôtel,* leaving the other two-thirds available for commissions to the provinces.[49] Both these *commissaires* and their seventeenth-century successors the intendants were chosen largely, almost exclusively, from among the *maîtres des requêtes,* but we knew little about their shadowy activity until the 1960 publication of Bernard Barbiche's article "Les commissaires députés pour le 'régalement' des tailles en 1598–1599."[50] Now we know that they frequently visited the provinces in the king's service, not to administer affairs there directly, but to exhort local officials to fulfill their responsibilities with an exactitude too often neglected, convey the king's sense of priorities, and report back to their royal master, through the chancellor, their evaluation of the local situation. Their function as the direct agents of the chancellor emphasizes that their origins lay in the traditions of juridical monarchy.

An important threshold in the gradual transition from juridical to administrative monarchy, Barbiche has recently argued, was crossed through Sully's triumph over Pomponne de Bellièvre in the king's favor in about 1605.[51] To this development Michel de Marillac made a modest contribution. As *commissaire* to Guyenne in 1598–99, he investigated how the local Estates collected the taille, in a province where the differing justice meted out to Huguenots and Catholics was also an issue. Both Henry and Sully read his unfavorable reports, which joined the other influences leading the king and his chief minister to take a harsh view toward provincial estates and local governance.[52]

Apart from his embassy to the court of Mantua in February 1612, about the time of his resignation from the mastership, next a mission to Bordeaux in December 1615, when he was a *conseiller d'état,* and then his attendance at the Assembly of Notables in Rouen in 1617–18, Marillac left no traces of official travel between 1601 and his entry into the royal council in 1624 that historians have so far mentioned. When he at last, in 1600, emerges in the documents as a *rapporteur* of the cases decided in the Conseil Privé, however, we can find him during the fall quarter in Grenoble, Provence, and Lyons for stretches of time of between one and six weeks in each place. But during the following decade, we find him traveling in this capacity only to Rouen briefly in August 1603, and otherwise leaving Paris for no more than short visits to Fontainebleau.[53]

His first year traceable as a *rapporteur* was also his busiest. During 1600, his signature appeared on 71 *arrêts,* which amounts to 16.44 percent of François Dumont's total of 432 *arrêts* in that year.[54] The masters were responsible for serving as *rapporteurs* in the Privy Council during one of the three formal quarters in each year, but Marillac signed fifteen *arrêts* in 1600 in the *quartier d'avril* and 56 *arrêts* in the *quartier d'octobre.* If one-third of the approximately fifty masters were reporting in any one quarter, then sixteen or seventeen officers would find themselves together on work in the Privy Council, and an equal share of that work would be 6.06 percent of the reporting. But in "his" quarter of his first active year as a *maître rapporteur,* Marillac participated in reporting 40.28 percent of the *arrêts,* and even in the earlier quarter he was, at 5.26 percent, handling almost his full share. Just over a third of these *arrêts* in 1600, 27, he handled alone, and on the 44 that he reported jointly with one to four colleagues, his signature appeared as the first, and therefore as the one primarily responsible, on 13.

He remained busy as a *rapporteur* during the next three years, but in each of them, "his" quarter was clearly that of January through March. All 32 of his *arrêts* in 1601 and all 39 of those in 1602 (11.63 percent and 5.88 percent of the total for the respective quarters) fell into the *quartier de janvier,* while of his 44 *arrêts* in 1603, 1 was reported in August and 6 were reported in the *quartier d'octobre,* leaving the other 37 in the first quarter of the year (5.9 percent of the total in that quarter). His work dropped dramatically in 1604, when he evenly divided 8 *arrêts* between the first and last quarters of the year (both proportions below 1 percent), and I can find no *arrêts* at all signed by him in the years 1605–7 (with the possible exception of 1 in March 1606). His work picked up modestly in 1608, with 2 in the April quarter and 3 scattered evenly across the three months of the October quarter. He concentrated his work into the first half of the next two years, leaning in both years to the *quartier de janvier*—16 and 22, respectively (both less than 3 percent of the whole)—with the remainder in both years in the *quartier d'avril*—8 and 5, respectively. With that, although he did not resign as a *maître des requêtes* until 1612, his reporting responsibilities ceased, except for one last *arrêt* in December of his last year, an *arrêt* that might even have been a responsibility executed some months after his resignation.

Beyond allowing us to assess Marillac's diligence, including how it compared with that of his peers, I am not yet sure what this picture signifies. An examination of the actual contents of Marillac's *arrêts* reveals no area of specialization, whether of religious or financial substance, social or regional origins of litigants, or type of legal question. He handled any of the juridical issues described by Albert Hamscher for the reign of Henry's grandson, and I am no closer than this scholar was to understanding how the chancellor decided the distribution of assignments to his *maîtres*.[55] It appears, however, that in some years he was more active in more than one quarter than would be accounted for merely by suggesting that *maîtres* stayed with the occasional cases that were carried over from one quarter to the next.

The distribution of work load is also difficult to assess at this time. My impression is that, during these twelve years, at least five other *maîtres* were present more often than Marillac, and reported more cases when present, while at least three that I noted appeared to do less reporting. Between early 1608 and late 1611, fewer cases were jointly reported than before and after those dates, and the maximum number of *maîtres* involved on one *arrêt* never exceeded four, whereas in earlier years six and seven signatures were not uncommon and as many as nine were reached on more than one occasion. I have found Marillac himself sharing the rapportage only twice after 1600 (in August 1603 and October 1604).

Work will therefore have to be done in other institutions served by the *maîtres des requêtes de l'hôtel du roi* to reveal what Marillac's other tasks might have been during these years. Did his commitment to religious devotions and institutions significantly distract him from his work? If so, did such distractions hurt or help his career? Marie's regency court, following Henry's assassination, was certainly characterized by a new religiosity, in which Marillac played an important part, and it was she who in 1612 made him a *conseiller d'état*. Today, we expect even governments to be anxious about the efficiency of their servants, but we are less tolerant, let alone encouraging, of religious convictions that intrude into the secular workplace than was the seventeenth century. Furthermore, the conventional pursuits of self-enrichment and conspicuous consumption no doubt distracted some of his colleagues from their proper work at least as much as his religious commitments distracted Marillac.

In any case, he was not permitted to withdraw from public life. He had felt no enthusiasm for Bellièvre's offer to make him a president of the Parlement de Paris more than five years earlier,[56] but Marie de Médicis wanted him to serve the royal council. Whereas most *maîtres* under the Valois had died in office, the early Bourbons began to draw on their expertise to serve them in more exalted posts. Of those becoming masters under Henry IV, 28 percent subsequently became *conseillers d'état,* and Marillac was among the approximately twenty masters so promoted by Marie.[57] He was part of a general opening of career opportunities for *maîtres des requêtes* in these years, as the royal council saw in them both the legal and financial competence required in difficult times and the compliance with royal desires lacking in most other judicial officials.[58] By 1619, he was serving in the *conseil des finances,* and in 1624 he became *surintendant des finances* jointly with another former master, Jean Bouchart, which made him one of eighteen *maîtres des requêtes* who eventually acquired high financial office in these years.[59]

Whereas Marillac's reputation for hard work cannot be demonstrated in the minutes and registers of the Conseil Privé for more than a quarter of his years as a master of requests, J. Michael Hayden identifies him as among the five hardest-working men who assisted Nicolas Brûlart de Sillery in the Conseil d'Etat et des Finances and in the Conseil Privé in 1614–15, the years of the meeting of the Estates General.[60] Was Marillac drawn to the greater degree of religiosity that surrounded Marie than he had found in the circle of her late husband? Can it be argued that Marillac easily fused his religious and political interests when the direction of the royal government appeared to bring them together, but lost interest when political considerations alone seemed to prevail? On the other hand, if future investigations substantiate an erratic pattern of work throughout Marillac's career, we shall have to consider purely psychological explanations as well as religious ones.

He was one of nine former masters who eventually became *gardes des sceaux,* when Richelieu and Louis XIII became dissatisfied with Chancellor d'Aligre in 1626, but he was not one of the two who came to possess the actual title of chancellor.[61] This seemed a more natural ministry for him than *surintendant des finances.* Indeed, despite the integrity that has earned Marillac praises from most previous historians, his competence in the supervision of finance and his ability to implement effective financial reforms have not withstood the recent careful scrutiny of Richard Bonney. In the two years of Marillac's tenure in finance, Bonney writes, "overall expenditure had arisen from about 34 million *livres* in 1624 to over 44 million."[62]

In contrast, Marillac's whole life could be seen as a preparation for the chancellorship. The offices of *parlementaire, maître des requêtes,* and *conseiller d'état et des finances,* together with his commissions to the provinces, had given him broad experience in the laws and institutions of justice in the kingdom. He had dealt with estates in Guyenne, Brittany, and elsewhere after 1595, with the Estates General in 1614–15, and with the Assembly of Notables in 1596–97 and in 1617–18—both meetings happening to be in Rouen. Thus, Louis XIII and Richelieu gave him the primary responsibility, after themselves, for the deliberations of the Assembly of Notables in 1626–27.[63] Out of the meetings of both Estates and Notables, and out of all this experience, grew the last great codification of the ancien régime, clearly driven by the goals of the cardinal, but largely the result of both the vision and the industriousness of the *garde des sceaux.*

Of all the prominent figures in the Catholic Renaissance in France, Marillac was one who most completely focused its diverse interests. As we have seen, he was a scholar, a contemplative active in the world, an organizer of religious institutions combining both piety and social beneficence, a well-placed individual who seems to have lacked the acquisitiveness conventional for his age and station. Indeed, his political attitudes seem almost a by-product of his rectitude and self-righteousness. Did they not derive from a sense that most others lacked his own probity and integrity and that affairs should be conducted in a manner allowing a just and vigorous king to monitor what his subjects did in his name, as much as from any self-conscious sense that political centralization was to be preferred to traditional particularism?

If Marillac shared the goals and religious style of Pierre de Bérulle, Mme Acarie, Vincent de Paul, and François de Sales, he also shared many of the political aspirations of the young bishop of Luçon. At the Estates General of 1614–15, Jean Armand Duplessis de Richelieu (1585–1642) urged the reception of the Tridentine decrees into France. Richelieu had already demonstrated his considerable organizational capacities in reforming what had been a badly neglected bishopric. Nestled under the shadow of La Rochelle, Luçon was fertile ground for the sowing of religious pamphlets, some of which were written by the young bishop himself. Though personally ambitious and acquisitive, and lacking the devout spiritualism of Marillac, whom he first met at the Estates General or upon his initial entry into the royal council in 1616, Richelieu had already won the committed friendship of François Joseph Leclerc du Tremblay, the Capuchin known as Père Joseph (1577–1638), who also had mystical tendencies. All these men embraced the Catholic Reformation at home and abroad, but they were soon to find disagreements over ways and means, especially as they differently read the implications for both France and the church of the international leadership claimed by Spain in that effort.

Marillac and Richelieu shared an interest in the *dévot* agenda for political reform, and they shared the social background that some have seen as being a significant motivation of that agenda.[64] Descended from the old sword nobility on their fathers' side, they were also descended from the new robe nobility—Richelieu through his mother's family and Marillac through the latterly shift in noble pursuits that his family had undertaken in abandoning the military career. These social groups stood to benefit from any financial retrenchment that governmental reform might achieve, if the issue were merely reduced taxes with the resulting potential to raise noble financial exactions. But if the issue became how taxes should be collected and by whom, or whether royal offices should be bought and sold and how they should be protected for their incumbents' heirs, then it was no longer so easy to see how broadly based class interests would benefit from *dévot*-inspired reforms.

But Marillac, more than Richelieu and more than other *dévots*, had the prior experience to know how such reforms would affect a broad range of governmental institutions. In this respect, he resembled the Arnauld family, *parlementaires* and religious, whose embracing of the later Jansenist movement has by historical convention severed them from association with the *dévots* of Marillac's generation. The father of the many famous Arnauld children, the original restorer of that Abbey of Port-Royal with which the children were associated throughout the seventeenth century, was Antoine Arnauld (1560–1619). As a *parlementaire* and then a councillor of state, he had a career that paralleled very closely the early professional life of Michel de Marillac, and that career helps us again to situate the latter at the very center of the religious, professional, political, and personal associations that constituted the Catholic Renaissance in France.

Thanks to the prewar studies of Georges Pagès and Jeanne Petit, and the postwar work of Roland Mousnier, J. Russell Major, and Richard Bonney, we now know a great deal more about Michel de Marillac, his colleagues, and the institutions through which he pursued his career than we once did. Doctoral dissertations by Colin Kaiser and me have also added to that understanding.[65] Here, I have attempted but the briefest sketch to bring those studies into touch with the beginnings of my current research into the whole life and career of Marillac.

An integrated, thorough study is not yet within our reach, but in the meantime we have well-known studies about his activities in the provinces in the 1590s and 1620s and at the heart of royal government in the 1620s. From my synthesis of his early career, family, and religious activities, I believe I have discerned that his religious attitudes gave him more than an agenda for reform. I think they gave him a moral and spiritual stance, an integrity, and a self-righteousness that made a rather modest and humble individual into a wielder of power with considerable determination, rigidity, and even intolerance. To the pluralism and freedoms of French society he posed a greater threat than did Richelieu, but his policies of reform and retrenchment, with his avoidance of external aggression, might well have left French government and society stronger and more resilient than did the work of the two cardinals. Further careful study will, I believe, transform this interpretation into demonstrated argument.

NOTES

For their careful reading of and perceptive suggestions for this piece, I would like especially to thank my colleague Professor Bruce C. Daniels; the editor of the book, Mack P. Holt; the anonymous readers of the University of Georgia Press; and my wife, Leuba S. Bailey. In addition, I owe a special debt to Professors Albert N. Hamscher and Kristen B. Neuschel for their thoughtful assistance, and to Ms. Beverly B. Hill for her help in reading some of the archival sources. Finally, I wish to thank the Social Science and Humanities Research Council of Canada and the University of Winnipeg for generous financial support.

1. J. Russell Major, *Representative Government in Early Modern France* (New Haven, 1980), passim, but especially chaps. 14 and 15.

2. Georges Pagès, "Autour du 'Grand Orage'—Richelieu et Marillac: Deux politiques," *Revue historique* 179 (January–March 1937): 63–97.

3. Georges Mongrédien, *La journée des dupes (11 Novembre 1630),* Trente Journées qui ont fait la France, 14 (Paris, 1961).

4. For example, Roland Mousnier, ed., *Le conseil du roi de Louis XII à la Révolution* (Paris, 1970); and idem, *La plume, la faucille et le marteau: Institutions et société en France du moyen âge à la Révolution* (Paris, 1970). Of course, Mousnier's early *Vénalité des offices sous Henri IV et Louis XIII* (Rouen, 1945; 2d ed., Paris, 1971) is a prominent exception, and Marillac does receive some attention in this study.

5. J. Russell Major, "Henri IV and Guyenne: A Study Concerning the Origins of Royal Absolutism," *French Historical Studies* 4 (1966): 363–83.

6. The still widely repeated date for Marillac's birth is 1563, but in his appendix, Edouard Everat corrects the date given in his own study, *Michel de Marillac, sa vie, ses oeuvres: Etude historique, juridique et littéraire* (Riom, 1894), 197; and the contemporary scholar Robert Descimon confirms the earlier date in "Qui étaient les Seize?" *Paris et Ile-de-France* 34 (1983): 187.

7. Much of the genealogical information derives from Charles Samaran, *Archives de la maison de la Trémoîlle* (Paris, 1928), 62, 79–80; from Père Anselme de Saint Marie, *Histoire généalogique et chronologique . . . ,* 9 vols. (Paris, 1726–33; reprint, New York, 1967), passim; and from *Documents historiques sur la famille de Marillac,* recueillis par les descendants de Jacques-Victor-Hippolyte de Marillac (Paris, 1908), passim.

8. Russell Major writes that of the four sons who entered the church, one became, "to the chagrin of the family, a Calvinist" (*Representative Government,* 489). I have not yet tried to determine which son that was.

9. See Mousnier, ed., *Conseil du roi,* 47–55, for much of this information on the first and second generation. The name of Charles's abbey comes from AN, "Insinuations du Châtelet" (hereafter ANIC) (20 March 1554), Y99, fol. 276v.

10. ANIC (22 December 1551), Y97, fol. 171.

11. ANIC (24 July 1549), Y95, fol. 177v.

12. ANIC (11 January 1551), Y96, fol. 127v.

13. ANIC (22 December 1551), Y97, fol. 171.

14. J.-B.-A. Boucher, *Histoire de la bienheureuse Marie de l'Incarnation dite dans le monde Madame Acarie,* new ed. (Paris, 1854), 1:217.

15. Descimon, "Qui étaient les Seize?" 187.

16. ANIC (10 May and 29 June 1588), Y130, fol. 277; (17 November 1587 and 12 August and 3 December 1594), Y134, fol. 104v, respectively—assuming that the earliest date on the second citation does not imply her already living in the rue de Paradis as well.

17. ANIC (17 November 1587), Y130, fol. 32v; (12 August and 3 December 1594), Y134, fol. 104v.

18. ANIC (10 April 1595), Y134, fol. 304; (27 August 1603 and 19 January 1605), Y143, fol. 387.

19. ANIC (16 October 1619), Y160, fol. 345; (20 May 1622), Y163, fol. 109v.

20. ANIC (26 August 1629), Y169, fol. 444; (26 March 1631), Y179, fol. 2.

21. Descimon, "Qui étaient les Seize?" 187.

22. Everat, *Marillac,* 7.

23. Descimon, "Qui étaient les Seize?" 187; Everat, *Marillac,* 18–19; ANIC (27 August 1603 and 19 January 1605), Y143, fol. 387.

24. Paul Hay du Chastelet, "Prose Impie" (1631), a poem in Latin that I can find only in *Journal de Richelieu* (Amsterdam, 1664), 58–60.

25. ANIC (2 January 1595), Y134, fol. 190v.

26. ANIC (10 April 1595), Y134, fol. 304.

27. ANIC (17 November 1587), Y130, fol. 32v; (12 August and 3 December 1594), Y134, fol. 104v.

28. ANIC (10 May and 29 June 1588), Y130, fol. 277.

29. ANIC (16 October 1619), Y160, fol. 345v.

30. Charles E. Williams, *The French Oratorians and Absolutism, 1611–1641,* American University Studies Series 9, History, vol. 47 (New York, 1989), 88, 92.

31. Boucher, *Marie de l'Incarnation,* 227.

32. *Ibid.,* 221.

33. Major, *Representative Government,* 491–92.

34. AN, V6 3–23 (Conseil Privé, Minutes d'Arrêts), V6 1171–94 (Registre d'Arrêts du Conseil Privé), and V6 1249–50 (Minutes d'états du Conseil Privé).

35. Orest Ranum, *Paris in the Age of Absolutism: An Essay* (New York, 1968), "Historical Cities," 130.

36. See Raoul Allier, *La cabale des Dévots, 1627–1666* (Paris, 1902; reprint, Geneva, 1970).

37. *Documents historiques sur la famille de Marillac,* 187–88. Marillac was eventually buried in the chapel he had personally maintained in their church.

38. See the "Mémoire de Michel de Marillac, garde des sceaux," in *Choix de chroniques et mémoires sur l'histoire de France [1589–1604],* ed. Pierre Victor Palma Cayet, avec notices biographiques par J. A. C. Buchon (Paris: A. Desrez, 1836), vol. 2, especially the major section, entitled "De la Ligue . . . ," pp. 521–30.

39. Ibid., 186; Léon Desjonquères, *Le garde des sceaux Michel de Marillac et son oeuvre législative*, Thèse pour le doctorat, Faculté de Droit de l'Université de Paris (Paris, 1908), 51.

40. "Mémoire de Marillac," 522. Boucher, *Marie de l'Incarnation*, dates this event to 1594 (p. 218).

41. "Mémoire de Marillac," 517–30.

42. Desjonquères, *Garde des sceaux*, 40–46.

43. Ibid., 49–51.

44. Everat, *Marillac*, 18; see also Major, *Representative Government*, 491.

45. Colin R. E. Kaiser, "The Masters of Requests: An Extraordinary Judicial Company in the Age of Centralization, 1589–1648" (Ph.D. diss., University of London, 1971), 62, 141, 160.

46. Ibid., 178.

47. Ibid., 189.

48. Ibid., 200–214. Kaiser writes that the early sources are missing concerning *épices*.

49. Ibid., 16–17.

50. Bernard Barbiche, "Les commissaires députés pour le 'régalement' des tailles en 1589–1599," *Bibliothèque de l'Ecole des Chartes* 118 (1960): 58–96.

51. Bernard Barbiche, "Henri IV, Sully et la première 'monarchie administrative,'" *Proceedings of the Western Society for French History* 17 (1990): 10–23.

52. Major, *Representative Government*, 273–74, 376; but see also his earlier article, "Henry IV and Guyenne."

53. Actually, during this decade, the Conseil Privé traveled not much farther or more frequently without Marillac than when he was present.

54. François Dumont, *Inventaire des arrêts du Conseil Privé: Règnes de Henri III et de Henri IV* (Paris, 1971), vol. 2, fasc. 1, pp. 187–253.

55. Albert N. Hamscher, *The Conseil Privé and the Parlements in the Age of Louis XIV: A Study in French Absolutism*, Transactions of the American Philosophical Society, vol. 77, pt. 2 (Philadelphia, 1987).

56. Major, *Representative Government*, 491.

57. Kaiser, "Masters of Requests," 235–36.

58. Ibid., 280–81.

59. Ibid., 260–61, 268, 278.

60. J. Michael Hayden, *France and the Estates General of 1614* (Cambridge, 1974), 13–14.

61. Kaiser, "Masters of Requests," 261.

62. Richard Bonney, *The King's Debts: Finance and Politics in France, 1589–1661* (Oxford, 1981), 121; see also pp. 116–21. Cf. Major, *Representative Government*, 498.

63. Jeanne Petit, *L'Assemblée des Notables de 1626–1627* (Paris, 1936), passim. I am grateful to Orest Ranum for directing my attention to this important study.

64. Williams, *French Oratorians*, 408, 423. Cf. Roland Mousnier, "French Institutions and Society, 1610–61," in *New Cambridge Modern History*, ed. G. N. Clark, vol. 4, *The Decline of Spain and the Thirty Years War, 1609–48/59*, ed. J. P. Cooper (Cambridge, 1970), 484–85; and Ranum, *Paris*, 230–34 (the most comprehensive and searching interpretation, though focused on the years 1630–50).

65. Kaiser, "Masters of Requests"; Donald A. Bailey, "Writers Against the Cardinal: A Study of the Pamphlets Which Attacked the Person and Policies of Cardinal Richelieu During the Decade 1630–40" (Ph.D. diss., University of Minnesota, 1973), 2 vols.

11. Parlements and Litigants

at the King's Councils During

the Personal Rule of Louis XIV:

The Example of *Cassation*

ALBERT N. HAMSCHER

Contrary to the conventional view of domestic politics in France during Louis XIV's personal rule (1661–1715), accommodation, compromise, and goodwill played a significant role in royal policies toward traditional institutions. This dimension of "royal absolutism" emerges clearly from an examination of a significant aspect of the relations between the hub of the central administration, the king's councils, and the most powerful and prestigious law courts of the realm, the parlements. Specifically, the councils possessed the authority in certain circumstances to nullify, either on their own initiative or on the request of individual litigants, the civil and criminal sentences that the parlements and other sovereign courts rendered in last resort. The councils' exercise of this right of judicial supervision and discipline, known as *cassation*, raised fundamental questions about the very nature and extent of the parlements' own authority in the administration of justice, and it was one of the issues that so sharply divided the monarchy and its highest judges throughout the first half of the seventeenth century. Complaints that the councils disregarded procedural formalities in rescinding parlementary sentences and engaged in an excessive and seemingly random interference in the *parlementaires'* judicial business figured prominently in the constitutional conflicts associated with the civil wars known as the Fronde (1648–53). After Louis XIV assumed responsibility for state affairs in 1661, however, the councils showed considerable restraint and moderation when dealing with the parlements on the subject of *cassation*, often resolving in favor of the judges many of the grievances they had expressed at mid-century.[1]

Normally examined within the context of legal and institutional history, litigation concerning *cassation* also had an important social component that makes its study appropriate in a volume devoted to "society and institutions." Most legal actions in *cassation* were initiated by private individuals, which meant that a durable settlement of differences between the councils and the parlements could never have been reduced to the preparation of formal regulations or to an abstract division of administrative responsibilities. Confronted with a steady stream of litigants, each having a unique set of legal problems to resolve, the councils were compelled on a daily basis not only to adjust to changing circumstances, but also to strike the delicate balance between providing access to petitioners for the redress of legitimate grievances, on the one hand, and defending the honor of the magistrates and the integrity of their judicial sentences, on the other. Litigants, then, were the unpredictable element in a resolution of the disputes between the councils and the parlements. For this reason, the jurisprudence and judicial procedures of the councils frequently aimed to impress upon litigants that the legal remedy of *cassation* was an extraordinary expression of the king's sovereign authority to be applied sparingly and within narrow limits.

The general contours of the conflicts between the councils and the parlements before 1661 are now well known.[2] During the ministries of Cardinals Richelieu and Mazarin, the parlements drew upon all their powers—including the judgment of litigation—to block the implementation of a broad range of royal financial and administrative policies they perceived as jeopardizing their wealth, functions, and prestige. The councils naturally responded to this opposition by changing the venue of sensitive litigation (often retaining cases for final judgment at the councils themselves), by resolving jurisdictional disputes in favor of more compliant tribunals (such as the Requêtes de l'Hôtel), and by nullifying the judicial sentences and administrative acts of the parlements. This activity in turn prompted the magistrates to protest against "abuses" in the councils' adjudication of *évocations*, *règlements de juges*, and *cassations*. To these grievances, the judges added other complaints of a purely procedural nature. On the subject of *cassation*, for example, the parlements resented the rescission of their judgments solely on the basis of a petitioner's request without all the parties in a disputed sentence having received the opportunity to present evidence; they also objected when a council suspended the enforcement of judgments rendered after full instruction in the courts while it considered the merits of a request for *cassation*. As a deterrent against chicanery, the parlements called for fines against litigants who initiated and then lost actions at the councils.[3]

The acrimonious disputes between the councils and the parlements presented a genuine danger to royal authority, not only because they jeopardized the enforcement of specific governmental programs, but also because they threw into bold relief serious constitutional issues, such as the problem of a "confusion of powers" among the principal institutions of the state that blurred lines of authority and thereby threatened political stability. The controversy also offered litigants an open invitation to fish in troubled waters. Because the stakes were so high, the monarchy's victory in the civil wars of the Fronde and the gradual decline of the political activities and influence of the parlements during Louis XIV's personal rule quite understandably led generations of historians to assess the fate of the magistrates after 1661 in negative terms, concluding that the consolidation and extension of royal power severely limited the ability of the parlements to defend their interests at the highest levels of the central administration.[4] While this view has merit in its broadest outlines, it lacks nuance, and this for two reasons.

First, the defeat of the Fronde did not enable the monarchy to ride roughshod over its former critics in the law courts. However much the king and his ministers aspired to silence judicial opposition in subsequent decades and to undermine still further the traditional restraints on the exercise of royal authority, they possessed neither the resources nor the assurance of widespread support to ignore completely the vested interests of the magistrates or to restructure judicial institutions in a fundamental way. As a result, royal control of the high judiciary in the second half of the seventeenth century depended as much upon compromise and skillful management as upon overt acts of discipline and administrative innovation. Second, interpretations resting exclusively on the most striking examples of the resurgence of royal power risk exaggerating the decline of the parlements after 1661 and overestimating the degree of coercion in the monarchy's relations with its highest judges. After all, the parlements were first and foremost courts of law; their principal responsibility was to serve as the leading appellate courts of the realm, judging both civil and criminal cases in last resort. So long as the monarchy's approach toward this aspect of the *parlementaires'* activities and interests remains unclear, our understanding of the nature of royal absolutism and its impact on the parlements will be incomplete and distorted.

There were, in fact, important forces for accommodation operating throughout the period 1661–1715. The king himself set the tone for a compromise. Louis XIV had no illusions that the conflicts between the parlements and the councils had been solely the fault of the former. Although the highest council over which he presided personally, the Conseil d'En haut, proclaimed in July 1661 the supremacy of conciliar decisions (*arrêts*) over the judicial sentences and administrative acts of the parlements, the king informed his principal advisers that he did not intend this supremacy to establish a virtual carte blanche for the councils to continue indiscriminately the practices that had so distressed the parlements in the past. He also noted on several occasions that the judicial reforms he contemplated would apply to the councils as well as to the ordinary judiciary.[5] But expressions of goodwill would have produced few concrete results had not the parlements themselves contributed substantially to a durable settlement of differences by curtailing their political activities and by considerably reducing their opposition to royal policies after 1661. Many aspects of this fundamental change in parlementary conduct remain obscure and constitute an important agenda for future research. But the results of this quiescence are clear: so long as the parlements trimmed their political ambitions—especially in the vaguely defined realm of "affairs of state"— and so long as they gradually abandoned their public criticism of royal programs—using instead more conventional channels (such as negotiating with individual ministers) to lobby for their interests—the central administration was little inclined to review their judicial decisions in a systematic way or to interfere with their caseloads on a large scale. The price the parlements paid for a successful settlement of their grievances against the councils was unquestionably a high one: a reduction of their political role in the state. But in return they received a renewed consideration for their traditional authority in the daily administration of justice.

The conduct of individual councils illustrates this trend. Presided over by the chancellor of France and composed of councillors of state (*conseillers d'état*) and masters of requests (*maîtres des requêtes*), the Conseil Privé was only a secondary or lesser council in the service of the monarchy. But it is the most important for our purposes because it specialized in judicial affairs and because it adjudicated most legal actions in *cassation*. A number of developments within this council augured well for improved relations with the parlements. Although the responsibilities of the chancellors in the general administration of the realm declined dramatically after 1661, their influence in judicial affairs remained considerable. In this respect, the parlements were fortunate to deal with chancellors (especially Michel Le Tellier [1677–85], Louis Boucherat [1685–99], and Louis Phélypeaux de Pontchartrain [1699–1714]) who pursued a common policy of reconciliation. They regularly consulted the magistrates about the formulation and implementation of judicial legislation, and they consistently defended the supervisory powers of the parlements over lesser tribunals. Within the Conseil Privé itself, they urged adherence to procedural rules, they kept the *parlementaires* informed about the status of individual cases (at times even explaining the rationale for the council's decisions), and they ensured that the parlements had both formal and informal avenues of recourse open to express their concerns and grievances.[6]

Such conduct struck a responsive chord among the council's membership. As one example, when in 1665 Jean-Baptiste Colbert solicited advice from several councillors of state about the possible direction of judicial reform, many echoed opinions the *parlementaires* themselves had expressed in the era of the Fronde. A future chancellor of France, Etienne d'Aligre, spoke of his "deference to the parlements on the issue of *cassation*," and other councillors emphasized that few legal grounds justified the council's nullifying parlementary judgments in last resort: *cassation* "ought to be accorded with great difficulty," stated Alexandre de Sève; "for the blatant [*formelle*] contravention of [royal] ordinances and conciliar *arrêts*, and not otherwise," in the words of François Verthamon.[7] Aligre and Sève also criticized the practice of suspending the enforcement of parlementary judgments when cases of *cassation* were pending at the council; Sève went so far as to condemn the procedure as "the greatest vexation that arises in the distribution of justice."[8] There was even support for the parlements' position that unsuccessful petitioners to the council should be fined and that the council should refrain from pronouncing *cassation* solely on the basis of a petitioner's request without allowing the other litigants involved in a disputed sentence to present evidence.[9]

The desire of the chancellors and their colleagues to ameliorate the conditions of this council's work also found tangible expression in a number of important legislative acts that applied primarily to the Conseil Privé, such as the ordinance of August 1669 and the regulations (*règlements*) of 27 February 1660, 3 January 1673, and 17 June 1687. Together, this legislation defined the council's membership, regulated the conduct of reporting magistrates and *avocats aux conseils,* established the conditions for initiating legal actions, and set forth the council's judicial procedures on the broad spectrum from the initial summons to the liquidation of court costs.[10]

Of all the powers the Conseil Privé exercised, none tested the judicial expertise and political acumen of its members more than *cassation.* This legal action was not an ordinary right of all litigants to pursue, but an extraordinary recourse to the king's sovereign power against judgments that in normal circumstances were nonappealable. A petitioner following this course both questioned the conduct of the magistrates in specific litigation and called into play the council's disciplinary powers over even the highest levels of the ordinary judiciary. Neither prospect pleased the *parlementaires,* with the result that each time the council examined a request for *cassation,* it had to take into account not only the interests of parties and the need to uphold respect for the law, but also the dignity of the high magistracy and the controversy that too liberal a policy of granting *cassations* might generate.

To complicate matters further, the monarchy never defined explicitly the grounds (*ouvertures*) for this legal action for fear of setting overly precise limits on the discretionary authority of its central institutions. In practice, the members of Louis XIV's Conseil Privé, like their counterparts in the eighteenth century, allowed for only a limited number of grounds for *cassation:* (1) when a court in entering judgment exceeded its jurisdiction; (2) when a judgment contravened royal legislation or the fundamental laws of the realm; (3) when a judgment violated well-established private law, either customary or Roman; (4) when serious errors occurred in judicial procedure or in the redaction of the judgment itself; (5) when obvious inequity ("iniquité évidente") characterized a judgment. As a general rule, claimed mistakes in a court's opinion on the merits of litigation—"mal jugé au fond"—were not grounds for nullification; otherwise, *cassation* would have assumed the character of an ordinary appeal.[11] If the grounds for *cassation* were few in number, however, they were sufficiently broad and ambiguous to require a high degree of interpretation in individual cases. Only by acting with restraint and consistency on this matter and by developing procedures aimed at discouraging frivolous attacks on the parlements' sentences could the Conseil Privé hope to accomplish its mission efficiently and with a minimum of political risk.

Finally, the fact that most legal actions in *cassation* involved litigants who enjoyed high social standing either on the national level or in their local communities provided yet another incentive for the Conseil Privé to proceed cautiously when adjudicating these cases. The *arrêts* of the council do not always define with precision the rank or profession of contesting parties. But they were clearly important people, those who could afford the cost of pursuing litigation both in a parlement and at the council—the king's own officials, members of the clergy and the nobility, and such urban notables as mayors, merchants, bankers, and so on.[12] As one way of winning the support of the "political nation" for the more disciplined regime Louis XIV and his principal advisers envisioned, it was obviously in the best interest of the Conseil Privé to eliminate disorder from its own proceedings and to assure litigants as well as the parlements that the council could render carefully prepared and legally sound decisions.

Determining how the Conseil Privé responded to all these considerations requires a basic familiarity with the decisions it issued in *cassation* and the information one can find in them.[13] A petitioner seeking the rescission of a parlement's judgment submitted to the council a request (*requête*) that summarized the attacked judgment and explained the reasons (*moyens*) for challenging it. The council responded with an *arrêt sur requête* that either granted or rejected the petitioner's demands outright or, more often, summoned all the litigants involved in the disputed judgment to contest the complaint fully in writing. In this latter instance, a second *arrêt*—a definitive one "between parties" (*contradictoire*)—eventually resolved the action. Unfortunately, because the council did not give the judicial reasoning (*motifs*) for its decisions, the *arrêts* do not indicate which circumstances in a given case led the council to find as it did. Nevertheless, the *arrêts sur requête* repeated in detail the contents of the requests submitted by petitioners. We thus have a record of the grievances the council was at least willing to consider as grounds for *cassation*, information that is indispensable for understanding how broadly the council conceived its authority to nullify parlementary judgments. As regards the *arrêts* between parties, in addition to giving the council's decision, they provide only a chronology of procedures followed in a case and a list of documents submitted in evidence; the *moyens* of parties are either absent or described only briefly. But these *arrêts* can lead one to *arrêts sur requête* issued earlier in an action.[14] Moreover, when combined with those *arrêts sur requête* that do give a final decision, the *arrêts* between parties indicate how often attempts to secure *cassation* succeeded.

During Louis XIV's personal rule, the Conseil Privé issued as many as 100,000 *arrêts* concerning all aspects of its jurisdiction. A primary sample of 1,511 of these *arrêts* (the equivalent of between six months and two years of this council's work) drawn from nine years between 1661 and 1715 yields several hundred *arrêts* pertaining to the parlements and the subject of *cassation*.[15] Most of these *arrêts* dealt with noncontroversial, routine, and relatively minor jurisdictional issues in which neither the conduct of the magistrates in judging litigation nor the legitimate right of the parlements to decide certain kinds of legal issues was in dispute. Limitations of space require that we set aside these cases.[16] If we concentrate instead on the more serious cases of *cassation*, those in which the complaining parties tapped the full range of grounds for nullification and in the process raised fundamental questions about the judges' conduct and authority, the sample contains 67 *arrêts sur requête* concerning the parlements. I have supplemented these *arrêts* with 10 *arrêts* between parties drawn from the primary sample and with an additional 7 *arrêts sur requête* traced from these 10.[17]

At first glance, these *arrêts* seem to defy systematic analysis because complaining parties tended to submit elaborate requests for *cassation* that raised a variety of grievances and legal issues. Indeed, 31 of the 74 *arrêts sur requête* mention two grounds for *cassation* while 8 *arrêts* refer to three. Thirty-five *arrêts* indicate only one ground, such as the violation of procedural rules, but within this single category petitioners normally cited many individual infractions to substantiate their complaints. Despite this problem, the *arrêts* can be examined in ways that reveal broad patterns in the council's jurisprudence. On one level, a simple overview of the final decisions in the *arrêts* is informative, suggesting as it does that most serious challenges to parlementary judgments were unsuccessful. Among the 67 *arrêts sur requête* and the 10 *arrêts* between parties drawn from the primary sample, 28 gave a final decision, and 17 of these (or 61 percent) denied the request for *cassation*. But the best method for gaining insight into both the nature of the grievances that petitioners raised and the council's response to different kinds of complaints is to examine the *arrêts* from the vantage point of the grounds for *cassation* they mention.

If we review the principal grounds for *cassation*, the paucity of complaints about the equity in parlementary judgments is among the most striking features of the council's *arrêts*. Only 12 of the 74 *arrêts sur requête* contain allegations that the parlements had decided unfairly the substantive issues in the litigation that came before them, and not a single petitioner expressed this grievance as the sole reason for seeking nullification of a parlement's sentence. Given the proclivity of losing litigants then as now to doubt the fairness of judgments rendered against them, the reluctance of petitioners to base their cases at the Conseil Privé exclusively on this complaint illustrates the council's basic respect for both the legal decisions that the parlements made in last resort and the great freedom that French magistrates traditionally enjoyed in weighing evidence in individual cases.

Petitioners themselves testified to the council's unwillingness to allow *cassation* to assume the character of an ordinary appeal on the merits of litigation. Bernard de Genevois, who sought the rescission of a judgment the Parlement of Paris had rendered against him in a contest over land possession, acknowledged that "the supplicant well knows that claims of injustice are not capable of destroying [parlementary] sentences if there are no other grounds for nullity and *cassation*," and Isaac Marchays, who believed the Parlement of Bordeaux had shown excessive leniency toward his opposite party in a prosecution for theft, granted that "even the most crying injustice does not alone constitute grounds for *cassation*, although it always determines His Majesty in favor of those who [also] draw on [royal] ordinances [to justify their complaints]." [18] Like all the other parties who appealed to the council's sense of fairness, these petitioners did so only to supplement additional, fully documented claims of judicial error.[19] But even this tactic was not particularly effective: of the 12 *arrêts sur requête* that raised questions of equity, 4 gave a final decision at this stage of the proceedings, and only 1 of these ordered *cassation* (none of the *arrêts* between parties in the sample dealt with this issue).[20] Moreover, when the council did consider questions of equity, it could do so to the advantage of the judges. Chancellor Pontchartrain's correspondence indicates that the council occasionally rejected requests for *cassation*, even when petitioners had fully proved their contentions, if the "merits of the case" or "principles of equity" dictated that a parlement's judgment should stand.[21] As both Genevois and Marchays assumed, there is no evidence to suggest that the council showed similar consideration for litigants by pronouncing *cassation* for reasons of inequity if other grounds for nullification were not well founded.

The *parlementaires* also endured few complaints regarding another important aspect of their discretionary authority: their right to interpret and apply in individual cases the private law of the realm. To be sure, parties rightly considered a violation of private law to be a legitimate cause for complaint before the Conseil Privé. Eleven of the 74 *arrêts sur requête* mention this issue, 8 petitioners feeling sufficiently confident to designate it as the sole ground for *cassation*. Upon close scrutiny, however, these cases were less onerous to the judges' interests than one might imagine. On the one hand, the council seems to have been no more liberal in pronouncing *cassation* in cases raising this grievance than in those involving allegations of inequity: of the 4 final decisions we have on these 11 actions (3 *sur requête* and 1 between parties), 3 rejected the request for nullification.[22] On the other hand, the issues in contention in these 11 cases were generally not of a nature either to undermine the magistrates' authority or to tarnish their reputations in a serious way.

In five cases, petitioners claimed that the parlements had violated laws that, in fact, the judges had only limited experience in applying. This situation could arise, for example, when a change of venue had sent a case from a tribunal in a region of Roman law, like the Parlement of Aix, to a court that normally decided cases on the basis of customary laws, like the Parlement of Paris. Because any act of transfer required the parlement receiving litigation to apply the law of the case's origin, occasional and honest mistakes were bound to occur.[23] Yet another case concerned the problem of "contrariété des arrêts," which arose when two sovereign courts rendered contradictory judgments between the same parties on the same substantive issues; that a petitioner would seek nullification of the judgment against him was understandable.[24] Three other cases involved clerics who maintained that parlementary sentences had violated either the constitutions of religious orders or canonical regulations governing the possession of benefices, documents that enjoyed the force of law in France. The parlements might well have resented such challenges to their legal decisions, but at least they could view quarrels with the clergy, which was notoriously jealous of its own privileges, as an ordinary feature of judicial life. More important, the three cases in question concerned strictly private litigation that did not raise fundamental questions about the parlements' general authority in religious affairs.[25] Only in the two remaining cases were the parlements alleged to have violated laws with which they should have been perfectly familiar, as in the case of Jean de La Care, who claimed that the Parlement of Paris had disregarded key provisions in the custom of Bourges when it called for a "useless" ordering of creditors in litigation involving an inheritance burdened with debt. But neither of these attempts to secure *cassation* succeeded.[26]

The Conseil Privé also proceeded cautiously in cases of *cassation* that raised fundamental questions about the limits of parlementary jurisdiction in judicial affairs. In one respect, the parlements were spared numerous challenges of this sort because their right to hear a broad range of civil and criminal cases was well established and widely recognized. But the lines of jurisdictional authority in early modern France overlapped sufficiently to leave ample room for heated disagreements even at the highest levels of the judiciary. Twenty-three of the 74 *arrêts sur requête* under consideration contain complaints that a parlement had exceeded its legitimate power in the course of judging litigation. We may set aside 12 of these cases because they entailed the routine or minor grievances referred to previously, the only reason they fall into the primary sample being that in these dozen actions such grievances were joined to other grounds for *cassation.*[27] Far more noteworthy were the 11 remaining cases, in which petitioners maintained that certain legal issues fell completely outside a parlement's competence. Thus the syndic of the clergy in the diocese of Quimper contended that when the Parlement of Rennes decided a case concerning a clergyman's *capitation* tax, it violated a contract between the king and the clergy of France that had awarded jurisdiction in such matters to local ecclesiastical institutions.[28] As another example, a judge in the town of Saint-Union in the Limousin, Etienne Lamy, contested the right of the Parlement of Bordeaux to hear appeals from the rulings that the provincial intendants issued in police matters.[29]

Without underestimating the threats that such challenges posed to the parlements' authority and pretensions, it is also important to recognize that recourse to *cassation* for serious jurisdictional reasons was a remedy pursued most often by a well-defined and privileged group, namely clerics and lesser royal officials anxious to defend their jurisdictional rights against parlementary encroachments. Seven of the 11 cases fall into this category (6 initiated by clergymen), and the high rate of success in these actions (3 of the 4 final decisions we possess pronounced *cassation*) indicates that when called upon the Conseil Privé acted to maintain an equilibrium between the various public authorities of the realm, especially when petitioners cited recent royal legislation to justify their jurisdictional claims (as was done in 5 cases).[30] But the quashing of some of their judgments did not jeopardize the parlements' general authority in religious affairs, which remained substantial throughout Louis's reign. Moreover, the council was apparently less receptive to ordinary litigants questioning the limits of parlementary jurisdiction in a fundamental way. The presence of only four such attempts in the primary sample reveals the reluctance of complainants to follow this course, and in only one of these cases did the petitioner raise a major point about jurisdiction as his only ground, and this involved a clear-cut instance of a parlement having issued an order in a case that another sovereign court had already judged in last resort.[31]

The Conseil Privé proved to be equally circumspect when considering *cassation* for the two grounds that petitioners cited most often in their complaints: errors in judicial procedure and violations of royal legislation. On the former matter, the appearance in April 1667 and August 1670 of the two famous ordinances on civil and criminal procedure, supplemented in later years by a host of additional acts, unquestionably provided litigants with an unprecedented opportunity to protest the conduct of the *parlementaires* before a superior authority and thereby increased the council's ability to subject parlementary sentences to judicial review.[32] In the decades before the 1660s, complaints of a procedural nature at the Conseil Privé were rare, no doubt because the paucity of existing royal legislation that set forth judicial procedures in a comprehensive fashion had given all the parlements wide latitude to develop their own particular usages.[33] This situation changed during Louis's personal rule, when complaints that the parlements had violated procedural rules became the most frequently cited ground for *cassation:* of the 74 *arrêts sur requête* under consideration, 50 (or 68 percent) raised this issue, and 20 of these *arrêts* mentioned it as the sole reason for a party's seeking relief from a parlementary sentence. Moreover, the council's willingness to receive such complaints was not limited to the early decades of Louis's reign, when most procedural legislation appeared: as with the other grounds for *cassation,* complaints of a procedural nature run uniformly through all nine years represented in the primary sample.

But if the council exhibited a general commitment to enforce compliance with the new legislation in the parlements, it had no intention of undermining the magistrates' ability to supervise their own conduct or of allowing disgruntled litigants to harass them about relatively minor infractions. Three aspects of this jurisprudence merit brief mention. First, there existed in French law a legal action known as *requête civile* that enabled the parlements in certain circumstances to retract their own judgments and to rehear litigation, and this without the mediation of the king's councils.[34] The ordinance of April 1667 defined the grounds for *requête civile* with precision, and for the most part these grounds were quite distinct from those for *cassation.* But in one important instance—the violation of the procedural rules set forth in the two codes—an aggrieved party had the option to pursue either a *requête civile* or *cassation.*[35] The Conseil Privé avoided a potentially troublesome overlap of conciliar and parlementary authority in this respect by adjudicating complaints about procedural irregularities only when it could claim clear jurisdiction. For example, if petitioners had already pursued *requêtes civiles* at the parlements, or if they cited in their complaints grounds for *cassation* in addition to purely procedural ones, the council's intervention was fully justified.[36] The same thing was true if parties cited only procedural violations in their complaints but referred to royal legislation other than, or in addition to, the two procedural codes.[37]

In fact, in only 4 of the 50 cases, in which petitioners referred solely to alleged violations of the ordinances of April 1667 and August 1670, could the council even be suspected of denying a parlement the opportunity to emend its mistakes. Yet a careful reading of these cases indicates that the council's interest in them was both appropriate and reasonable. An example is the case of Julien de La Gonnière, who maintained that the Parlement of Rouen had violated provisions in both procedural codes not only when it permitted a lesser tribunal, the bailliage of Coutances, to judge a case of verbal injury according to procedures intended for more serious criminal offenses, but also when it failed during appellate procedures to correct an important error committed by the judges at Coutances (La Gonnière claiming that one of these judges had been ineligible to participate in his trial).[38] It so happens that this party lost his bid for *cassation,* yet the fact remains that his case raised sufficiently serious charges of procedural irregularity to warrant the council's allowing him to bypass a *requête civile*. But the existence of only 4 such cases in the entire primary sample indicates how rarely the Conseil Privé chose to exercise this option. In any case, the council certainly knew how to distinguish those cases it should adjudicate: upon receiving requests for *cassation* that met the criteria for a *requête civile* and did not raise larger questions about the judges' conduct, the council simply converted the petitioner's request into a *requête civile* and remanded the case to the appropriate parlement.[39]

A second and especially creative way in which the Conseil Privé approached the task of enforcing the new procedural legislation in the parlements was for the chancellors to inform the judges about the procedures that the council considered to be particularly important and whose violation was likely to result in *cassation*. Sometimes this correspondence took the form of circular letters, as when Boucherat warned eight provincial parlements in 1687 that the council was determined to nullify judgments rendered in violation of royal legislation that both limited the types of litigation that the courts could judge in expensive special sessions and prohibited the magistrates from requiring litigants to deposit judicial fees prior to the final judgment of cases.[40] At other times, the chancellors discussed specific cases pending at the council, occasionally explaining in detail to a parlement why the council had nullified one of its judgments. In 1711, for example, the Parlement of Toulouse ordered the arrest and imprisonment of a solicitor (*procureur*), Antoine Gravière, for having ignored a deliberation of the court and continued procedures in a case after the deadline for such activity had expired. In his request to the council, Gravière raised seven separate objections to the Parlement's conduct, claiming (among other things) that he was never properly informed about the court's deliberation and its results, that the deadline the judges wished to enforce lacked legal foundation, and that procedural rules dictated that only persons accused of having committed serious crimes should suffer imprisonment during trial. The council overturned the Parlement's rulings in this case. But in a series of letters addressed to the court's first president, Pontchartrain indicated precisely which of Gravière's grounds had convinced the council to act as it did (the issue of unwarranted imprisonment being the most crucial).[41]

One should not exaggerate the extent to which such correspondence gave the parlements even unofficial access to the council's deliberations. The chancellors exercised great discretion in deciding when to contact the parlements, and even Pontchartrain, who excelled in preparing clear and informative letters, wrote about only a few cases of *cassation* each year. The council had no intention of divulging the judicial reasoning behind more than a handful of its decisions, and it never restricted its own freedom of action by leading the magistrates to believe that procedural violations that were not the subject of special comment would be exempt from *cassation*. With this said, however, the chancellors' letters did open an important line of communication between the Conseil Privé and the parlements, lifting in at least a few cases the veil of secrecy that surrounded decision making in the council and thereby enabling the judges to avert some challenges to their judgments before they occurred.[42]

Finally, without question the best method by which the Conseil Privé could enforce royal legislation on judicial procedure without provoking serious conflict with the parlements was to consider nullifying their judgments only for the most "important" (to use a favored word of the era) procedural infractions. Exactly what in the council's view constituted an important as opposed to a minor violation of judicial procedure obviously varied from one case to another according to the particular circumstances involved. This situation, when coupled with the absence of the council's judicial reasoning in its *arrêts*, prevents us from ever defining with absolute precision criteria that were themselves constantly changing. If the letters of the chancellors shed at least some light on this problem, it seems that when the council reviewed allegations of procedural error, it took into account not only the gravity of the violation in principle—whether a court had flagrantly transgressed widely accepted norms of judicial conduct, for example, or whether the judges had ignored previous warnings by the council—but also the extent to which a specific infraction had determined the final outcome of litigation before a parlement.[43] The council certainly exercised its discretionary power within sufficiently narrow limits to prevent charges of procedural irregularity from becoming an easy route to *cassation*. Of the 50 cases in which this issue appeared either alone or with other grounds for *cassation*, we have 15 final decisions (11 *sur requête* and 4 between parties), and only 5 of these pronounced nullification (7 parties lost their bid for *cassation* while 3 others were advised to pursue a *requête civile* before a parlement).[44]

Turning to the final ground for *cassation*—the violation of royal legislation (excluding that pertaining to judicial procedure discussed above)—familiar patterns emerge in the council's conduct. To be sure, the Conseil Privé did not dissuade litigants from making complaints of this type. Twenty-one of the 74 *arrêts sur requête* under consideration mention this issue, 9 of them citing it as the sole reason for a petitioner's recourse to the council.[45] But if the council gave litigants wide latitude to submit requests for *cassation*, at the same time it not only made the actual nullification of sentences difficult to achieve, but it also attempted to limit the instances when *cassation* would apply. On the one hand, the rate of success in these cases was hardly more impressive than that associated with the other grounds for *cassation*. The 21 cases include 10 final decisions (6 *sur requête* and 4 between parties), half of which pronounced nullification. This is a modest number if we bear in mind that 2 of the 5 victories involved royal legislation concerning jurisdiction, which we have already noted the council was anxious to enforce.[46] On the other hand, an examination of the dates of legislation that petitioners cited in their complaints reveals that the Conseil Privé was most interested in defending royal acts of recent vintage, those that were presumably well known to the *parlementaires*. Seventeen of the 21 *arrêts sur requête* referred to legislation issued after 1654, and only 5 parties claimed that the *parlementaires* had violated royal decrees that had appeared before that date.[47] The Conseil Privé apparently gave litigants little incentive to comb the legal heritage of

France for ancient or esoteric statutes upon which to build a case against the parlements' judicial decisions.

In addition to fashioning a jurisprudence that respected the parlements' interests, the Conseil Privé also smoothed points of friction with the judges and at the same time improved its efficiency by implementing significant reform of its own judicial procedures. Owing to the large number and complexity of the council's procedures, a full and systematic review of even those pertaining exclusively to *cassation* is beyond the scope of this essay.[48] But several developments that reveal the council's efforts to respond favorably to the parlements' grievances of mid-century and to inform litigants that requests for *cassation* were not to be taken lightly can be summarized succinctly. Beginning in 1673, for example, the council established substantial mandatory fines (normally ranging from 150 to 300 livres) against petitioners who initiated cases of *cassation* and then either lost these cases or desisted from them without good cause.[49] The council also abandoned altogether the practice of retaining some cases for final judgment after having nullified the judicial sentences of the parlements; upon ordering *cassation,* the council either sent the parties to another parlement for retrial or, less frequently, simply pronounced nullification and left the parties to their own devices.[50]

The council was less inclined to abandon its policy of occasionally pronouncing *cassation* solely on the basis of a petitioner's request without calling all the litigants in a disputed sentence to contest the complaint fully in writing. After all, if the issues in a complaint were clear and could be resolved immediately by an *arrêt sur requête,* it made little sense to burden a petitioner's adversaries with the expense and inconvenience of additional proceedings. But the council followed this course with great discretion, especially in the more serious cases of *cassation.* Of the 67 *arrêts sur requête* in the primary sample, only 20 (or 30 percent) resolved the action at this stage of the proceedings, and in only 8 of these 20 cases did the council rule in favor of the complaining party (9 *arrêts* rejected outright the request for *cassation* while 3 others converted actions into *requêtes civiles* for the parlements to adjudicate).[51] In addition, for those few individuals who did see a parlementary judgment in their favor overturned without their having had the opportunity to contest the matter at the council, a procedure known as *opposition* enabled them to request the council to reconsider its decision.[52] The *parlementaires* as well could pursue this remedy if they believed that the council had nullified one of their sentences too precipitously.[53]

The parlements also received satisfaction on the issue of the council's practice of suspending at times the enforcement of their judgments while actions in *cassation* were pending. The procedure itself, known as *surséance*, was juridically sound because the possibility always existed that the immediate enforcement of a parlementary sentence might do irreparable harm to a petitioner with a potentially strong case: in these circumstances, considerations of equity outweighed the risk of offending the magistrates.[54] But once again the council acted with restraint: in only 15 percent of the cases (8 of 54) in the primary sample that proceeded beyond an *arrêt sur requête* did the council order a *surséance*, and only 1 of these cases appears after 1676.[55] By the second decade of Louis's personal rule, then, any incentive for litigants to pursue *cassation* as a way to delay the enforcement of parlementary judgments against them had evaporated.

If the inspiration for procedural reform within the Conseil Privé came in part from the judges' complaints in the era of the Fronde, the chancellors and their colleagues also worked on their own initiative to refine the judicial procedures associated with *cassation*. Beginning in 1660, for example, all requests for *cassation* had to be signed not only by the petitioner's principal *avocat aux conseils*, but also by 2 additional consultants selected from among the council's 50 senior *avocats*, a requirement that clearly aimed to reduce the number of requests for *cassation* submitted to the council by having the *avocats* refuse to sign, and thereby weed out, those with little merit.[56] How many potential actions in *cassation* were cut short in this fashion is, of course, impossible to determine. Certainly, there is good reason to suspect that the rule fell short of meeting the council's expectations—after all, the council's *avocats* had purchased their offices, and it was thus in their own financial interest to encourage rather than to discourage litigation.[57] Insofar as the parlements were concerned, however, the requirement of prior consultation, like the regulations that subjected losing litigants to mandatory fines, worked only to the judges' advantage: any formality that made a litigant's recourse to the council more difficult tended to enhance the independence that the *parlementaires* enjoyed in exercising their judicial functions.[58]

Moreover, once a request for *cassation* passed this hurdle, it then came under the careful scrutiny of several committees permanently attached to the Conseil Privé whose purpose was to allow small groups of council members to examine cases in advance of the council's formal sessions. Having been designated by the chancellor as a case's reporting magistrate charged with reviewing evidence and preparing an oral report for the entire council, a master of requests first discussed the case with his colleagues in an "assembly of masters of requests." He then met with one of several *bureaux* staffed with five to seven councillors of state, a procedure that both widened the circle of council members familiar with a case and provided the reporting magistrate with an additional opportunity to clarify his views through group deliberation.[59] If, after a formal council meeting, a case proceeded beyond the stage of an *arrêt sur requête,* this "double" examination occurred again before the Conseil Privé rendered a final decision by an *arrêt* between parties.[60] By 1685, one of the bureaus specialized in reviewing cases of *cassation.* Unlike the assemblies of the masters of requests and the other bureaus of councillors of state, its role was not purely advisory in all instances—if, upon initially receiving a request for *cassation,* the reporting magistrate and the members of this bureau agreed unanimously that the request lacked merit, they could prepare an *arrêt sur requête* to this effect and have the chancellor sign it without consulting the entire council.[61] The bureau of *cassations* was very busy: "in effect," according to Chancellor Pontchartrain, "the most tiring and disagreeable of all." But he also noted that this bureau "more than all the others [contributes to] the welfare of justice and [protects] the honor of the courts whose judgments are attacked."[62]

A final example of the judicial procedures associated with *cassation* also illustrates the council's efforts to review carefully cases pertaining to the parlements. Like the council's own *arrêts,* the sentences of the parlements did not mention the judicial reasoning, or *motifs,* behind the magistrates' judgments.[63] As a result, when members of the council examined requests for *cassation,* they lacked any precise indication why a court had decided a given case in a particular way. If, at the stage of an *arrêt sur requête,* the council believed that such information was necessary to resolve an action, it could solicit from the appropriate parlement a report explaining the *motifs* for the disputed sentence.[64] The council acted with circumspection on this matter. Owing to both its prestige and its proximity to the council, the Parlement of Paris, whose jurisdiction included nearly half of the realm, was actually exempt from the procedure—a reporting magistrate at the council was expected to visit this court and collect information orally.[65] When the other parlements did submit reports, these were held in strict confidentiality: contesting parties did not have access to them, nor did the *arrêts* between parties that terminated cases reveal their contents. Moreover, the council did not solicit *motifs* in most cases. Of the 74 *arrêts sur requête* under consideration, 20 provided final decisions while 13 others involved the Parlement of Paris; of the remaining 41, 17 (or 41 percent) called for *motifs*.[66] The chancellors' correspondence also indicates that carefully prepared and well-reasoned reports could rescue a sentence from potential nullification even if a petitioner had technically established a ground for *cassation*.[67]

The spirit of accommodation toward the parlements that was so evident in Louis XIV's Conseil Privé can also be observed in the activities of other councils. At the summit of conciliar organization stood the three *conseils de gouvernement*, so called because the king sat personally on these bodies with various combinations of his ministers, secretaries of state, and other leading royal officials and advisers. Together, these councils—the Conseil d'En haut, the Conseil des Dépêches, and from 1661, the Conseil royal des Finances—issued *arrêts en commandement* (some 35,000 in the period 1661–1715), which constitute a second source of conciliar decisions for tracing royal policies concerning the parlements and *cassation*.[68] These *arrêts* fell into two broad categories: those "sur requête," which responded to petitions filed by individuals or corporate groups, and those "de propre mouvement," which the councils issued on their own initiative without necessarily having been formally requested to intervene. The members of the *conseils de gouvernement*, meeting either in formal session or on an individual basis with the king, considered all manner of domestic and foreign affairs. Although their functions were primarily executive rather than judicial in nature, and despite the Conseil Privé's status as the principal forum for adjudicating actions in *cassation*, the high councils could assume jurisdiction over such cases, especially if they concerned royal finances or other public affairs.

In fact, during the decades preceding Louis XIV's assumption of personal rule, the *conseils de gouvernement* participated frequently in the process of *cassation*. For example, a sample of eight years between 1643 and 1660 yields 1,385 *arrêts en commandement*, or a yearly average of 173 *arrêts*. Of these, 111 *arrêts* nullified the judicial sentences and administrative acts of the parlements, for an annual average of 14 *cassations*.[69] All but a few of these *cassations* had an obvious political purpose, such as overcoming attempts by the parlements to interfere with the collection of royal taxes or to supervise the conduct of the provincial intendants.[70] In later years, however, as the parlements tempered their political ambitions and gradually abandoned their public opposition to royal policies, the role of the high councils in issuing *cassations* declined dramatically. Thus, although a sample of eight years between 1675 and 1710 yields a substantial 5,832 *arrêts* (an average of 729 *arrêts* per year), only 23 of these *arrêts* (an annual average of 3 *arrêts*) nullified a parlementary decision.[71] This decline signaled the resurgence of royal authority during Louis's reign and the emergence of more compliant parlements. But the king and his principal advisers, having achieved this objective, did not press their advantage: so long as the parlements expressed their views and grievances through acceptable and conventional channels, such as negotiating with individual ministers, the king's highest councils showed little interest in ruling on complaints about parlementary judgments. They were content to leave the bulk of this task to the Conseil Privé, with all the safeguards that this implied for the judges' interests.

Why did Louis XIV's highest councils order *cassations,* even if only infrequently? In 9 of the 23 cases (6 of them "de propre mouvement"), the councils were motivated by the same considerations that had predominated in earlier years: either the parlements failed to enforce important royal policies or they seriously overstepped their legitimate authority. In 1683, for example, the intendant of Guyenne, who exercised broad powers for billeting the royal troops who passed through his area of jurisdiction, ordered the royal and municipal officials of Tartas not to interfere in this matter. When these officials appealed this order to the Parlement of Bordeaux, and when the magistrates there agreed to hear the appeal, an *arrêt en commandement* nullified the Parlement's decision as having been made "par juge incompétent."[72] But the paucity of *cassations* with clear political intent during the period of Louis's personal rule stands in sharp contrast to the situation that had prevailed in the era of the Fronde, when a single year could witness over a dozen such nullifications.

The remaining 14 *cassations* concerned private rather than public affairs, all but 2 of them having been issued "sur requête" on the basis of complaints filed by individuals. Never very numerous even before 1661, instances of *cassation* concerning private litigation seem to have arisen in three special circumstances. First, it certainly helped if the complaining parties had connections in high places. Six of the 14 *cassations* involved people whose status was sufficiently high to attract the attention of the *conseils de gouvernement:* prominent nobles of the sword like the comte de l'Aubespine as well as leading officials in the king's own administration, including councillors of state and judges in the sovereign courts.[73] Second, a high council might pronounce *cassation* when it wished to encourage a parlement to apply consistently specific points of law. In 1687, for example, the Parlement of Paris had decided litigation in such a way that a

15-year-old girl, through the intercession of her adult fiancé, was able to set aside her father's will and to contract a marriage despite the opposition of her legal guardian and other blood relatives. The *arrêt* that annulled this sentence stated explicitly that the judges had violated several ordinances of the realm and had ignored the father's will, which stipulated that the girl could not marry without her guardian's permission.[74] Third, a *conseil de gouvernement* could nullify a sentence if the allegations against the *parlementaires* were particularly serious, as occurred in 1683 when an *arrêt en commandement* suspended from his functions a magistrate at the Parlement of Pau for having made numerous and significant procedural errors while serving as a *commissaire* charged with collecting evidence in a case.[75] The interdiction of a judge in a sovereign court was serious business, and to my knowledge an *arrêt en commandement* always ordered it.

Given their primarily executive functions and an inherent flexibility in their methods of work, the *conseils de gouvernement* did not undertake procedural reform comparable to that seen in the Conseil Privé. But the high councils could use the judicial procedures that the Conseil Privé followed as a matter of course. They occasionally solicited the *motifs* for parlementary judgments, and although they rarely called all the litigants in a disputed sentence to contest a complaint fully in writing—something that was common at the Conseil Privé—the *arrêts en commandement* do contain some references to the practice.[76] Certainly, private individuals whose requests for *cassation* came before the high councils could be required to follow the rules regarding consultation with three *avocats aux conseils* and the payment of fines if their requests failed.[77] No bureaus of councillors of state were permanently attached to these councils to examine all the cases that came before them, and contact between the high councils and the assemblies of masters of requests was infrequent. Nevertheless, the principal members of the high councils—the controller general of finances, the chancellor, and the secretaries of state—all had their own "ministerial bureaus" to receive and sort correspondence, to coordinate investigations on the local level, and to prepare reports for their superiors in advance of council sessions and private meetings with the king.[78] If a case was particularly complicated, a group of councillors of state might be called upon to serve as "commissaires d'avis," examining evidence and offering a collective opinion prior to a final decision.[79] Finally, the fact that the *conseils de gouvernement* at times transferred cases pending before them to the Conseil Privé for final resolution according to all the procedural rules shows that the king and his principal advisers exercised discretion in choosing which cases to decide themselves.[80]

A third and final source of conciliar decisions that reveals the crown's position on the subject of *cassation* is the *arrêts simples* "en finance" issued by the various council bodies that together directed the financial administration of the realm: the Conseil royal des Finances (which also issued *arrêts en commandement*); the Conseil d'Etat et des Finances (until its disappearance by the 1690s); the ordinary *commissions* of Grande and Petite Direction; and most important as the reign progressed, the many bureaus that served the controller general of finances.[81] These *arrêts* were numerous—perhaps some 130,000 for the period 1661–1715—but they are the least important for our purposes because the *parlementaires'* limited jurisdiction in financial affairs coupled with their growing submission to royal policies during the course of Louis's personal rule meant that the council bodies that issued these *arrêts* did not normally concern themselves with the judicial activities of the parlements.

A sample of 316 *arrêts* drawn from two years (1674 and 1710) includes only 3 cases involving requests for the nullification of parlementary judgments.[82] In one, the tax farmer in charge of collecting levies on the delivery of mail contended that the Parlement of Rouen had exceeded its authority by investigating corruption in the king's postal service; royal legislation, he asserted, had awarded jurisdiction in this matter to the provincial intendants.[83] In another, a litigant claimed to have uncovered errors in a judgment the Parlement of Rennes had rendered in a suit pertaining to the inheritance of royal offices.[84] The third case concerned a Parisian banker named Jean Nicolas, who was a party in litigation pending before *commissaires* appointed by the council. He maintained that the Parlement of Paris had overstepped its authority when it ignored this prior arrangement and assumed jurisdiction over his legal disputes.[85] What is remarkable about these complaints is not the reasons for nullification that these parties offered: allegations that the parlements had violated royal legislation or had exceeded their proper jurisdiction were legitimate and conventional grounds for *cassation*. What stands out instead is that the *arrêts* ruling on these requests displayed the same concern to avoid making hasty decisions that was evident in the Conseil Privé and in the *conseils de gouvernement*. Only in the case of the tax farmer did the *arrêt* nullify a parlement's sentence on the party's request without calling for additional procedures. The attempt to overturn the sentence of the Parlement of Rennes actually failed, and this only after both sides in the dispute had presented evidence. As for the banker's case, the *arrêt* did not give a final decision; it simply summoned his adversaries to contest his complaint fully in writing.

It is certainly true that during the period of Louis XIV's personal rule the controller general of finances and his collaborators became increasingly independent in administering the king's finances and made many decisions among themselves without consulting one of the councils—"par voie bureaucratique" in the words of Michel Antoine.[86] But there is no reason to suspect that this development made the nullification of parlementary sentences easier to achieve. The *arrêts simples* "en finance" provide additional evidence that in matters pertaining to the administration of justice, the desire to seek an accommodation with the parlements was widespread among all the branches of the king's Council.

Efforts by Louis XIV's councils to respect the legitimate rights of litigants without undermining the judicial authority of the parlements formed an important part of a broader royal policy regarding the kingdom's highest courts of law. After 1661, there was a growing recognition in the highest circles of government that the monarchy's limited resources and bureaucratic apparatus should be directed toward controlling certain crucial sectors of the state's activities—war, financial policy, and a few areas of domestic administration. For the more "ordinary" aspects of governing the realm, the king's traditional officials should be left a free hand, unharassed by overzealous superior authorities. The spirit of innovation inherent in Louis XIV's absolutism was thus balanced by a conservative commitment to work through rather than to destroy traditional institutions.[87]

NOTES

Grants and fellowships from the Institute for Advanced Study, the National Endowment for the Humanities, the American Philosophical Society, and Kansas State University made possible the research and writing of this article.

1. Limitations of space prevent even a selective listing of the many historical works that describe the activities of the royal councils in the ancien régime or that figure prominently in the ongoing debate about the nature of royal absolutism in Louis XIV's France and the place of the parlements in this debate. Interested readers should consult the bibliography and historiographical references in Albert N. Hamscher, *The Conseil Privé and the Parlements in the Age of Louis XIV: A Study in French Absolutism,* Transactions of the American Philosophical Society, vol. 77, pt. 2 (Philadelphia, 1987), a book that describes the organization and composition of Louis XIV's councils, discusses in detail the sources for their study, and explores the jurisprudence of the various councils on a broad range of legal issues. Let it suffice here to mention an important addition to the literature on council life in Louis's reign—David Parker, "Sovereignty, Absolutism

and the Function of the Law in Seventeenth-Century France," *Past and Present*, no. 122 (1989): 36–74—and to underscore that a careful reading of two works by Michel Antoine should precede all manner of research on the royal councils: *Le conseil du roi sous le règne de Louis XV* (Geneva, 1970), and *Le fonds du conseil d'état du roi aux Archives Nationales* (Paris, 1955). The best introduction to *cassation* is Antoine, *Conseil du roi*, 289–91, 446–47, 525–36. See also R. Martinage-Baranger, "Les idées sur la cassation au XVIIIe siècle," *Revue historique de droit français et étranger* 47 (1969): 244–90; Emile Chénon, *Origines, conditions et effets de la cassation* (Paris, 1882); and Jean Plassard, *Des ouvertures communes à cassation et à requête civile* (Paris, 1924). These three works and those by Antoine focus primarily on the eighteenth century (Chénon and Plassard considering later eras as well), and only Antoine has consulted manuscript sources, the others relying instead on an examination of royal regulations and the writings of jurists.

2. For an overview of these conflicts, see Roland Mousnier, *Les institutions de la France sous la monarchie absolue,* 2 vols. (Paris, 1974, 1980), vol. 2, bk. 8, chaps. 1–3. The substantial historical literature on the Fronde rebellions often refers to the parlements' conflicts with the councils. See the bibliographies in A. Lloyd Moote, *The Revolt of the Judges: The Parlement of Paris and the Fronde, 1643–1652* (Princeton, 1971); and in Albert N. Hamscher, "Ouvrages sur la Fronde parus en anglais depuis 1970," *XVIIe Siècle,* no. 145 (1984): 380–83. Throughout this essay, the term "parlement" applies to the 12 parlements existing in 1715—Aix-en-Provence, Besançon, Bordeaux, Dijon, Grenoble, Metz, Paris, Pau, Rennes, Rouen, Toulouse, Tournai/Douai—as well as to three other tribunals that enjoyed parlementary authority in their areas of jurisdiction—the *conseil provincial* of Artois and the *conseils souverains* of Alsace and Roussillon.

3. For example, see the memoranda prepared in the 1650s by the *parlementaires* of Aix, Bordeaux, and Paris in BN, MSS fr. 17288, fols. 523–37v; 17315, fols. 104–5v, 106–7, 139–52v, 167–73v; 18467, fols. 212–13, 214–16v; nouv. acq. fr. 7982, fol. 334A–H; and MSS Joly de Fleury 1051, fols. 19–23v.

4. As one significant example, writing in 1947 (and reiterating his views in 1980), Roland Mousnier, whose work on the history of French institutions has been very influential, reviewed the opposition of the parlements to the councils in the era of the Fronde and concluded: "But this was in vain. All these practices continued and gradually increased. *Evocations générales* and *de propre mouvement,* the sovereign judgment of individual cases in first and last resort, the suspension and *cassation* of [parlementary] sentences of all kinds, especially those concerning the observation of edicts and ordinances, multiplied." "Le conseil du roi de la mort de Henri IV au gouvernement personnel de Louis XIV," *Etudes d'histoire moderne et contemporaine* 1 (1947): 66; idem, *Institutions,* vol. 2, bk. 8, chaps. 2–4.

5. For the *arrêt* of 8 July 1661, see François-André Isambert et al., eds., *Recueil général des anciennes lois françaises depuis l'an 400 jusqu'à la révolution de 1789,* 29 vols. (Paris, 1822–33), 17:403–5. For Louis's views, see his *Mémoires for the In-*

struction of the Dauphin, ed. and trans. Paul Sonnino (New York, 1970), 26; Jean de Boislisle, ed., *Mémoriaux du conseil de 1661,* 3 vols. (Paris, 1905–7), 2:233; and Jean-Baptiste Colbert, *Lettres, instructions et mémoires,* ed. Pierre Clément, 7 vols. (Paris, 1861–82), 6:371.

6. These generalizations emerge from a thorough reading of the major collections of the correspondence dispatched by these three chancellors: BN, MSS fr. 5267 and 21118 (Le Tellier; these two volumes are nearly identical in content); AN, V1 577–85 (Boucherat, for the years 1685–91 only); and BN, MSS fr. 21119–42 (Pontchartrain).

7. BN, MSS Clairambault 613, pp. 13, 478–79, 565.

8. Ibid., 13, 478.

9. Ibid., 45 (Louis Le Maistre de Bellejambe), 498 (anonymous), 567 (Verthamon), 588–89 (anonymous).

10. Isambert et al., eds., *Anciennes lois* 17:375–79 (1660, abbreviated version; complete text in AN, V6 400), 18:341–52 (1669); AN, E 1770, fols. 3–21 (1673); ibid., 1840, fols. 201–29 (1687). The most readily accessible collection of regulatory acts pertaining to the Conseil Privé through 1698—including the *règlements* of 1660, 1673, and 1687, as well as ten others—is Philippe Bornier, *Conférences des ordonnances de Louis XIV,* 2 vols. (Paris, 1729), 2:808–64.

11. The clearest statement we have on the grounds for *cassation* is a memorandum prepared by Councillor of State Pierre Gilbert de Voisins for Louis XV in 1767, published in full in Michel Antoine, "Le mémoire de Gilbert de Voisins sur les cassations: Un épisode des querelles entre Louis XV et les parlements (1767)," *Revue historique de droit français et étranger* 36 (1958): 1–33. My contention that the grounds for *cassation* in force during Louis XIV's reign were identical to those stated by Gilbert de Voisins is based on my own examination of conciliar *arrêts* and not on the works of jurists, who on this matter were not particularly well informed.

12. Of the 74 petitioners in the sample of the Conseil Privé's *arrêts sur requête* to be examined shortly, I noted the social-corporate identity of 58, who fall roughly into the following categories: the king's own officials and related professions (2 *avocats,* a *notaire,* etc.)—21; nobles and military officers—14; members of the clergy—13; mercantile and municipal elites—6; and miscellaneous (including a single *tailleur d'habits*)—4. Despite a certain overlap of some of these categories, the results substantiate Parker's terse but correct observation that "the higher reaches of the legal system were almost axiomatically the preserve of the upper classes." "Sovereignty," 68. Parker himself has determined the status of the plaintiffs who appear in the Conseil Privé's *arrêts* concerning *cassation* during the months of January and February 1680 (AN, V6 653), and his findings are similar in this respect: three nobles (chevaliers), a merchant's widow, a member of the clergy, the syndic of a community, and a seigneurial judicial official (the status of two of nine plaintiffs being unknown). I thank Dr. Parker for sharing with me this information.

13. The *minutes* of the *arrêts* of the Conseil Privé for the personal rule of Louis XIV are arranged chronologically in cartons: AN, V6 422–836. The studies by Antoine and Hamscher cited above in note 1 offer a detailed discussion of the location, types, official wording, and interpretation of these *arrêts* and those of the other royal councils.

14. Sometimes the correspondence of the chancellors can be integrated into the process of tracing the *arrêts* issued in a given case. For example, on 22 July 1710, Pontchartrain notified the Parlement of Bordeaux that one of its judgments had recently been nullified because it violated the ordinance of August 1669, tit. 1, art. 17 (BN, MSS fr. 21142, fols. 1145v–48). A search in the council's archives leads to the pertinent *arrêt*, one between parties dated 21 July (AN, V6 819, no. 24); this *arrêt* in turn mentions an *arrêt sur requête* dated 27 March 1708 that originally introduced this case at the council, and it is located in V6 811 (no. 18).

15. The sample: AN, V6 544 (dossiers for 13, 18, 22, 24, and 28 [nos. 56–66 only] September 1668); V6 554 (dossiers for 3, 6, 9, and 10 [nos. 54–69 only] July 1669); V6 626 (dossiers for 14 and 23 April and 7, 16, 20, 21, and 28 May 1676); V6 686 (dossiers for 13, 20, and 27 February and 9, 13, 20, and 27 March 1685); V6 755 (dossiers for 9, 23, 24, 26, 28, and 30 September and 19, 21, and 25 October 1695); V6 802 (all dossiers, September–December 1705); V6 805 (dossier for 5 July 1706); V6 831 (dossier for 19 March 1714); and V6 834 (all dossiers, December 1714–March 1715). I chose the nine years represented in this sample in order to include *arrêts* from the tenure of each of Louis's chancellors and to take account of the appearance over time of the major regulatory acts guiding the council's conduct. The *arrêts* themselves were chosen at random.

16. For instance, a parlement risked *cassation* if it judged litigation even though one or more of the parties held letters patent (such as those of *état*, *répit*, or *commitimus*) that either postponed litigation for a specified time period or awarded special jurisdiction in a case (see, for example, AN, V6 626, 23 April 1676, no. 8). Because such cases did not raise fundamental questions about the judges' integrity or overall jurisdiction, they generated little tension between the parlements and the Conseil Privé. For a full discussion of these "routine" cases of *cassation*, see Hamscher, *Conseil Privé*, 42–46.

17. Two of the 10 *arrêts* between parties were issued "sur les requêtes respectives," and they are also included in the 67 *arrêts sur requête*. In these cases, both the petitioner and his opposing party submitted requests, and the council then resolved the dispute with a single *arrêt*, in effect combining an *arrêt sur requête* and an *arrêt* between parties in the same document.

18. AN, V6 686, 9 March 1685, no. 17; V6 834, 25 February 1714, no. 3.

19. For additional cases in which claims of inequity supplemented other grounds for *cassation*, see AN, V6 544, 18 September 1668, no. 36; V6 554, 3 July 1669, no. 23; and V6 802, 16 October 1705, no. 6. In one case, a petitioner was so reluctant to mention "injustice" as a formal ground that he referred to it only in passing, "par manière de remonstrance." V6 686, 27 March 1685, no. 22.

20. And in this single instance (AN, V6 544, 18 September 1668, no. 35) the council remanded the case to the court whose judgment it had just nullified (the Parlement of Paris), something it did rarely and almost certainly would not have done had it suspected that the *parlementaires* were incapable of judging fairly this petitioner's litigation.

21. For example, Pontchartrain to Montholon and Bermonville, both at the Parlement of Rouen, 6 March 1701, BN, MSS fr. 21120, pp. 266–70.

22. In the single case in which *cassation* was ordered, it is impossible to determine the weight the council gave to the claimed violation of law because the petitioner, an abbess from Aix, also offered other grounds for nullification, including alleged violations of judicial procedure: AN, V6 802, 14 September 1705, no. 1.

23. AN, V6 554, 18 September 1668, no. 1; V6 686, 27 February 1685, no. 17; V6 802, 7 September 1705, no. 4. Two of the five cases did not arise from the formal transfer of litigation from one court to another, but from the principle that even in the ordinary course of judging litigation the parlements had to apply the custom of the region where the objects of litigation were located: V6 626, 16 May 1676, no. 9; V6 831, 19 March 1714, no. 1.

24. AN, V6 554, 3 July 1669, no. 5.

25. In addition to the *arrêt* cited above in note 22, see AN, V6 626, 20 May 1676, no. 17; and V6 834, 3 December 1714, no. 16.

26. AN, V6 755, 9 September 1695, no. 11. For the other case, which involved a petitioner's claim that the Parlement of Bordeaux had ignored a customary statute of limitations for the prosecution of crime, see V6 726, 31 January 1691, no. 3 (traced from V6 755, 26 September 1695, no. 22).

27. For example, see AN, V6 686, 27 February 1685, no. 6; and V6 755, 9 September 1695, no. 41.

28. AN, V6 834, 14 January 1715, no. 2.

29. AN, V6 802, 14 September 1705, no. 3.

30. In addition to the *arrêts* cited in the previous two notes, see also AN, V6 544, 13 September 1668, no. 16; V6 554, 3 July 1669, no. 13; V6 802, 7 September 1705, no. 13 (see with V6 796, 28 April 1704); V6 834, 31 December 1714, no. 11; and V6 834, 28 January 1715, no. 8 (see with V6 822, 15 June 1711, no. 8).

31. AN, V6 626, 16 May 1676, no. 42. For the other three cases, see V6 554, 10 July 1669, no. 58; V6 626, 21 May 1676, no. 10 (see with V6 622, 16 October 1675); and V6 834, 14 January 1714, no. 3.

32. The two ordinances are in Isambert et al., eds., *Anciennes lois* 18:103–80, 371–423. A compendium of later acts is Daniel Jousse, ed., *Recueil chronologique des ordonnances, édits et arrêts de règlement cités dans les nouveaux commentaires sur les ordonnances des mois d'avril 1667, août 1669, août 1670, et mars 1673*, 3 vols. (Paris, 1757).

33. A summary examination of 571 *arrêts* from various dossiers in AN, V6 215 (12 February–15 March 1647) and 319 (11–28 February 1656) uncovered only one

case in which the petitioner's principal complaint dealt with a claimed violation of judicial procedure: V6 319, 18 February 1656, no. 127.

34. For a clear description of this legal action and its procedures, see Bornier, *Ordonnances de Louis XIV* 1:337–72; and Marc-Antoine Rodier, *Questions sur l'ordonnance de Louis XIV du mois d'avril 1667* (Toulouse, 1777), 638–90.

35. Grounds for *requête civile*, which were set forth in the ordinance of 1667, tit. 35, arts. 34–36, included such issues as fraud by a litigant's opposite party, the issuance of a judgment based on forged documentary evidence, inconsistent provisions in a given judgment, and most important for our purposes, "si la procédure par nous ordonnée n'a point été suivie." See also Plassard, *Ouvertures communes*, chap. 2.

36. For example, see AN, V6 686, 9 March 1685, no. 17; V6 802, 7 September 1705, no. 4; V6 831, 19 March 1714, no. 13; and V6 834, 31 December 1714, no. 21.

37. For example, see AN, V6 802, 18 September 1705, no. 4; and V6 834, 3 December 1714, no. 15.

38. AN, V6 834, 17 December 1714, no. 8 (see with V6 830, 19 March 1714, no. 5). For the other three cases, see V6 755, 28 September 1695, no. 19; V6 802, 14 September 1705, no. 28; and V6 802, 7 December 1705, no. 4.

39. For example, see AN, V6 544, 18 September 1668, no. 35; and V6 686, 13 March 1685, no. 11.

40. Boucherat to the first presidents of the parlements, 8 November 1687, AN, V1 580, pp. 234–35. For examples of letters of general intent addressed to individual parlements, see Le Tellier to Fieubet (Toulouse), 18 December 1679, BN, MSS fr. 5267, pp. 142–43; and Pontchartrain to the Parlement of Rennes, 17 June 1707, ibid., 21141, fols. 737–43v.

41. Pontchartrain to Bertier, 1 June, 9 November, and 6 December 1711, BN, MSS fr. 21134, fols. 468–70v, 904–5v, 976–77v (see with AN, V6 822, 8 May 1711, no. 22). For a similar communication, see Pontchartrain to Gassandy (Aix), 25 September 1705, BN, MSS fr. 21124, fols. 566v–68v (see with AN, V6 802, 14 September 1705, no. 1).

42. Indeed, a request for *cassation* did not even have to be successful to elicit comments from Pontchartrain about individual cases, whether these involved claimed violations of judicial procedure or other grounds for nullification. See, for example, his letters to La Tresne and Dalon (Bordeaux, 26 and 31 January 1701), to Le Mazuyer and the Parlement of Toulouse (7 February 1710), and to Doroz (Besançon, 18 July 1711), BN, MSS fr. 21120, pp. 111–13, 136–37; 21131, fols. 215v–18v; 21134, fols. 609–11v.

43. To observe the council operating within these criteria, see the letters cited in the preceding notes as well as the letters of Pontchartrain to Morant (Toulouse, 31 March 1700), to La Bedoyère (Rennes, 12 November 1702), and to Le Bret (Aix, 24 April 1714), ibid., 21119, pp. 247–48; 21121, fols. 531v–33v; 21139, fols. 375v–76v.

44. For examples of successful attempts to secure *cassation:* AN, V6 802, 14 September 1705, nos. 1, 28; V6 831, 19 March 1714, no. 23 (see with V6 828, 29 May 1713, no. 26). For unsuccessful attempts: V6 834, 3 December 1714, nos. 5, 15. For conversions to *requêtes civiles:* V6 686, 27 February and 13 March 1685, nos. 23, 11.

45. The spectrum of royal acts the parlements were alleged to have violated in their legal decisions was actually quite broad, ranging from such legislative monuments as the marine ordinance of April 1681 to more specific laws like the edict of February 1683 that regulated the disbursement of sums resulting from the sale of crown offices. Even official acts of very limited scope, such as letters patent of 1655 confirming the statutes of the saddlers' guild of Rennes, attracted the attention of litigants. See, for example, AN, V6 802, 16 October 1705, no. 6; V6 831, 19 March 1714, no. 8; and V6 834, 3 December 1714, no. 17.

46. AN, V6 802, 7 September 1705, no. 13 (see with V6 796, 28 April 1704); V6 802, 14 September 1705, no. 3.

47. Nor was the pre-1654 legislation cited obscure. Adrun Moret, for example, alleged that the Parlement of Paris had violated an ordinance of 1551 on the attachment of real property (*saisie réelle*), a well-known piece of legislation: AN, V6 834, 3 December 1714, no. 2.

48. The subject is treated at length in Hamscher, *Conseil Privé,* chap. 6. As a result, the notes that follow are highly selective regarding the sources they mention.

49. In Bornier's collection of acts (*Ordonnances de Louis XIV*), see the principal regulations on this subject: *règlement* of January 1673, arts. 62, 68; *arrêt* of 27 October 1674; *règlement* of June 1687, art. 44; and the *arrêt* of 3 September 1698. See also the *arrêt* of 3 February 1714 (AN, E 1974) in conjunction with Pontchartrain to Le Pelletier, 19 December 1713, BN, MSS fr. 21138, fols. 1107–10.

50. In the entire primary sample of 1,511 *arrêts,* the Conseil Privé retained final jurisdiction over only 2 cases, both jurisdictional disputes (*règlements de juges*): AN, V6 686, 20 February 1685, no. 45; V6 755, 23 September 1695, no. 14.

51. For example, see AN, V6 686, 27 February 1685, no. 23; V6 802, 14 September 1705, no. 28; and V6 834, 3 December 1714, no. 5. Note that the council's members had no monetary incentive to prolong litigation: unlike ordinary judges, they did not assess personal fees, or *épices,* for their work.

52. For examples of parties having successfully done this, see AN, V6 554, 3 July 1669, no. 32; V6 626, 16 May 1676, no. 35; and V6 834, 3 December 1714, no. 18.

53. For example, see the *procureur général*'s report to the Parlement of Grenoble on 7 September 1715, AD, Isère, B 2313, fols. 81–82; and letters by Pontchartrain to Bertier (Toulouse, 9 November 1711) and to Le Bret (Aix, 24 April 1714), BN, MSS fr. 21134, fols. 904–5v, and 21139, fols. 375v–76v (see with AN, V6 822, 18 May 1711, no. 22; and V6 831, 26 March 1714, no. 5).

54. The *règlements* of January 1673 (art. 65) and June 1687 (art. 40) prohibited

surséances in principle, but allowed them "by the express order of His Majesty," an escape clause that enabled the council's members to use the procedure when they deemed it necessary, something, according to Pontchartrain, "which they almost never do." Letter to Mirat (Bordeaux), 2 March 1714, BN, MSS fr. 21139, fols. 197v–98v.

55. And this case involved a suspension that was automatic, the pertinent *arrêt* having joined the request for *cassation* to a pending action for a change of venue (*évocation de justice*): AN, V6 802, 22 December 1705, no. 2. Moreover, even in the 1660s and 1670s it seems that the council ordered an occasional *surséance* only when allegations against a parlement were especially serious—for example, that it had exceeded its jurisdiction in a major way. See AN, V6 544, 13 September 1668, no. 16; and V6 554, 3 July 1669, no. 13.

56. See the *règlements* of February 1660, art. 14, and June 1687, art. 43, as well as the *arrêt* of 3 February 1714 cited above in note 49.

57. In 1710, for example, Pontchartrain denounced the "spirit of chicanery of all kinds" and the "shameful greediness" he detected in the conduct of some of the council's *avocats*, "either in multiplying costs and augmenting dockets for the most insignificant affairs or in taking on the worst cases and then using the falsest colors to sustain them." Pontchartrain to the syndic of the community of *avocats aux conseils*, 7 December 1710, BN, MSS fr. 21142, fols. 1198–99v. In 1713 he claimed that too many *avocats* were willing to sign requests for *cassation* "without having seen anything." Letter to Le Pelletier cited above in note 49.

58. Parties who felt confident about their complaints did not object to the rule: Mathurin Goeslin saw it as a way to prevent chicanery and "to defend the integrity of *arrêts contradictoires*." AN, V6 544, 18 September 1668, no. 33.

59. The committee structure of the Conseil Privé was complex and it evolved considerably over time. For details, see Antoine, *Conseil du roi*, 152–55, 306–8; and Hamscher, *Conseil Privé*, 81–89.

60. The participation of a bureau is mentioned at the end of an *arrêt*'s introductory section (*exposé*); the assembly of masters of requests is rarely, if ever, noted in cases of *cassation*, its activity being presumed without official mention. For examples of a bureau's participation, see AN, V6 831, 19 March 1714, no. 13; and V6 834, 17 December 1714, no. 8. Sometimes several bureaus examined the same case, but at different stages of the proceedings: V6 822, 15 June 1711, no. 8; V6 834, 28 January 1715, no. 8.

61. The procedure is mentioned in René Guillard, *Histoire du conseil du roy depuis le commencement de la monarchie jusqu'à la fin du règne de Louis le grand* (Paris, 1718), 95. For an early mention of this bureau, see AN, V6 686, 27 February 1685, no. 6.

62. Pontchartrain to La Reynie (who presided over this bureau in the late 1690s and early 1700s), 12 December 1708, BN, MSS fr. 21128, fols. 1098–99v.

63. For an informative overview of this aspect of judicial life in ancien régime France, see Tony Sauvel, "Histoire du jugement motivé," *Revue du droit public et de la science politique en France et à l'étranger* 71 (1955): 5–53.

64. For a general discussion of the procedure, especially in the eighteenth century, see Tony Sauvel, "Les demandes de motifs adressées par le conseil du roi aux cours souveraines," *Revue historique de droit français et étranger* 35 (1957): 529–48.

65. For this principle, see First President of the Parlement of Paris Lamoignon to Procureur General Harlay, 30 September 1666, BN, MSS fr. 17413, fol. 33. If the issues in a petitioner's complaint were clear, *motifs* were unnecessary: Pontchartrain to Le Bret (Aix), 24 April 1714, ibid., 21139, fols. 375v–76v.

66. The council's archives contain many cases raising identical grounds for *cassation* but differing in whether they entailed a call for *motifs*. For example, compare AN, V6 626, 20 May 1676, no. 17, with V6 831, 19 March 1714, no. 1: both raise a violation of law as grounds for *cassation*, but only the former includes a call for *motifs*.

67. For example, Pontchartrain to De Lasse and to La Bedoyère (Rennes), 5 May 1700, BN, MSS fr. 21119, pp. 361–63.

68. The *minutes* of all but a few of these *arrêts* for the period of Louis XIV's personal rule are arranged chronologically in four parallel series of volumes, each corresponding to a secretary of state: AN, E 1712–1982. A useful descriptive index, 100 small manuscript volumes in length and prepared in the eighteenth century, is AN, *inventaire 50: Répertoire chronologique et analytique des arrêts du conseil des dépêches des années 1611 à 1710* (available on 20 rolls of microfilm from the Service International de Microfilms in Paris and from the Center for Research Libraries in Chicago). Although the title refers only to the Conseil des Dépêches, this index's entries actually give the volume reference and a brief description of every *arrêt en commandement* located in series E for the years 1611–1710 (thus *all* the *conseils de gouvernement* are represented).

69. Statistics drawn from the *Répertoire* for the years 1643, 1645, 1648, 1651, 1653, 1656, 1658, and 1660. I chose (at random) years between 1643 and 1660, first, because *cassations* were a hotly contested subject in the two decades before Louis XIV assumed personal rule, and second, because few *arrêts en commandement* exist for the years before 1640. For a method to recognize *cassations* in the *Répertoire*, see Hamscher, *Conseil Privé*, 136.

70. See, for example, *Répertoire* 2:124; 3:100, 110, 142; 4:141, 215, 260, 280; 6:22, 51, 53, 62, 67, 98, 134, 214, 216, 220; and so on through the index for the sample years.

71. Statistics drawn from the *Répertoire* for the years 1675, 1683, 1687, 1690, 1695, 1708, 1709, and 1710. All the controllers general of finances, chancellors, and secretaries of state who served Louis XIV after 1675 are represented in this sample; I chose the particular years at random.

72. AN, E 1822; *Répertoire* 53:281 (30 April). For other examples of "political" *cassation,* see the *arrêts* of 20 November 1675 (E 1781; *Répertoire* 38:309), 1 April 1683 (E 1822; *Répertoire* 53:210), and 19 March 1687 (E 1843; *Répertoire* 62: 151).

73. For example, see the *arrêts* of 22 December 1687 (AN, E 1843; *Répertoire* 63:341), 10 December 1708 (E 1944; *Répertoire* 97:458), and 8 May 1709 (E 1946; *Répertoire* 98:166).

74. *Arrêt* of 24 October 1687 (AN, E 1841; *Répertoire* 63:227). See also the *arrêt* of 17 September 1708 (E 1946; *Répertoire* 97:356).

75. *Arrêt* of 5 June 1683 (AN, E 1816; *Répertoire* 53:379). See also the *arrêt* of 20 November 1675 (E 1781; *Répertoire* 38:310).

76. For examples of a call for *motifs,* see the *arrêts* of 10 January 1687 (AN, E 1839; *Répertoire* 62:22) and 26 September 1690 (E 1859; *Répertoire* 69:205). For examples of contests between litigants, see the *arrêts* of 6 April 1675 (E 1781; *Répertoire* 37:254) and 23 November 1687 (E 1843; *Répertoire* 63:277).

77. For an example of a fine, see the entry for 29 April 1675 in *Répertoire* 37: 309. For the participation of *avocats,* see the *arrêts* of 25 June and 23 September 1668 in Bornier, *Ordonnances de Louis XIV* 1:clii–cliii, cciv–ccviii.

78. For an overview of these bureaus in the eighteenth century, see Antoine, *Conseil du roi,* 309–19.

79. For example, see the *arrêts* of 10 December 1708 and 8 May 1709 cited above in note 73.

80. For examples from just the year 1708, see *Répertoire* 97:277, 279, 282, 315, etc.

81. The *minutes* of *arrêts simples* "en finance" issued between September 1661 and September 1715 are arranged chronologically in volumes: AN, E 348B–879.

82. The sample: AN, E 500 (October 1676) and 859A (2–20 January 1714). I chose these volumes at random.

83. AN, E 500, fol. 269 (17 October 1676). Two days later another *arrêt* (fols. 333–34) voided some procedures the Parlement of Paris had initiated in a criminal case over which the *lieutenant général de police* had jurisdiction; this was not, however, the *cassation* of a parlementary judgment.

84. Ibid., fols. 148–53v (3 October 1676).

85. AN, E 859A, fols. 23–24v (2 January 1714). Note that on this date another *arrêt* (fols. 14–18) nullified just that portion of a judgment rendered by the Parlement of Dijon that failed to order a fine required by statute in convictions regarding contraband tobacco; the substantive portion of the sentence, however, remained in force.

86. Antoine, *Conseil du roi,* 319, 399. See also Gary Bruce McCollim, "Council Versus Minister: The Controller General of Finances, 1661–1715," *Proceedings of the Annual Meeting of the Western Society for French History* 6 (1978): 67–75.

87. In other contexts, several recent studies offer perceptive comments about

the conservative aspects of Louis's reign, whether in the king's own thinking or in the nature of his policies. For example, see William Beik, *Absolutism and Society in Seventeenth-Century France: State Power and Provincial Aristocracy in Languedoc* (Cambridge, 1985), 31, 279–81, 303, 333–34; Richard Bonney, *Political Change in France Under Richelieu and Mazarin, 1624–1661* (Oxford, 1978), 448–51; Daniel Dessert, *Argent, pouvoir et société au grand siècle* (Paris, 1984), chaps. 14–15; Sarah Hanley, "Engendering the State: Family Formation and State Building in Early Modern France," *French Historical Studies* 16 (1989): 4–27; Sharon Kettering, *Patrons, Brokers, and Clients in Seventeenth-Century France* (New York, 1986), 213–14, 224, 231; Andrew Lossky, "The Absolutism of Louis XIV: Reality or Myth?" *Canadian Journal of History* 19 (1984): 1–15; J. Russell Major, *Representative Government in Early Modern France* (New Haven, 1980), 634–36, 663–72; Roger Mettam, *Power and Faction in Louis XIV's France* (Oxford, 1988), chaps. 1, 4–5; and David Parker, *The Making of French Absolutism* (London, 1983), 136–45.

Bibliography of the Works of J. Russell Major

COMPILED BY GARRETT L. MCAINSH

The books, articles, and essays listed below show the development of J. Russell Major's scholarly career as an interpreter of Renaissance France. They reveal the long-term concentration of his interest in the structure of monarchy and in the subtle shifts between the actual powers of the crown and the perceived rights of subjects. His most important contribution has been his insistence on the importance of the long-ignored role of representative institutions in the monarchy's operation. In this work Major also demonstrates his growing curiosity about the social structure upon which the French monarchy rested, particularly about the role of the aristocracy. Viewed as a whole, these works manifest how much of our present understanding of the French monarchy and society we owe to Major's meticulous scholarship.

The list of doctoral dissertations appended to this bibliography reflects another facet of Russell Major's distinguished scholarly career. As a teacher he has introduced a number of younger scholars to the exhilaration and the pains of disciplined research. The titles of these dissertations indicate the ways in which he has imbued his students with his own curiosity while guiding their research.

I. BOOKS, ARTICLES, AND REVIEWS

1951
The Estates General of 1560. Princeton: Princeton University Press. Reprint. New York: Johnson Reprints, 1970.

1954
"The Third Estate in the Estates General of Pontoise, 1561." *Speculum* 19:460–76.

1955
"The Payment of the Deputies to the French National Assemblies." *Journal of Modern History* 27:217–29.
Review of *An Introduction to Seventeenth-Century France,* by John Lough. *American Historical Review* 60:418–19.

1956

"The Electoral Procedure for the Estates General of France and Its Social Implications, 1483–1651." *Medievalia et Humanistica* 10:131–50.

1957

"The Renaissance Monarchy: A Contribution to the Periodization of History." *Emory University Quarterly* 13:112–24. Reprinted in *The "New Monarchies" and Representative Assemblies: Medieval Constitutionalism or Modern Absolutism?* edited by A. J. Slavin, 77–84. Boston: D. C. Heath, 1964.

1959

Review of *Le bailliage royal de Montferrand (1425–1556),* by André Bossuat. *American Historical Review* 64:436–37.

Review of *The Paris of Henry of Navarre As Seen by Pierre de l'Estoile: Selections from His Mémoires-Journaux,* edited and translated by Nancy Lyman Roelker. *American Historical Review* 64:703.

1960

The Deputies to the Estates General in Renaissance France. Madison: University of Wisconsin Press. Reprint. Westport, Conn.: Greenwood Press, 1974.

Representative Institutions in Renaissance France, 1421–1559. Madison: University of Wisconsin Press. Reprint. Westport, Conn.: Greenwood Press, 1983.

1961

"The Loss of Royal Initiative and the Decay of the Estates General in France, 1421–1615." *Album Helen Maud Cam* 2:245–59. Reprinted in *Die Geschichtlichen Grundlagen der Modern Volksvertsetung,* edited by Heinz Rausch, 1:359–73. Darmstadt: Wissenschaftliche Buchgesellschaft, 1980.

Review of *The Royal Funeral Ceremony in Renaissance France,* by Ralph E. Giesey. *Journal of Modern History* 33:185–86.

1962

"The French Monarchy as Seen Through the Estates General." *Studies in the Renaissance* 9:113–25. Reprinted in *Government in Reformation Europe, 1520–1560,* edited by Henry J. Cohn, 43–57. New York: Macmillan, 1971; and (in Italian translation) in *Lo Stato moderno,* edited by Ettore Rotelli and Pierangelo Schiera, 2:245–56. Bologna: Società Editrice il Mulino, 1973.

Review of *La Guerre de Cent Ans vue à travers les registres du Parlement (1337–1369),* by Pierre-Clément Timbal et al. *American Historical Review* 68:186.

Review of *The Juristic Basis of Dynastic Right to the French Throne,* by Ralph E. Giesey. *American Historical Review* 67:776.

1963

Review of *Les Ducs de Bourbon pendant la crise monarchique du XVe siècle: Contribution à l'étude des apanages,* by André Leguai. *Speculum* 38:642–43.

Review of *The French Secretaries of State in the Age of Catherine de Medici*, by N. M. Sutherland. *Renaissance News* 16:121–22.

Review of *Recherches sur les effectifs des armées françaises des Guerres d'Italie aux Guerres de Religion, 1494–1562*, by Ferdinand Lot. *American Historical Review* 68:516.

Review of *Tribunaux et gens de justice dans le bailliage de Senlis à la fin du Moyen Age (vers 1380–vers 1550)*, by Bernard Guenée. *American Historical Review* 69:195–96.

1964

"The Crown and the Aristocracy in Renaissance France." *American Historical Review* 69:631–45. Reprinted in *Lordship and Community in Medieval Europe*, edited by F. L. Cheyette, 240–54. New York: Holt, Rinehart, and Winston, 1968.

"French Representative Assemblies: Research Opportunities and Research Published." *Studies in Medieval and Renaissance History* 1:181–219.

Review of *The Six Bookes of a Commonweale*, by Jean Bodin (a facsimile reprint of the English translation of 1606), edited by Kenneth Douglas McRae. *Journal of Modern History* 36:52–53.

1965

Review of *Assemblies and Representation in Languedoc in the Thirteenth Century*, by Thomas N. Bisson. *American Historical Review* 70:1083–84.

1966

"Henry IV and Guyenne: A Study Concerning the Origins of Royal Absolutism." *French Historical Studies* 4:363–83. This article was awarded the William C. Koren, Jr., Prize by the Society for French Historical Studies. Reprinted in *State and Society in Seventeenth-Century France*, edited by Raymond Kierstead, 2–24. New York: Franklin Watts, 1975.

The Western World: Renaissance to the Present. Philadelphia: J. B. Lippincott. This work was also published in two parts under the titles *Civilization in the Western World: Renaissance to 1815* and *Civilization in the Western World: 1815 to the Present*, as well as in a two- and three-part format in collaboration with G. P. Cuttino and Robert Scranton titled *Civilization in the Western World*.

1967

"Popular Initiative in Renaissance France." In *Aspects of the Renaissance*, edited by A. R. Lewis, 27–41. Austin: University of Texas Press.

Review of *Seventeenth-Century France*, by G. R. R. Treasure. *Renaissance Quarterly* 20:251–52.

1968

"A Doctoral Program for College Teachers." *American Historical Association Newsletter* 7:36–40.

1969

"The Renaissance Monarchy as Seen by Erasmus, Seyssel, and Machiavelli." In *Action and Conviction in Early Modern Europe: Essays in Memory of E. H. Harbison,* edited by Theodore K. Rabb and Jerrold E. Seigel, 17–31. Princeton: Princeton University Press.

1970

The Age of the Renaissance and Reformation. Philadelphia: J. B. Lippincott.

Review of *The Parlement of Paris,* by J. H. Shennan. *Journal of Modern History* 42:95–96.

Review of *Queen of Navarre: Jeanne d'Albret, 1528–1572,* by Nancy Lyman Roelker. *Journal of Modern History* 72:389–90.

1971

The Western World: Renaissance to the Present. 2d ed. Philadelphia: J. B. Lippincott.

1972

"The Assembly at Paris in the Summer of 1575." In *Post Scripta: Essays on Medieval Law and the Emergence of the European State in Honor of Gaines Post,* edited by Joseph R. Strayer and Donald E. Queller, 699–715. Rome: Studia Gratiana.

1973

Review of *The Fiscal System of Renaissance France,* by Martin Wolfe. *Journal of Modern History* 65:480–81.

1974

Bellièvre, Sully, and the Assembly of Notables of 1596. Transactions of the American Philosophical Society, n.s., vol. 64, pt. 2. Philadelphia: The Society.

Review of *Jean Bodin and the Rise of Absolutist Theory,* by Julian Franklin. *American Historical Review* 79:504–5.

1975

Review of *Prosecuting Crime in the Renaissance: England, Germany, France,* by John H. Langbein. *Journal of Interdisciplinary History* 6:321–22.

1976

"There Is Also a Time to Tell a Story." *Reviews in European History* 2:20–23.

1977

Review of *Society in Crisis: France in the Sixteenth Century,* by J. H. M. Salmon, and *Radical Reactionaries: The Political Thought of the French Catholic League,* by Frederic J. Baumgartner. *Renaissance Quarterly* 30:238–40.

1978

Review of *Les Bourgeois Gentilshommes: An Essay on the Definition of Elites in Renaissance France,* by George Huppert. *Renaissance Quarterly* 31:392–94.

1979

Review of *The Development of the Modern State: A Sociological Introduction,* by Gianfranco Poggi. *American Historical Review* 84:422.

1980

Representative Government in Early Modern France. New Haven: Yale University Press.

1981

"Noble Income, Inflation, and the Wars of Religion in France." *American Historical Review* 86:21–48.

Review of *Philosophy and the State in France: The Renaissance to the Enlightenment,* by Nannerl O. Keohane. *Renaissance Quarterly* 34:234–36.

1983

Review of *Francis I,* by R. J. Knecht. *Journal of Modern History* 55:712–13.

1984

Review of *Origins of Legislative Sovereignty and the Legislative State,* by A. London Fell. *American Historical Review* 89:1296–97.

Review of *Paris City Councillors in the Sixteenth Century: The Politics of Patrimony,* by Barbara Diefendorf. *American Historical Review* 89:131.

Review of *The State, France, and the Sixteenth Century,* by Howell A. Lloyd. *Renaissance Quarterly* 37:82–84.

Review of *The Young Richelieu: A Psychoanalytic Approach to Leadership,* by Elizabeth Wirth Marvick. *Journal of Interdisciplinary History* 15:337–38.

1985

Review of *The Parlement of Poitiers: War, Government, and Politics in France, 1418–1436,* by Roger G. Little. *American Historical Review* 90:940.

Review of *Richelieu and Olivares,* by J. H. Elliott. *Journal of Modern History* 57:718–20.

1986

"The Revolt of 1620: A Study of Ties of Fidelity." *French Historical Studies* 14:391–408.

Review of *Mazarinades: La Fronde des mots,* by Christian Jouhaud. *American Historical Review* 91:933–34.

Review of *Popular Culture and Elite Culture in France, 1400–1750,* by Robert Muchembled. *Sixteenth Century Journal* 17:523.

1987

"Bastard Feudalism and the Kiss: Changing Social Mores in Late Medieval and Early Modern France." *Journal of Interdisciplinary History* 17:509–35. This article was awarded the William C. Koren, Jr., Prize by the Society for French Historical Studies and the Nancy Lyman Roelker Prize by the Sixteenth Century Studies Conference.

Review of *Cardinal Richelieu: Power and the Pursuit of Wealth,* by Joseph Bergin. *Journal of Modern History* 59:583–85.

Review of *Change and Continuity in the French Episcopate: The Bishops and the Wars of Religion, 1547–1610,* by Frederic J. Baumgartner. *Renaissance Quarterly* 40:782–84.

Review of *From Valor to Pedigree: Ideas of Nobility in France in the Sixteenth and Seventeenth Centuries,* by Ellery Schalk. *Renaissance Quarterly* 40:123–25.

1988

"French Representative Assemblies." *Dictionary of the Middle Ages* 10:316–28.

The Monarchy, the Estates, and the Aristocracy in Renaissance France. London: Variorum Press.

Review of *The European Crisis of the 1590s: Essays in Comparative History,* edited by Peter Clark. *Renaissance Quarterly* 41:486–88.

Review of *Louis XIII: The Making of a King,* by Elizabeth Wirth Marvick. *Journal of Interdisciplinary History* 19:328–30.

Review of *Women, Production, and Patriarchy in Late Medieval Cities,* by Martha C. Howell. *Journal of Interdisciplinary History* 19:103–4.

1989

Review of *The D'Aligres de la Rivière: Servants of the Bourbon State in the Seventeenth Century,* by D. J. Sturdy. *Journal of Modern History* 61:163–64.

Review of *The King and the City in the Parisian Royal Entry Ceremony: Politics, Ritual, and Art in the Renaissance,* by Lawrence M. Bryant. *Journal of Modern History* 61:377–78.

1990

Review of *The Duel in European History: Honour and the Reign of Aristocracy,* by V. G. Kiernan. *American Historical Review* 95:485.

II. DOCTORAL DISSERTATIONS
DIRECTED BY J. RUSSELL MAJOR

1956

"The First Girondin Ministry, March–June 1792: A Revolutionary Experiment," by Charles A. Leguin.

1961
"A History of the Estates of Poitou," by Joseph M. Tyrrell.

1968
"The Government of Béarn, 1472–1494," by Eva Stone Duncan.

1969
"Introduction and Translation of Jean Bodin's *Colloquium Heptaplomeres de Rerum Sublimium Arcanis Abditis* (Books I–IV)," by Marion Daniels Kuntz.

1973
"French Provincial Opinions at the Time of the Fronde," by Walter E. Brown.
"The Relations Between the Crown and the Parlement of Paris After the Fronde, 1653–1673," by Albert N. Hamscher.
"Richelieu and the Estates of Brittany, 1624–1640," by Kenneth M. Dunkley.
"Social Structure and Social Change Among the Nobility of the *Election* of Bayeux, 1463–1666," by James B. Wood.

1974
"English Views of France During the Renaissance, 1470–1600," by Garrett L. McAinsh.

1975
"The Cahiers of the Parishes of the Balliwick of Chartres Prepared for the Estates General of 1576," by Alan G. Arthur.

1982
"The Nobility of Seventeenth-Century Aix-en-Provence," by Donna Bohanan.
"A Prince of the Blood in the French Wars of Religion: François de Valois, Duke of Alençon and Anjou, 1555–1584," by Mack P. Holt.

1988
"Anatomy of a Fortune: The House of Foix-Navarre-Albret, 1517–1610," by S. Amanda Eurich.
"Rouen and the New World: Rouennais Investors in Commerce with North and South America, 1559–1629," by Gayle K. Brunelle.

1991
"Henry IV and the Towns: Royal Authority Versus Municipal Autonomy, 1589–1610," by Annette Finley-Croswhite.

Contributors

DONALD A. BAILEY is a professor of history at the University of Winnipeg, Canada. After completing undergraduate degrees from both the University of Saskatchewan and the University of Oxford, he received his Ph.D. in 1973 from the University of Minnesota, where he studied with John B. Wolf. He has published several articles and is currently working on a major study of Michel de Marillac.

WILLIAM BEIK received his Ph.D. from Harvard University in 1969. After having taught at Northern Illinois University for twenty years, he was appointed an associate professor of history at Emory University in 1990. He is the author of numerous articles as well as the prize-winning book *Absolutism and Society in Seventeenth-Century France: State Power and Provincial Aristocracy in Languedoc* (Cambridge: Cambridge University Press, 1985). He is currently preparing a book on popular protest in seventeenth-century France.

DONNA BOHANAN received her Ph.D. from Emory University in 1982 and is currently an associate professor of history at Auburn University. She has written several articles and is the author of *The Nobility of Seventeenth-Century Aix-en-Provence: A Privileged Elite in Urban Society* (Baton Rouge: Louisiana State University Press, forthcoming). She is presently working on a comparative study of the nobility in Provence and Brittany in seventeenth-century France.

GAYLE K. BRUNELLE received her Ph.D. from Emory University in 1988 and is currently an assistant professor of history at California State University-Fullerton. She has written several articles, as well as *Rouen and the New World: Rouennais Investors in Commerce with North and South America, 1559–1629* (Kirksville, Mo.: Sixteenth Century Journal Publishers, forthcoming). She is working on a book on Spanish merchants in Rouen and Nantes in the sixteenth century.

ANNETTE FINLEY-CROSWHITE received her Ph.D. from Emory University in 1991. She has written several articles and is presently preparing a book on Henry IV's policies toward the Protestant, league, and royalist towns at the end of the religious wars.

ALBERT N. HAMSCHER received his Ph.D. from Emory University in 1973 and is currently a professor of history at Kansas State University. He is the author of numerous articles as well as two books: *The Parlement of Paris*

After the Fronde, 1653–1673 (Pittsburgh: University of Pittsburgh Press, 1976), and *The Conseil Privé and the Parlements in the Age of Louis XIV: A Study in French Absolutism* (Philadelphia: The Society, Transactions of the American Philosophical Society, vol. 77, pt. 2, 1987). He is working on a study of the state, finance, and the prosecution of crime in France, 1670–1789.

SARAH HANLEY received her Ph.D. in 1975 from the University of Iowa, where she studied with Ralph E. Giesey. She is currently a professor of history at the University of Iowa. The author of a number of articles as well as *The Lit de Justice of the Kings of France: Constitutional Ideology in Legend, Ritual, and Discourse* (Princeton: Princeton University Press, 1983), she is currently preparing a book on gender and the state in early modern France.

MACK P. HOLT received his Ph.D. from Emory University in 1982. After having taught at West Texas State, Harvard, and Vanderbilt universities, he is now an associate professor of history at George Mason University. In addition to a number of articles, he is the author of *The Duke of Anjou and the Politique Struggle During the Wars of Religion* (Cambridge: Cambridge University Press, 1986) and *The French Wars of Religion, 1562–1629* (Cambridge: Cambridge University Press, forthcoming). He is presently preparing a book on the social impact of the Wars of Religion in the province of Burgundy.

GARRETT L. MCAINSH received his Ph.D. in 1974 from Emory University, where he wrote a dissertation entitled "English Views of France During the Renaissance, 1470–1600." He has authored several articles and has taught for more than fifteen years at Hendrix College in Conway, Arkansas, where he is currently a professor of history.

OREST RANUM received his Ph.D. in 1960 from the University of Minnesota, where he studied with John B. Wolf. After having taught at the University of Southern California and Columbia University, he is now a professor of history at the Johns Hopkins University. In addition to numerous articles, he is the author of *Richelieu and the Councillors of Louis XIII* (Oxford: Oxford University Press, 1963), *Paris in the Age of Absolutism: An Essay* (New York: John Wiley & Sons, 1968), and *Artisans of Glory: Writers and Historical Thought in Seventeenth-Century France* (Chapel Hill: University of North Carolina Press, 1980) and the editor or coeditor of more than half a dozen books of essays. He is currently preparing a major reinterpretation of the Fronde.

ELLERY SCHALK received his Ph.D. in 1970 from the University of California at Berkeley, where he studied with William Bouwsma. He has taught at the University of Texas at El Paso since 1971 and is now chair of the history department. In addition to editing a book of essays, he has written several articles and one book, *From Valor to Pedigree: Ideas of Nobility in France in the Sixteenth and Seventeenth Cen-*

turies (Princeton: Princeton University Press, 1986). He is presently at work on a study of the league in Marseilles.

JAMES B. WOOD received his Ph.D. from Emory University in 1973 and is presently chair of the history department at Williams College in Williamstown, Massachusetts. The author of a number of articles as well as *The Nobility of the Election of Bayeux, 1463–1666: Continuity Through Change* (Princeton: Princeton University Press, 1980), he is currently completing a book entitled *The Army of Charles IX*.

Index